Woman as Hero in Old English Literature

Woman as Hero
in Old English Literature

JANE CHANCE

SYRACUSE UNIVERSITY PRESS 1986

Copyright © 1986 by Syracuse University Press
Syracuse, New York 13210

All Rights Reserved

First Edition

The paper used in this publication meets the minimum requirements of American National Standard for Information Sciences—Permanence of Paper for Printed Library Materials, ANSI Z39.48-1984. ∞

Library of Congress Cataloging-in-Publication Data

Chance, Jane, 1945–
    Woman as hero in Old English literature.
    Bibliography: p.
    Includes index.
    1. Anglo-Saxon literature—History and criticism.
2. Women in literature.   3. Heroines in literature.
4. Heroes in literature.   5. Sex role in literature.
I. Title.
PR179.W65C4   1985   829'.90352042   85-17288
ISBN 0-8156-2345-3 (alk. paper)
ISBN 0-8156-2346-1 (pbk. : alk. paper)

To
Jackson J. Campbell
and
Joseph B. Trahern, Jr.

By the same author, as Jane Chance Nitzsche
The Genius Figure in Antiquity and the Middle Ages
Tolkien's Art: A 'Mythology for England'

as Jane Chance
Co-ed., *Approaches to Teaching Sir Gawain and the Green Knight*
Co-ed., *Mapping the Cosmos*

JANE CHANCE is Professor of English at Rice University, Houston, Texas.

Contents

Preface

Y EARS AGO, in an attempt to understand the reasons for the *Beowulf*-
poet's inclusion of the middle section of the poem and to account for
the depiction of Grendel's Mother as a monstrous woman, I became
interested in the role played by aristocratic women in Anglo-Saxon society
and literature. What intrigued me most in the epic was the description of
the monster's inversion of feminine social values in Germanic heroic
terms. This anomaly eventually led to an investigation of other Old
English works in which women served as heroes or participated actively in
society. With this social, psychological, and historical perspective of the
woman as hero, the shape of Old English poetry and culture has become
clearer to me, colored as it is by the values and imagery of the Germanic
duguð or *comitatus*—the band of retainers and their lord—even within
the context of a Christian view of reality. This study traces the outlines of
this perspective in relation to the women characters and types offered in
historical and literary works of the period and thus supplements the work
of earlier scholars. Stanley Greenfield, Alvin A. Lee, Edward B. Irving,
Jr., Alain Renoir, John Gardner, and others have already demonstrated the
coexistence of the native heroic with the learned religious tradition in the
literature, without whose insights so many of my own conclusions would
not have been possible.

I am indebted to Rice University's Fondren Library and especially
the Interlibrary Loan Department for recovering difficult texts; for the
preparation of the manuscript I am also grateful to Rice University, Allen
Matusow, Dean of Humanities, and the English Department for supply-
ing funds for typing, checking of references, proofreading and indexing.

Many thanks are due to the friends, colleagues, and students who have read or heard portions of the manuscript and who have provided helpful suggestions or support, among them Kristine G. Wallace, Daniel P. Deneau, Edward B. Irving, Jr., Thomas Cable, Helen Damico, Lois Roney, Gretchen Mieszkowski, Madeline Fleming, Alexandra Hennessey Olsen, Sharon Farmer, Ted Reed, and Dean James. I am especially grateful to Rita M. Copeland and Julian N. Wasserman for suggestions and comments. Finally, I would like to express deep gratitude to Jackson J. Campbell of the University of Illinois, from whose *Beowulf* seminar the inspiration for this study derived, and to Joseph B. Trahern, Jr., who taught me Anglo-Saxon. To them this volume is dedicated.

Material in this book has appeared previously in various forms. The first chapter was originally delivered in shortened form as a paper, "The Role of the Queen as *Freoðuwebbe* in the Anglo-Saxon Court," at the Conference on the Medieval Court, University of Houston, 3 March 1983. The second chapter, on images of the Virgin Mary in *Christ I*, was delivered as a paper entitled, "The Unity of *Christ I:* The Use of Variation in Images of the Virgin Mary," at the Ninth Annual Conference of the Southeastern Medieval Association, University of Virginia, Charlottesville, 7 October 1983. The fourth chapter, on the Saint, Abbess, and Chaste Queen, was first delivered as a paper, in the Old English Language and Literature Division session of the Modern Language Association annual meeting on 28 December 1980, and later published in *Allegorica* 5 (1980): 139–48. The sixth chapter was first presented as "*Uncer Giedd Geador:* Anglo-Saxon Woman as *Scop* in *The Wife's Lament* and *Wulf and Eadwacer*" at the Seventeenth International Congress on Medieval Studies, the Medieval Institute, Western Michigan University, Kalamazoo, Michigan, on 6 May 1982. Chapter 7, on Grendel's Mother in *Beowulf,* was originally delivered as a paper at the Third Annual Conference on Medieval Studies sponsored by John Carroll University, Cleveland, Ohio, 11 October 1976, and again by invitation at the Southeastern Medieval Association conference sponsored by Virginia Commonwealth University, Richmond, Virginia, 25 March 1977. It was later published in different form as "The Structural Unity of *Beowulf:* The Problem of Grendel's Mother," in *Texas Studies in Literature and Language* 22 (1980): 287–303. Permission has been granted by the University of Texas Press and by *Allegorica* to reprint the two previously published articles in altered form.

The translations throughout are my own, unless otherwise indicated; their bald literalness sacrifices grace of expression for fidelity to the poet's meaning, an admittedly heinous stylistic fault that I hope will be forgiven in the higher interest of clarity.

Houston, Texas   JANE CHANCE
March 1985

Introduction

Næs ða dead þa gyt,
ealles orsawle; sloh ða eornoste
ides ellenrof oðre siðe
þone hæðenan hund, þæt him þæt heafod wand
forð on ða flore.—*Judith*, 107–11a.[1]

⌐T⌐HE TERM *"ides ellenrof"* means "exceedingly brave or powerful woman" and in the lines cited above refers to the heroic Judith at the moment she cuts off the head of the "heathen hound" Holofernes, in the Old English version of the Apocryphal Old Testament Book of Judith. An unusual conjunction of the word *ides* (normally reserved for more ordinary aristocratic women) and *ellenrof* (normally reserved for warriors found in *Waldere, Andreas, Juliana,* and *Exodus*), this epithet provides the impetus for this study of heroic women in Old English literature.

It is by now a commonplace that Germanic heroic diction and imagery color even the most religious of Anglo-Saxon poems: Christ or Saint Andreas as a warrior battles against evil adversaries in the same *comitatus* terms in which epic heroical poems depict the clash of armies. The most brilliant example of such depiction occurs perhaps in *The Dream of the Rood,* in which the Cross views himself as a retainer of Christ committed to serving him valorously but ironically by remaining strong during the Crucifixion. What is less apparent is that such diction and imagery predominate in poems focusing on women—poems like the saints' lives; the biblical poems *Genesis B,* the *Advent Lyrics,* and the apocryphal *Judith;* the Cynewulfian poems *Juliana* and *Elene;* the elegies *Wulf and Eadwacer* and *The Wife's Lament.* The application of heroic images to women also occurs in other poems that do not at first glance exclusively focus on women, like the gnomic poems, the riddles, and *Beowulf.* Given the relative paucity of extant literature from the Anglo-Saxon period, these works featuring major woman characters seem many in number. What startles even more is the strength of the female characterization, given the literary social ideal of the aristocratic woman as primarily a passive, peaceful, and colorless addition to society. Such an ideal does not accord with several recent historical studies of the role of women in the Anglo-Saxon period that have concluded that such women were more masterful and independent than their post-Norman conquest counterparts.[2] The task of this study, then, is to examine freshly the sources and to ask new questions about the appearance of women in the literature of the period.

Many of these women are portrayed as heroic figures, either in terms of the Germanic *comitatus* tradition of retainers in relation to their lord or the Christian tradition of the warrior of God. However, those portrayed as Germanic are treated pejoratively because passivity rather than heroism generally epitomized the ideal Anglo-Saxon woman—a peacemaker and mother. This study argues that the primary conventional secular role of Anglo-Saxon woman demanded her passivity and peacemaking talent, an ideal perfectly fulfilled in the social and religious archetype of the Virgin Mary (who represented all ages of, and roles available to, Anglo-Saxon women). While there were very many nearly-ideal Anglo-Saxon wives and queens who attempted to weave peace but who failed because of external (political) factors, they were not castigated for their failure; only those women who failed because of internal (psychological) factors—and failed by deliberately inverting the passive ideal—were blamed by others or themselves. Frequently, they were identified as lascivious, heathen, and rebellious—hence modeled upon Eve. These two social roles of woman, typified by the biblical contrast between Eva/Ave, find literary expression in Anglo-Saxon characters who range from the failed, possibly adulterous women of *The Wife's Lament* and *Wulf and Eadwacer*, and the monstrous mother of Grendel in *Beowulf* modeled on Eva, to the chaste (but heroic) figures and saints Judith, Juliana, and Elene modeled on Ave. What is interesting is the way in which Anglo-Saxon poets explain the secular and religious ideal for woman by using both Germanic and Christian images and concepts.

This study attempts a comprehensive examination of all the major appearances of women in all genres of Anglo-Saxon literature, from the chronicle to the epic. It focuses, however, on the types of the heroic woman figure, with only a brief look at the conventional ideal of the peacemaking woman to provide a context for the later discussion. By contrast, most of the recent literary studies have either delineated or emphasized only this social ideal, with general literary articles defining, surveying, and classifying examples of female characterization,[3] and less specialized literary studies focusing on women in single poems.[4]

Chapter 1 defines the secular convention of the peacemaker by examining its appearance in early works like Tacitus' Latin *Germania* and the Anglo-Saxon gnomic and moralistic poems, with some attention to minor references in other works of literature. The conventional image depends in part upon the peacemaking and peace-weaving role of the aristocratic woman, or *ides*, and the more common-born but similarly faithful mate, such as the Frisian wife. In marital unions involving both types, there is an underlying bond between man and woman which resembles the bond of loyalty between lord and retainer and which is predicated on the reward of treasure for valor and faithfulness.

Chapter 2 defines the Anglo-Saxon secular and ecclesiastical ideal for women. The virgin mother Mary in *Christ I* ideally fulfills all of the roles normally available to women—young girl, virgin, bride, and mother—and ultimately triumphs as the Queen of hosts, the Church herself. However, even in this role she assumes a guise relevant to Anglo-Saxon society; she is the "bracelet-adorned bride" whose bold thinking propels her to become the spouse of God. These varied roles thus unify the twelve apparently disparate lyrics of *Christ I* through the formal principle of variation.

Chapter 3 presents other biblical and patristic role models for Anglo-Saxon women, all types of Mary. The protagonists of the religious epics—Juliana, Judith, and Elene—exemplify degrees of chastity from pure virginity (Juliana) to chaste widowhood (Judith) and chaste conjugality (Elene). Each illustrates heroic behavior through sanctity, whether as a figure of the soul or *anima* battling vices, as a type of Christ or of God *(miles Christi* or *Dei)* battling the Devil, or as a figure of the Church *(Ecclesia)* battling its enemies. All three roles together suggest the three levels of allegory—tropological, allegorical, and anagogical.

Chapter 4 examines hagiographical and historical examples of administrators, rulers, teachers, and politically active women. The exceptional queens who embodied such examples were touted and beatified for singular continence or chastity (in some cases despite marriage) and for great piety. The latter group was permitted an active political role in kingdoms as chaste rulers or strong abbesses, and some became saints who were even allowed to adopt heroic behavior (even masculine clothing) once their chastity and sanctity had been attested. The remainder of the chapter investigates theological and patristic explanations for the existence of these two extremes which associate the chaste and pious woman with masculine rationality and the irreligious and lascivious queen as descendant of Eve with feminine concupiscence and the Devil. Most queens who embodied such examples were castigated for a lack of chastity and Christianity in their usurpation of power.

Chapter 5 examines the equation drawn in the previous chapter between rebelliousness and concupiscence as explained through the character of Eve in *Genesis B*. Depicted as a virgin who, like the Virgin Mary, is visited by an angelic messenger, Eve nevertheless differs from Mary in her disobedience to God. Eve's disobedience finds an Anglo-Saxon as well as a theological correlative: she is portrayed additionally as the peace-weaver who usurps her husband's role out of anxiety to maintain peace, in this case between Adam and the Lord. The poet is careful to use heroic diction and imagery throughout to pinpoint Eve's fall in contemporary Anglo-Saxon terms.

The next two chapters turn to appearances of women in the major secular works as types of Eve. Chapter 6 examines the elegies *Wulf and Eadwacer* and *The Wife's Lament*, which portray two Anglo-Saxon women posed in the roles of the masculine *scop* to sing a song of lament, their grief caused by men who have abandoned or punished them. The imagery and diction used throughout is that of the minstrel, and the metaphors found therein that explain their situations belong to the tradition of the *scop* at court as seen in *Widsith* and *Deor*. Although both figures may have involuntarily failed as types of the Anglo-Saxon woman peace-weaver, the use of the *scop* image and role, and similarly heroic masculine behavior to convey the image and role, becomes ultimately ironic.

The seventh and last chapter, on *Beowulf*, explains the puzzling structure of the secular epic by examining the role of Grendel's Mother in the middle section of the poem. Grendel's Mother monstrously inverts the image of the Anglo-Saxon queen because she behaves in a heroic and masculine way. She thus serves as a foil for other failed women, like Thryth, and contrasts with more positive images of women, like Wealhtheow and Freawaru, all of whom appear primarily in the middle section of the poem dominated by the female monster. She also resembles the politically active but socially and morally castigated queens of the chronicles and legendary histories discussed in the second chapter, exceptions to the ideal of the conventional peacemaker. These exceptions are explained by Eve, who in *Genesis B* failed God and her husband by eating the apple and thus, as an Anglo-Saxon peacemaker anxious to maintain peace between Adam and God, usurps her husband's role as decision-making retainer. So also in *Beowulf*, Grendel's Mother functions as a type of Eve. Further, in her arrogation of a masculine role, she is linked with the speakers of *Wulf and Eadwacer* and *The Wife's Lament* who as *scopas* sang a song of failure at peacemaking. But in her parody of the role of the Virgin Mary in her vengeful mission over the loss of her son, she also monstrously inverts an image regarded by the Anglo-Saxons as a religious ideal.

In summary, the definition of that conventional peacemaker described by the early Tacitus and the gnomic poems and displayed in wills, writs, charters, chronicles, and legendary histories is reflected in the more positive social images of *Beowulf*. They find their role model in the Virgin Mary of *Christ I*, who ideally fulfills all of the roles available to women. But in *Beowulf*, the peacemaking queens invariably suffer disaster and tragedy, if not torture and rape like Juliana and other chaste saints. And bellicose females like Thryth and Grendel's Mother—failures like the female narrators of *The Wife's Lament* and *Wulf and Eadwacer*—seem to represent the same type as Eve in *Genesis B*. The *Beowulf*-Poet perhaps agrees that a female protagonist can avert horrible consequences for her warlike behavior only when she functions as a heroic emblem of the Church or like the warrior of Christ battling the Devil—like Judith, Juliana, and Elene in the religious epics.

There were thus two archetypes of women that ordered the Anglo-Saxon social world. Both figures were drawn from the Bible; their depiction was colored by Germanic heroic imagery and values—Eve as overly-aggressive retainer, and Mary as the perfect maiden, wife, mother—and heroic and militant Ecclesia figure. With these two contrasting types were grouped various literary characters, historical figures, and saints. What they shared, however, was in some way, literally or figuratively, heroic behavior. And yet, clearly, feminine heroism was not countenanced by Anglo-Saxon society. This study of *ides ellenrof* begins with a definition of this feminine social—non-heroic—ideal.

Peace-Weaver, Peace Pledge

The Conventional Queen and Ides

T HE ANGLO-SAXON SOCIAL IDEAL of the aristocratic woman, or *ides*, depended upon her role as a peacemaking queen, which was achieved fundamentally through her function as a mother. Child-bearing became a specific means of making peace between two tribes by literally mingling their blood; because of this political function, the aristocratic woman was often termed a "peace-pledge" or *friðusibb*. Socially, within the tribe, the female mead-bearer's passing of the mead-cup first to the most noble warrior and then to other members of the *duguð* and *geoguð* formed a more ritualistic and symbolic way of making peace, similar to her role of giving gifts to valued members of the tribe, and was in part responsible for the epithet "peace-weaver," *freoðuwebbe*. Finally, the *ides* manifested personal qualities characteristic of the peacemaker: in addition to being cheerful in dealing with others, she was also close-mouthed, loving, loyal, and most of all, wise. Common-born wives perhaps played a less significant social and political role, but they too inculcated what might be termed *comitatus* values, much diluted—that is, they were required to be faithful, as a retainer was faithful to his lord, and chaste. These definitions of the *ides* role can be found in the gnomic poems, or maxims, or in isolated references in the literature of the period, and are derived from Germanic concepts similar to those enunciated in Tacitus' *Germania*.

The word *ides* common to Old English and to West Germanic (possibly even Germanic) probably meant "noble woman, lady," rather than merely a woman: in the Old English *Genesis* it appears for Eve (896), for the wives of Cain and Lamech (1054 and 1076), for Sarah and for Hagar, her Egyptian handmaid (1728), and for the women of Sodom and Gomorrah who are described as "monig/blachleor ides" ("many a pale-faced

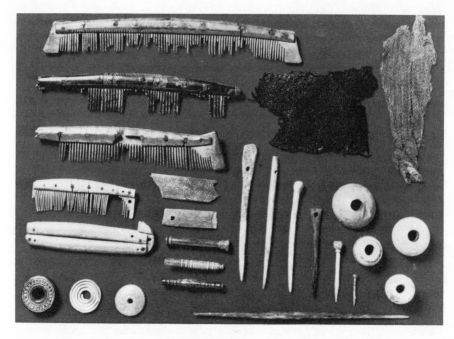

The Anglo-Saxon peace-weaver's implements: spindle whorls, sewing needles, dress pins, woolen textile fragments, and antler and bone combs. Tenth century, taken from the Coppergate Excavations at York. Photo by Mike S. Duffy, York Archaeological Trust.

lady") to show their sadness when being led to rape and ravishment (1969b–72b).[1] In these references, Eve, Cain's wife, and Hagar are also described as *freolecu mæg*, "noble woman," with Hagar termed so by Sarah when she wants Abraham to beget an heir upon her. In *Beowulf* the word is applied to the queens Wealhtheow (620, 1168, and 1649) and Hildeburh (1075, 1117), as well as to Offa's wife Thryth who later became a good queen, even though she was not when she married him (1941).[2] While earlier West Germanic usages of the word may have held prophetic or holy connotations,[3] by the seventh or eighth centuries *ides* probably had diminished to "important or noble woman," as in the examples from *Genesis* which can be construed as neither holy nor prophetic. Additionally, the word appears in two other contexts which reduce its complimentary connotations even further. In the Riddle following 75, *ides* appears in a single line, "Ic ane geseah idese sittan," literally, "I saw a woman sitting alone," but because it may be appended to Riddle 75, which lists "elk" *(eolk)* as its solution, it is possible that it refers to a female elk and not to a noble woman at all.[4] Further, as we shall see in the last chapter of this study, *ides* is also used ironically to describe the monstrous "woman," Grendel's Mother in *Beowulf.*

The *ides'* chief role was to effect peace between two tribes through marriage and children. Thus the phrase *friðusibb,* or "protecting peace," "peace pledge," translates Grein-Wülker's Latin terms *tutela pacis, tutela pacifica,* in Bosworth-Toller's *Anglo-Saxon Dictionary,* and refers specifically to the queen Wealhtheow as the protecting peace of nations, *friðusibb folca,* in *Beowulf* 2017, who as wife of Hrothgar and queen of the Danes united the Danes with the Helmings. In the same poem, although Hildeburh is not called by that epithet, she similarly (at least initially) unites the Danes and Frisians; Freawaru too plans to pledge peace between the Danes and Heathobards. Peace as an ideal must have been strong within a society for which war remained a constant threat.[5] Indeed, there exist five columns of compounds beginning with *freoðu-, freoðo-, frið-,* or *friðu-,* in Bosworth-Toller. Frequently, of course, such a peace mission failed because of the childlessness of the wife or the death of her children. This loss concealed a double grief, that of the mother for her child and, more symbolically, that of the peace pledge for her own failure. Hildeburh lamenting her son's death in *Beowulf* provides one example, but there are frequent allusions to grieving mothers elsewhere, as in *The Fortunes of Men* in *The Exeter Book,* in which "weeps the woman, who sees the brands enfold her child" ("reoteð meowle, / seo hyre bearn gesihð brondas þeccan," 46b–7).

Even within her tribe the noble woman was required to maintain peace just as her noble husband was required to further battle. According to *Maxims I,* the most important and straightforward definition of the role of the *ides,*

> War, battle, must grow
> in the earl, and the wife must thrive,
> beloved among her people, must be light-hearted.

> (Guð sceal in eorle,
> wig geweaxan, ond wif geþeon
> leof mid hyre leodum, leohtmod wesan. 83b–5)

Her ways of achieving this goal within the tribe were several: she might serve as wise counselor, all the time being close-mouthed about the counsel ("him ræd witan / boldagendum bæm ætsomne," 91b-2, and "rune healdan," 86a); she might be "rum-hearted" with horses and treasures in rewarding the valiant men of the tribe ("rumheort beon / mearum ond maþmum," 86b–7a); and finally, she might distinguish among the men of the tribe by first presenting the lord with mead and then passing the cup to the ranking members of the *duguð*, or old retainers, and the *geoguð*, or young retainers, as does Wealhtheow in *Beowulf* and also the ideal consort described in *Maxims I*. She must

> . . . in mead-state
> before the band of warriors   everywhere at all times
> the lord of the nobles   greet first,
> the first cups   to the lord's hand
> the mead-bearer present.

> (. . . meodorædenne
> for gesiðmægen   symle æghwær
> eodor æþelinga   ærest gegretan.
> forman fulle   to frean hond
> ricene geræcan. 87b-91a)

Finally, she exemplified peace and peacemaking in her character. The lightheartedness of the queen, for which she was beloved by her people, would be manifested by an aristocratic woman whatever her social and political role. All three of these roles of the *ides* are epitomized in the label of *freoðuwebbe*, or peace-weaver. This word describes Ealhhild, the "faithful peace-weaver" who sought the home of the Gothic king Eormanric, "the savage faithless one," in *Widsith* (line 6) and who was eventually murdered by him, and also, ironically, Thryth in *Beowulf* (1942), who herself murdered those suitors who stared at her too insistently. The *Beowulf*-poet interjects into the Thryth digression that "such a custom is not queenly for a woman to perform, though she be beautiful, that the peace-weaver after a pretended injury deprive the dear man of life":

> Ne bið swylc cwēnlic þēaw
> idese tō efnanne,   þēah ðe hīo ænlicu sȳ,
> þætte *freoðuwebbe*   fēores onsæce
> æfter ligetorne   lēofne mannan. (1940b–43)

The peacemaking function of woman, here invoked ironically by terming Thryth a "peace-weaver," or *freoðuwebbe*, is appropriately denoted by the concept of "weaving." The Anglo-Saxons were acquainted with advanced methods of weaving involving the use of the shuttle, the shedding operation, and the toothed batten, as evidenced by three Old English riddles (35, "Battle Shirt," 56, "Web in the Loom," and 70, "Shuttle").[6] The significance of such a knowledge deepens an understanding of woman's role as peace-weaver through her lightheartedness, gentleness, and possibly that constructive eloquence used in counseling. For, the shuttle, which probably replaced the needle very early, makes a singing as it (or the warp-threads) sounds, described by the ancients as *sono* or *strido;* for this reason, "because of their similarity loom and lyre were closely associated in the minds of the ancients."[7] Thus the peace-weaver might also be termed a singer of peace in her "weaving." Such poetic transfer explains the laments of the women in *The Wife's Lament* and *Wulf and Eadwacer* who, as we shall later discover, adopt the role of a *scop* in singing of their failures as peace-weavers. However, the term "peace-weaver" is not always used to designate a woman; in *Elene* (88), *friðowebba* describes an angel as *pacis tector:* he "up locade,   swa him se ar abead, / fæle *friðowebbe*" ("he looked up as the messenger, faithful peace-weaver, bade him").[8] The secular role of "weaving" peace—here the idea of the creative loom-working activity is conjoined with the abstract quality—analogizes the heavenly function of the angel as intermediary between man and God, just as woman acts as intermediary, at least politically and socially, between tribe and tribe, retainer and lord, or individual to individual.

Her bond with her husband as well as with the warriors of her tribe was expressed symbolically through the giving of treasure, not only during hall-ceremonies when mead was poured as we have already seen, but also initially when she was "bought" as a bride. *Maxims I* (lines 81–3) notes that, "A king must with goods buy a queen, with beakers and bracelets; both must first be liberal with gifts":

> Cyning sceal mid ceape   cwene gebicgan
> bunum ond beagum;   bu sceolon ærest
> geofum god wesan.

Later, in lines 125–31, *Maxims I* re-emphasizes as appropriate the use of gold on the man's sword and rare fabric and treasure, like bracelets, for the *cwen* or the *bryd* (it also mentions as gifts the shield for the warrior; books for the scholar; the host for the holy man; and sins for the heathen). Such gifts of treasure reinforced that bond between king and queen analogous to that between king and retainers and between queen and retainers. The bond between lord and *duguð* was predicated upon valor in battle and loyalty provided by the retainers and rewards of treasure and wise protection provided by the lord, as Tacitus' first-century *Germania* attests,[9] and the bond between queen and *duguð* was predicated upon the maintenance of peace in the hall and within the tribe by the retainers, and rewards of treasure and peacemaking by the queen. Between king and queen there must have existed a similar *comitatus* bond: he rewarded her with treasure for her peacemaking and wise counsel and for her loyalty to him.

That such a bond was at least vestigially heroic in character is made clear by the Germanic origins of the Anglo-Saxon dowry. In Chapter 18 of Tacitus' *Germania*, the husband offers to his wife oxen, horses, shields, and spears, symbolic of the heroic life in which she is expected to share:

> A woman must not imagine herself free to neglect the manly virtues or immune from the hazards of war. That is why she is reminded, in the very ceremonies which bless her marriage at its outset, that she is coming to share a man's toils and dangers, that she is to be his partner in all his sufferings and adventures, whether in peace or war. That is the meaning of the team of oxen, of the horse ready for its rider, of the gift of arms. On these terms she must live her life and bear her children. She is receiving something that she must hand over unspoilt and treasured to her children, for her sons' wives to receive in their turn and pass on to the grandchildren.

> (Ne se mulier extra uirtutum cogitationes extraque bellorum casus putet, ipsis incipientis matrimonii auspiciis admonetur uenire se laborum periculorumque sociam, idem in pace, idem in proelio passuram ausuramque: hoc iuncti boues, hoc paratus equus, hoc data arma denuntiant. Sic uiuendum, sic pariendum: accipere se quae liberis inuiolata ac digna reddat, quae nurus accipiant rursusque ad nepotes referantur. Pp. 294–95)

This very interesting heroic expectation by a Germanic husband is rarely echoed in Old English literature, with the exception perhaps of Hildegund's exhortation to battle in the fragmentary epic *Waldhere* (ca. 750). Even this famous plea for Waldhere to wield in battle the "work of Weland," the "choicest of treasures," is offered not by his wife but by his lover. Similarly, in the *Germania* men at battle are incited to greater valor by the laments and wailing of their nearby wives and children who later apply bandages to their battle wounds and give their men "food and encouragement" (Chapter 7).

But the *ides* is not herself expected to be valorous in battle, as we have seen, which frequently makes her a victim of marauding tribes in Anglo-Saxon society and the literature belonging to that period. *Genesis A* speaks of the four kings who sought Sodom and Gomorrah, when "Many a pale-cheeked woman must go forth trembling to a stranger's breast; the defenders of brides and bracelets fell, sick with wounds":

> Sceolde forht monig
> blachleor ides bifiende gan
> on fremdes fæðm; feollon wergend
> bryda and beaga, bennum seoce. (1969b–72)

In this reference it is significant that the fallen lords who should be protecting their wives from assault are termed "defenders of brides and bracelets," "wergend / bryda and beaga," as if to underscore ironically their heroic and contractual failure (this Old English rendition of a biblical poem also uses other *comitatus* metaphors in describing the angels as *þegnas* and their band as *þeoden*, in line 15). A much later reference, in Wulfstan's *Sermon to the English,* describes a man being forced to look on as his wife or daughter is raped; Wulfstan's call to virtue for Doomsday's sake conceals an implicit Germanic call to valor and defense of the passive and weak woman he should protect.

The *ides* must be not only passive and peacemaking, but usually also chaste and often holy, qualities that compelled her husband to keep her from assault by marauders. In the *Germania,* women used this vulnerability and their husbands' fears concerning that vulnerability to encourage their men to fight more fiercely (Chapter 8).

It stands on record that armies wavering on the point of collapse have been restored by the women. They have pleaded heroically with their men, thrusting their bosoms before them and forcing them to realize the imminent prospect of their enslavement—a fate which they fear more desperately for their women than for themselves. It is even found that you can secure a surer hold on a state if you demand among the hostages girls of noble family. More than this, they believe that there resides in women an element of holiness and prophecy, and so they do not scorn to ask their advice or lightly disregard their replies.

(Memoriae proditur quasdam acies inclinatas iam et labantes a feminis restitutas constantia precum et obiectu pectorum et monstrata comminus captiuitate, quam longe impatientius feminarum suarum nomine timent, adeo ut efficacius obligentur animi ciuitatum quibus inter obsides puellae quoque nobiles imperantur. Inesse quin etiam sanctum aliquid et prouidum putant, nec aut consilia earum asper- nantur aut responsa neglegunt. P. 284)

The chastity of an *ides* was threatened not only by the desires of her tribe's enemies but also by her own desires; unbecoming conduct, to say nothing of adultery, led to censure if not disgrace. *Maxims I* (lines 63–5) warns that "a woman must remain at her table; a wandering woman makes words spring up, often she makes light of a man with her sins, a man speaks of her contemptuously, often unsettles her cheek":

> Fæmne æt hyre bordan geriseð;
> widgongel wif word gespringeð,   oft hy mon wommum bilihð,
> hæleð hy hospe mænað,   oft hyre hleor abreoþeð.

In *Maxims II* (lines 43b–5a), in Ms. Cotton Tiberius B.i, a puzzling admonition advises that "a woman must visit her lover discreetly if she does not want people to think that one buys her with gifts":

> Ides sceal dyrne cræfte,
> fæmne hire freond gesecean,   gif heo nelle on folce geþeon
> þæt hi man beagum gebicge.[10]

The final half-line, "þæt hi man beagum gebicge," "that one buys her with gifts," can mean that she does not wish to bring it about among the people that she should be married and therefore she must seek out for herself a lover by "dyrne cræfte," "secret means"; or it can mean that she may be married, even if she is not of good reputation among the people, if she finds a lover for herself by means of magic; or, and this is perhaps the clearest of the three possibilities, it can mean that she may be regarded as a prostitute if she does not visit her lover discreetly.[11] Whatever the exact meaning, an *ides* must not sully her reputation or her chastity. In the *Germania* (Chapter 19), Tacitus notes that a husband was permitted to punish a wife's infraction by shaving off her hair, stripping her, sending her from his house, and flogging her through the village. Tacitus con- cludes that wives "must not love the husband so much as the married state" ("ne tamquam maritum sed tamquam matrimonium ament," p. 296). Despite these harsh rules and stern admonitions, the *ides* did not always remain chaste within or outside of marriage. Possibly adulterous behavior is described in the two elegies *The Wife's Lament* and *Wulf and Eadwacer*, even if not strictly voluntary (in the latter poem, a wife or lover is imprisoned and made love to by another man). And the many obscene riddles in Anglo-Saxon challenge the idea of the chastity of women: in these humorous poems with double entendres, women often exhibit great sexual pleasure, especially in "Onion" (25), "Dough" (45), "Key" or "Key-hole" (91), and many others.[12]

The value of chastity and the concept of loyalty to mate that supported it were also witnessed in more common-born women. The famous "Frisian Wife" passage in *Maxims I* defines the ideal wife welcoming home her seafarer-husband; she washes his clothes and virtuously keeps his faith, both activities which ensure cleanliness and purity:

> The dear one is welcome
> to the Frisian wife,   when the ship stands at rest;
> his vessel has come   and her man is home,
> her own food-giver,   and she invites him in,
> washes his garment stained with sea-weed   and gives him new
>   ones,
> pleasant it is for him on land   whom his love constrains.
> A woman shall with her man hold a compact,   often she makes light
>   of a man with vices,
> many a one is more steadfast in mind,   many a one is more curious,
> she makes froth with strange men,   when the other travels afar.

> (. . . leof wilcuma
> Frysan wife,   þonne flota stondeð;
> biþ his ceol cumen   ond hyre ceorl to ham,
> agen ætgeofa,   ond heo hine in laðaþ,
> wæsceð his warig hrægl   ond him syleþ wæde niwe,
> liþ him on londe   þæs his lufu bædeð.
> Wif sceal wiþ wer wære gehealdan,   oft hi mon wommum beliho;
> fela bið fæsthydigra,   fela bið fyrwetgeornra,
> freoð hy fremde monnan,   þonne se oþer feor gewiteð. 94b–102)

The caring for the seafarer's physical needs parallels the care of the house, hearth, and fields delegated to women, old men, and weaklings in the *Germania* (Chapter 15).

Few other references to common-born women exist in Anglo-Saxon literature except for very general references to the necessity of women to bear and raise children, although these responsibilities are actually listed in *Maxims I* and *The Fortunes of Men* as those of both man and woman.

Maxims I (lines 23b–5a) declares simply that "Two are mates; a woman and a man must bring into the world a child by birth" ("Tu beoð gemæccan; / sceal wif ond wer   in woruld cennan / bearn mid gebyrdum." *The Fortunes of Men*, which twice mentions women mourning at the pyres of their sons, prefaces the list of fates of men with a long description of a man and a woman bringing forth a child into the world, dressing, training, and caressing him, feeding, adorning, and bestowing gifts upon him, only to leave him to "hwæt him weaxendum   winter bringað" (9). Presumably a woman of lower class would be responsible for fewer and simpler duties than her aristocratic sister—child-rearing, cloth-making, cooking and cleaning, and then the more important and abstract duties to her husband, such as virtuousness, chastity, and fidelity.

Virtue—in a Germanic and secular sense and not necessarily in a Christian and religious sense—pervades the various definitions and descriptions of the Anglo-Saxon woman. She remains a loyal, generous, wise, loving, and cheerful peacemaker, a personification of secular virtue partly because her physical and spiritual demeanor reflects on the man who has bought her with his treasures. She shares both in the loyalty of the retainer to his lord and the generosity and wisdom of the lord to his followers. However, unlike a retainer or lord, she is also passive and loving.

Unfortunately, women who fulfill this ideal role in Anglo-Saxon literature are usually depicted as doomed and tragic figures, frequently seen as weeping or suffering—we think of Hildeburh bemoaning the loss of her son and her brother, torn between the pulls of two tribes; of the Geat woman mourning the hero's loss at the end of *Beowulf;* of the unfortunate Ealhhild in *Widsith* who is executed by her husband Eormanric only for being loyal and generous to him; of Beadohild in *Deor,* who is both raped and impregnated and whose brothers are killed by the smith Weland, their skulls made into decorative objects; of the moaning Mæthhild who suffers for love of Geat in the same poem; of the Wife in *The Wife's Lament* and the anonymous woman of *Wulf and Eadwacer* who voice to the wind their complaints of tyrannous consorts or lovers. It appears that the very passivity of the bride and peace pledge leads inexorably to disaster, both in Anglo-Saxon and in Germanic literature.

> Women frequently play a central role in Germanic heroic song: The Burgundian Guðrun, the Gothic Swanhild, the Frankish Brunhild, Hildeburh in the Finn story, the un-named wife in the Ingeld lay, and many more. Not that they are important as women; but they are, by their marriage or other association with a man, the link between two clans, and thus help to spark off the trouble.[13]

But in addition, women represent perfect foils for the masculine heroes who suffer the conflicting demands of Germanic valor—*comitatus* values—and of Christian virtue. To be a peace pledge, for the Anglo-Saxon poet, emblematized the tension between passivity and aggression, between social and antisocial behavior, between passion and reason (in that only women, according to Tacitus, openly wept); and ultimately, within more Christian contexts, that is, between the values of this world and the next, if peace is understood in an earthly and an otherworldly sense. While peace was not possible continually in this world, whatever the actions of the peace pledge and peace-weaver, because of its fallen nature, Anglo-Saxon woman nevertheless modeled herself upon the ideal exemplar of the Virgin Mary, the epitome of both secular and ecclesiastical perfection, as we shall see in the next chapter.

2

The Virgin Mary of *Christ I* as Secular and Ecclesiastical Feminine Ideal

T HREE MAJOR BIBLICAL MODELS for the Anglo-Saxon woman existed in the figures of Eve, the Virgin Mary, and Judith, the last taken from the Apocryphal book of the Old Testament with the same name. Each contributed to and was assimilated into the literary culture in a slightly different way, although each was also linked, implicitly and explicitly, to the other, especially in the patristic writings of the early centuries after Christ's death. According to the latter, in giving birth to Christ the Virgin ameliorated the curse placed upon Eve after the Fall. Such writings explicitly contrasted Mary and Eve as virgins, making virginity the highest feminine theological virtue. Saint Jerome accordingly draws a portrait of a family of angels on earth whose kinship depends on the virtue of chastity:

> Death through Eve: life through Mary. And so too the richer gift of virginity flowed to women, because it began from a woman. As soon as the Son of God descended upon the earth, He instituted a new family for Himself so that He who was adored by angels in heaven might also have angels on earth. Then it was that the continent [*continens*] Judith cut off the head of Holofernes.[1]

Although both Eve and Mary were wives and mothers (with Judith herself merely a chaste widow in the Apocrypha), they were both linked by the patristic commentators through their virginity. For example, Saint Cyril of Jerusalem notes that, "since through Eve, a virgin, came death, it behoved that through the Virgin, or rather from a virgin, should life

The Virgin with Child, from the eighth- to ninth-century *Book of Kells*, fol. 7v. The interlace pattern in the border underscores her signification as archetypal peace-weaver. Photo permission of the Board of Trinity College, Dublin.

appear."[2] Saint Irenaeus (A.D. 120–200) also remarks that the virgin Eve's disobedience is rectified by the Virgin Mary's obedience.[3] To this parallel others were added: both women were originally innocent and holy; both were espoused; both listened to the words of angels, the Tempter and Gabriel; both cooperated with man, fallen Adam and the Divine Son; both became mothers. Eventually the Virgin Mary was typified as a Second Eve, a typology so widespread that it was adopted by the three patriarchates of Rome, Alexandria, and Antioch and also many other commentators.[4] As an exemplar for women, the Virgin Mary offered a model of chaste behavior. Origen in his commentary on Luke notes that, "and in the same way that sin began from a woman, and finally came around even to man: thus the beginning of salvation had its origin from women, so that the rest of women, putting aside the fragility of their sex, might imitate the life and conversation of these blessed women."[5] The perpetual virginity of Mary in particular attracted those women who had relinquished marriage and motherhood for the Church.

The Virgin Mary played a prominent role in Anglo-Saxon England; indeed, the importance of any female saint in England depended in part on her literary and religious relationship with the Virgin.[6] In Anglo-Latin and Anglo-Saxon literature the two women occasionally appear in tandem. *De virginitate*, written by Aldhelm in 680, cites Mary as the Second Eve who fulfills many of the normal roles of woman.[7] The second part of *Christ and Satan*, on the Harrowing of Hell, introduces an apocalyptic Eve who confesses she angered God by eating the apple in a misguided attempt to find happiness, a holy dwelling, and the possession of heaven; now she prays for mercy from God by mentioning the imprisonment of Satan in Hell and by reminding Him that He was brought into the world through her daughter Mary to aid men.[8] The late tenth-century *Blickling Homily* entitled *Annunciatio S. Mariae* compares the two women in particular through their conception of children and childbirth:

> Eve conceived through carnal lust, Mary in her womb conceived the merciful and the innocent Christ. Eve bore tears in her womb, Mary brought forth through herself the everlasting joy for all the world, Eve brought forth her child in pain because she had conceived in sin. The Holy Ghost sowed the pure seed in the undefiled womb (of Mary), wherefore she, being a virgin became a mother, because, being a virgin, she had conceived.

> (Eua cende þurh firenlust. Maria cende þone mildheortan & þone un-sceþþendan Christ on hire innoþe; Eua bær tearas on hire innoþe. Maria brohte þurh heo þone ecean gefean eallum middangearde; Eua

cende hire bearn on sare; forþon þe heo on synnum ge eacnod wæs.
Se Halga Gast seow þæt clæne sæd on þone unbesmitenan innoþ;
forþon heo fæmne cende, forðon heo wæs fæmne geeacnod.)9

The most famous and interesting Old English depictions of Mary
and Eve, however, occur in *Christ I* (or the *Advent Lyrics*) and *Genesis B*,
even though the women do not both appear together as characters. *Christ
I* as the first of three individual parts of the Exeter Book *Christ* covers the
Annunciation of Christ during the season of Advent and thus was probably
written by a different poet than that of the other two parts, on the
Ascension and Doomsday. *Genesis B* represents a medial segment (235–
851) of the 2935-line poem of *Genesis* that differs from the longer adaptation of portions of the book of Genesis (continuing past the sacrifice of
Isaac) in that *Genesis B* focuses only on the fall of the angels and the
temptation and fall of man and in that it is based on an Old Saxon
original.10 From *Christ I* comes the many-faceted figure of the Virgin
Mary, who will be discussed in this chapter, leaving the problematic
character of Eve to be discussed in a later chapter. Both poems con-
sciously, if only implicitly in the case of *Genesis B*, draw upon patristic
contrasts between the two women to inform the characterization of their
female heroes and thus to enhance the imagery and structural unity of the
poems.

Christ I is comprised of twelve lyrics or lyrical poems based on the
Church antiphons for Advent, each of which begins with an "O" in Latin
or "Eala" in Old English. Scholars have generally agreed that its poet was
different from that of the other two books of the Exeter Book *Christ*,
Christ II on the Ascension (adapted from a homily by Pope Gregory the
Great), written by Cynewulf, and *Christ III* on Doomsday, by an anonymous poet. However, despite its separateness from the other two parts of
Christ, because it consists of twelve lyrics based on different Advent
antiphons its unity as a single work has been debated: are the individual
poems lyrics at all, do they form a unified and cohesive sequence, or must
each be examined individually, and of course how closely does each
adhere to its Antiphon source—how original is each?11

Even though various editions of the *Advent Lyrics* have been published,12 individual lyrics have received little critical attention, with the
exception of Poem 7, "Eala ioseph min," a dialogue between Mary and
Joseph that has posed a considerable problem for readers because of the
difficulty of attributing lines to the principal speakers.13 But when the
lyrics are examined closely for links with one another, a thematic and
structural variation of subjects emerges. Of the twelve, each mentions

either Christ or the Virgin Mother almost in a pattern of variation; further, many of the lyrics are based on metaphors for Christ or the Virgin derived from the Old rather than the New Testament, indicating the necessity for a typological reading and underscoring the time of the sequence, at the Advent of Christ (and hence the moment history shifted from the "old" to the "new," with all the implications that follow from that contrast). The first lyric portrays Christ as a temple, the second manifests Christ as a key and introduces his mother as a young maiden. In the third, her image looms behind the Holy Jerusalem described as a Virgin Dwelling for Christ, and in the fourth she emerges as the Virgin Mother. Following the fifth and sixth, which respectively praise Christ as "Eala earendel," the sun and the star, and as "Emmanuel," O God of Souls, Poem 7 returns to Mary with Joseph confronting her as the Virgin Spouse in "Eala ioseph min," that cryptic antecedent of many medieval dramas. Poem 8 describes Christ as a child, followed by Poem 9 which presents Mary as Bride of Christ (anticipated by Isaiah as the Door of Life). After the petition to the Lord in Poem 10 and the discussion of the Trinity in Poem 11, Poem 12 proceeds with its appeals to both Christ and the Virgin as they are invoked for help to mankind.

No previous critical study of *Christ I* has focused on Mary in particular or identified the variations in her image as keys to the unity of the lyrics.[14] In addition, considering only those lyrics dominated by Mary, variation among her images occurs. In Poem 2, the Virgin appears in all of her possible roles, as a young girl or *seo fæmne geong*, as a maiden or a *mægð*, a mother or *meder*, a bride or *bryd*, all significant images of the Anglo-Saxon *wif* which will be developed individually in the respective later lyrics in which she appears. Thus in Poem 3 Mary is typified as Jerusalem (also a type of Paradise). In Poem 4 she represents the Virgin Mother of Christ. In Poem 7 she is the Virgin Spouse of Joseph and in 9 the Virgin Spouse of Christ as a type of the Church. The progression of roles seems to begin with the most human and natural, in the image of the young girl in Poem 2, and end with the most divine, abstract, and allegorical, in the typology of Ecclesia in Poem 9. In a sense, all of the images of Mary and of Christ return to mankind in the last lyric, Poem 12, when their help is petitioned for mankind.

The introductory second lyric is thus the key to the succeeding appearance of Mary in the sequence because of its multiple roles and images, which serve as an epitome of the later individual images in different lyrics. This Anglo-Saxon version of the Antiphon "O clavis David," or "Eala þu reccend," introduces Mary first as a mere "young girl," *seo fæmne geong* (line 18), a woman selected from many and even described here through the roles available during a lifetime to most women. The difference between Mary and other women centers on her having been chosen by Christ from among all others. Note in this passage the italicized variations for the word "woman," each incrementally adding a different nuance, from the young girl (*seo fæmne geong,* line 18b) to the virgin or maiden (*mægð,* 19a), the mother (*meder,* 19b), the bride (*bryd,* line 21b), and to the woman (*wif,* 23b):

> The *girl was young,*
> a *virgin* sinless,   whom he chose for a *mother.*
> That happened   without the favors of man,
> that through the birth of a child   the *bride* became greater.
> Nothing similar to that,   either before or since,
> has been the reward of *woman*   in the world.

> (Wæs *seo fæmne geong,*
> *mægð* manes leas,   þe he him to *meder* geceas.
> Þæt wæs geworden   butan weres frigum
> þæt þurh bearnes gebyrd   *bryd* eacen wearð.
> Nænig efenlic pam,   ær ne siþþan,
> in worlde gewearð   *wifes* gearnung. 18b–23)

That Mary epitomizes not only the perfection of all womanhood (impossible for other women to attain) but also the fulfillment of all womanly roles is not original with the *Christ I* poet. The Church Fathers and early commentators such as Ambrose and Fulgentius, as well as Anglo-Latin writers like Aldhelm, saw in her the perfection of all woman-kind through her perpetual virginity. Because of her virginity she was thus chosen to reward all women in the world in this Anglo-Saxon lyric. Saint Fulgentius (A.D. 468–533), Bishop of Ruspe in Africa, in his paean to Mary summons all women to the Virgin, who inculcates all stages of female human nature:

> Come, virgins, to the Virgin; come, those conceiving, to the one who has conceived; come, those delivering, to the one who has delivered; come, those nursing, to the one who has nursed; come, mothers, to the Mother, come, maidens, to the Maiden. All the same stages of nature the Virgin Mary undertook in our Lord Jesus Christ, so that she might relieve all women who fled to her for help, and so the new Eve might restore each class of women which came to her by keeping her virginity, just as the new Adam our Lord Jesus Christ renewed each class of men.

(Venite, virgines, ad Virginem, venite, concipientes, ad con-
cipientem, venite parturientes ad parturientem, venite, matres, ad
matrem, venite, lactantes, ad lactantem, venite, juvenculae, ad juve-
nculam. Ideo omnes istos cursus naturae virgo Maria in Domino
nostro Jesu Christo suscepit, ut omnibus ad se confugientibus feminis
subveniret, et sic restauraret omne genus feminarum ad se venien-
tium nova Eva servando virginitatem, sicut omne genus virorum
Adam novus recuperat Dominus noster Jesus Christus.)[15]

As the perfect Incarnation of all women, she appropriately becomes the
Virgin Mother of all women. A similar idea is expressed by Aldhelm in the
Anglo-Latin *De virginitate* (A.D. 680), wherein she is the "perpetual virgin
. . . the daughter-in-law of her Father, the mother and sister of the Son
and at the same time his bride and blessed handmaid, the mother-in-law
of holy souls, the queen of the heavenly citizens."[16] The "perpetual
virginity" of Mary set her off from other daughters-in-law, mothers, sisters, brides, handmaids, mothers-in-law, queens. One possible reason for
this itself derives from the Bible, in which especially the virgin plays an
important and praiseworthy role. Saint Ambrose explains that

> Many women has Holy Scripture brought out to light; but the
> palm of public salvation it has given to virgins alone. In the Old
> Testament it is a virgin who led the Hebrew people, hemmed in by
> land and sea, dry shod through the waters. In the Gospel it is a Virgin
> who gave birth to the Maker and Redeemer of the world. The Church
> is a virgin, whom the Apostle so greatly desired to espouse as a chaste
> virgin to Christ. The daughter of Sion is a virgin. A virgin is that city
> of Jerusalem which is in heaven. Whereinto enters nothing common
> or unclean. Virgin too is she whom Jesus calls, to whom too He said:
> *"Thou art come from Libanus, My Spouse."*[17]

The first role of Mary stressed in Poem 2 is that of *seo fæmne geong*,
in line 18b, the young girl, the maiden or virgin (*maegð*, 19a). It is
appropriate to begin with a girl whose very youth marks her as common
and ordinary, not only to contrast her later apotheosis with this more
humble state and thus illustrate how she was chosen among many, but also
because, acccording to Saint Jerome in his commentary on Isaiah 7:14,
"virgin" in Hebrew means "young girl, hidden and set apart," "puellam,
adolescentulam, absconditam et secretam."[18] The youth of the Virgin
reminds the poet of other growing things, so that *wisna fela* in line 26a,

"many a thing," literally "many a shoot," possibly refers to the word play on *virgo* through *virga* to suggest the rod of Jesse (from Isaiah 11:1) and Mary's ancestry.[19] The line reads, "Þær wisna fela wearð inlihted," 26, or "There many a thing [lit. shoot] became illumined," the phrase *wisna fela* referring especially to the prophecies which were covered by earth and later made to sprout. But the line also refers to Mary's pregnancy as a mystery or spiritual gift which sprouts on earth. When she too is considered as a young girl "hidden" who will be "illumined" through the mystery of her pregnancy, the poet's emphasis in the lyric on sprouting, growth, and planting metaphors becomes clear.

In the third lyric there appears no explicit mention of Mary but instead an invocation of Jerusalem as "O Hierusalem, civitas Dei summi," or in Anglo-Saxon, "Eala sibbe gesihð, sancta hierusalem." However, the poet wants Jerusalem to be understood as a type of Mary, as the following (initially puzzling) passage makes apparent:

> He takes his dwelling in you,   as it was before long ago
> the wise prophets   said in words;
> made known the birth of Christ,   spoke to you joy,
> brightest of cities.

> (Nimeð eard in þe,   swa hit ær gefyrn
> witgan wisfæste   wordum sægdon;
> cyðdon cristes gebyrd,   cwædon þe to frofre,
> burga betlicast. 14–17a)

As the literal birthplace of Christ—envisioned in chains or fetters ("benda," line 19b) as a result of the sin of the first man—Jerusalem also occupies the role of holy Jerusalem, "sancta hierusalem," native seat of angels, "engla eþelstol" (line 3a). But because Christ was also literally born from the Virgin, where he might be said to "take his dwelling," the Virgin becomes identified with Jerusalem as well as an emblem of Paradise, the holy Jerusalem.[20] The connection centers on Mary's mediating role between the two Jerusalems, the old city of the past and prophecy and the future city of redemption. The young girl of Poem 2 mediates between the fallen world and Paradise.

The fourth lyric moves from "seo fæmne geong,/ maegð," to *meder* and the role of the Virgin Mother who will bring about the redemption of Jerusalem. In "O virgo virginum," "Eala wifa wynn," or "O joy of women," Mary discourses with a Son of Jerusalem or "sunu solimae" (21a) and his daughter, as if explaining how Mary will redeem old Jerusalem (the Son and his daughter) by bearing a child (the New Son) without intercourse. The subject is the Virgin Mother, who for this reason is termed "noblest of women," "fæmne freolicast" (2a), or "joy of women," "wifa synn" (1a). The miracle depends upon how a virgin can also be mother, how two disparate roles can be combined, or how the old and the new city of Jerusalem can be bridged. Again and again the poet says she bore a child without intercourse ("gebedscipe," line 6b), at least not according to human ideas ("æfter monwisan   mod ne cuðes," line 7). Thus her virgin motherhood linked the power of heaven with pure humanity:

> Indeed truth [trust] in you
> dwelled worthily,   now you the power of heaven
> bore in your bosom,   and did not become fouled,
> oh mighty maidenhood.

> (Huru treow in þe
> weorðlicu wunade,   nu þu wuldres þrym
> bosome gebære,   ond no gebrosnad wearð
> mægðhad se micla. 12b–15a)

This miraculous role of Virgin Mother results in the birth of the Child who will give eternal life for death in contrast to the birth of the "children of men" to human mothers who will give only further births for death:

> As all men's children
> sow in sorrow,   so again they ripen,
> given birth for death.

> (Swa eal manna bearn
> sorgum sawað,   swa eft ripað,
> cennað to cwealme. 15b–17a)

Mary as a model woman is thus questioned by the "son of Jerusalem" and his daughter, whose silence presumably pays appropriate attention to her as Mother. In her responses the Virgin Mother contrasts herself with Eve, the first virgin and mother, through allusions to the curse laid upon the female sex that she will ameliorate and in some sense "redeem":

Do you ask through curiosity   how I had virginity,
held my purity,   and also became a glorious mother
of the son of God?   For that to man is not
a known mystery,   but Christ revealed
in David's   dear kinswoman
that the sin of Eve   is all nullified,
the curse cast off,   and glorified is
the humbler sex.

(Fricgað þurh fyrwet   hu ic fæmnan had,
mund minne geheold,   ond eac modor gewearð
mære meotudes suna?   Forþan þæt monnum nis
cuð geryne,   ac crist onwrah
in dauides   dyrre mægan
þæt is euan scyld   eal forpynded,
wærgða aworpen,   ond gewuldrad is
se heanra had. 22–29a)

The contrasts between the first and second Eves, or the two virgins, have been explored previously; it is clear that the second virgin in her obedience to God saved all of mankind, not only womankind, as for example noted by Saint Irenaeus:

> In accordance with this design [of saving the human race] Mary is found obedient, saying, *Behold Thy handmaid, O Lord.* Whereas, Eve was disobedient, since she obeyed not whilst yet a virgin. Eve, moreover—having Adam for her husband, though still a virgin— through being disobedient, became the cause of death, both to herself and to the whole human race. Whereas Mary, having a husband fore-anointed, and yet a virgin, by yielding obedience, became both to herself and to the whole human race the cause of salvation.[21]

Mary's role as *salvatrix* of mankind is similarly enunciated by Eve in *Christ and Satan II*.[22] But the *Christ I* poet specifically narrows her regenerative role to that for "se heanra had" (line 29a), the "meaner sex," through her motherhood and her rehearsal of the role of Eve. This emphasis also is found in a comment by Saint Cyril of Jerusalem (A.D. 315–386), who remarks that "Eve being born from Adam's side without a mother, Jesus Christ was born from His Mother without father. For the female sex owed a debt to man; and this Mary paid by giving birth to Jesus Christ of herself alone, by the Holy Ghost, through the power of God."[23] Further, just as the Church Fathers saw a parallel between Eve and Mary in the dialogues each held with an angelic messenger who either tempted and subverted (in the case of Eve) or who raised up by means of the Annunciation (in the case of Mary),[24] so also a similar dialogue occurs here between Mary, in the role of angelic "messenger," and the Son of Jerusalem and his silent daughter, in the role of the maid Mary who will be raised up. The inversion of roles emphasizes the poet's focus on the regenerative womanhood of Mary. Finally, the poet declares through Mary that "the sin of Eve is all turned away" (or dammed up, *forpynded*, line 27b), presumably by Mary, who was often termed, in the light of Canticles 4:12, a fountain sealed. So Saint Jerome finds the Virgin "*A garden enclosed, a fountain sealed:* from which same fountain flows the river, according to Joel (3:18), that irrigates the torrent, either of ropes or of thorns—of the ropes of sinners, by which they were bound before; of the thorns which suffocated the seeds of the paterfamilias."[25] Water as a regenerative symbol has often been associated with the female principle of the *genetrix* as in the case of Venus' birth from Saturn's foamy genitals and of baptism and renewal associated with Christ. But here the water serves to divert and control sin.

Such a spiritual victory for Mary as emblem of woman is heralded by the *Christ I* poet when he regards this "blessed maiden" ("sio eadge mæg," 17b) as "symle sigores full, sancta maria" (18), or "ever full of victory." The phrase "full of victory," or "sigores full," when applied to Mary is reminiscent of the phrase "sigewif" of Metrical Charm 8, "For a Swarm of Bees," a term meaning "victorious women" for the bees who are invited to settle and fall to earth. That is, in the last four lines of this short charm, the petitioner cries to the bees,

> Settle, victorious women,   fall to earth!
> Never fly wild   to the woods.
> Be you as mindful   of my good,
> as certain men   of meat and of home.
>
> (Sitte ge, sigewif,   sigað to eorþan!
> Næfre ge wilde   to wuda fleogan.
> Beo ge swa gemindige   mines godes,
> swa bið manna gehwilc   mete and eþeles.[26])

The Valkyrie-like bees[27] who rush through the air as mediators between heaven and earth resemble the similar feminine *mediatrix* Mary in her role as intercessor, particularly Mary as woman triumphant in stamping out the sin of Eve.

Her means of triumph, to return to Poem 4, occurs through her role as Virgin Mother. Poems 5 and 6, positioned between Poems 4 (on Mary as Virgin Mother) and 7 (on Mary as Virgin Spouse), provide an appropriate transition through their focus on her Son. Both Isaiah 7:14 and Matthew 1:52 announce that, "Behold a Virgin shall conceive in her womb and bear a Son, and his name shall be called Emmanuel, which is interpreted, 'God is with us.'" Thus it is appropriate that the fifth lyric begins, "Eala earendel,   engla beorhtast," in reference to Christ as a star, brightest of angels, and the sixth, "Eala gæsta god," "O God of spirits," or from the Latin, "O Emmanuel." Indeed, Poem 6 continues the apostrophe to Emmanuel by declaring, "how you wisely with the name, justly, were called Emmanuel" ("hu þu gleawlice / mid noman ryhte   nemned wære / emmanuhel," 1b–3a).

Poem 7, "Eala ioseph min," which is not based on an Antiphon, contrasts with Poem 9: here Mary represents the Virgin Spouse of Joseph, but in Poem 9 she represents the Virgin Spouse of God as a type of the Church. In both lyrics the emphasis falls upon the issue of the espousal. Yet why did she need to be married at all if God intended her to remain a perpetual virgin?[28] In Poem 7, as a pregnant Virgin Spouse she has created a psychological dilemma for her angry and disgruntled husband, upset because he does not know what to do. Here we imagine him deliberating: either he will reveal her adultery and she will be stoned, or he will keep silent because he loves her and thereby break the law.[29] The law that he confronts is that of the Old Testament, and she, in her innocence of any adultery and awareness of the reality of her situation, will respond to him through the spirit of the New. His complaint is literal: he has been "dome bereafod," reft of reputation (5b),

because I about you   have heard words,
great sorrows   and hurtful speeches,
injuries, heard,   and to me they speak insults,
many angry words.

(forðon ic worn for þe   worda hæbbe
sidra sorga   ond sarcwida,
hearmes gehyred,   ond me hosp sprecað,
tornworda fela. 6–9a)

When she misunderstands, believing he is denigrating himself, and tries to comfort him by declaring that she has never found any sin in him (13b–18a), he then makes his complaint more explicit, by admitting that the injury has affected not only his public reputation but also his personal

honor. "I have received too much bale for this brideship" ("Ic to fela
hæbbe / Þæs byrdscypes   bealwa onfongen," 18b–19), in that he originally received a "pure virgin" ("fæmnan clæne," 24b) without stain
("womma lease," 25a) and now all is changed. Whether concerned about
public reputation or personal honor, however, Joseph remains faithful to
the Law and the Letter. Mary saves him from this pernicious literalism—
in anticipation of the later salvation of man performed by Christ—by
revealing the truth, that she has never known *gemæcscipe* with any man,
that in reality Gabriel informed her she would be the Virgin mother of the
Child of God (36). Mary here becomes a spiritual messenger instructing
fallen man, analogous to the angel Gabriel instructing Mary, or even the
Tempter "instructing" the soon-to-fall Eve. That is, she represents the
Spirit confronting and triumphing over the Letter, or the New Testament
over the Old.

Indeed, she educates him in how to read God's Word by the Spirit
instead of by the Letter. Joseph had mentioned that it was well-known
that he had received a pure virgin from the bright temple of God, "of þam
torhtan   temple dryhtnes" (23), literally referring to his espousal in God's
temple. But Mary tells him she is herself the Temple of God inhabited by
the Holy Spirit, there to bring him joy because she literally houses the
Word of God but also because she will mother Christ.

> Now I am his temple
> made without spot,   in me that Holy Ghost [lit. Comfort-Spirit]
> has dwelt,   now you entirely might abandon
> bitter sorrow-care.

> (Nu ic his tempel eam
> gefremed butan facne,   in me frofre gæst
> geeardode,   nu þu ealle forlæt
> sare sorgceare. 43b–44a)

The image of Mary as Temple of God was believed by patristic commentators to derive from Proverbs 9:1, "Wisdom hath built herself a house"
and Psalms 17:12, "his tabernacle round about him."[30] Nevertheless, the
image itself suggests the fulfillment of the Old Testament in the New, a
lesson propounded by Mary herself to her pupil husband. Her Augusti-
nian education of Joseph actually concludes with a reminder of the meaning of typological symbolism. The Old Testament (and its literalism, its
legalism) will be fulfilled in the New Testament (and its figurative levels,
the Word of Christ), or "Prophecy has to be in Himself truly fulfilled"

("Sceolde witedom / in him sylfum beon soðe gefylled," 49b–50). This pregnancy thus signals Joseph's conversion from the Old Man to the man new in Christ—a conversion available to all men.

The last major lyric in which Mary appears, and the most complicated in the entire sequence, is Poem 9, "Eala þu mæra," based on the Antiphon "O mundi Domina," "O great One of the world." Mary here appears as the Virgin Queen triumphant, "seo clæneste cwen ofer eorþan" (2), who rules over the heavenly, earthly, and infernal hosts (8–12). Thus in the poem's two parts she is described as the Bride of the most excellent Lord of the sky ("bryd . . . / þæs selestan swegles bryttan" (6b–7), and as the opened gate or door through which Christ entered and through which man and God may communicate.

As the Virgin Bride of God, she is depicted as both the Anglo-Saxon "bracelet-adorned Bride" and the patristic figure of Ecclesia, in a curious wedding of levels of meaning. As the Anglo-Saxon virgin bride, the archetypal peace-weaver, she comes to resemble a heroic-minded warrior in her "bold-thinking" decision (þristhycgende, line 14b) to give herself to God:

> Therefore you [Mary] alone   of all men
> resolved gloriously,   thinking boldly,
> that you your maidenhead   brought to God,
> gave without sin.   None like that came,
> no other   out of all the men,
> bride bracelet-adorned,   who the bright gift
> to heaven-home   with pure spirit
> afterwards sent.
>
> (Forþon þu þæt ana   ealra monna
> geþohtest þrymlice,   þristhycgende,
> þaet þu þinne mægðhad   meotude brohtes,
> sealdes butan synnum.   Nan swylc ne cwom
> ænig oþer   ofer ealle men,
> bryd beaghroden,   þe þa beorhtan lac
> to heofonhame   hlutre mode
> siþþan sende. 13–20a)

This Anglo-Saxon metaphor of the *bryd beaghroden* (18a) reminds the reader of the first lyric, the only other poem in the sequence that has been noted to manifest Germanic *comitatus* metaphors. In that lyric, Christ was sketched as the chief of "that great hall" now in ruins, but he was also portrayed as a craftsman who will restore the hall of the human body.

Doomed men awaiting him serve as wanderers in exile pressed by hateful hell-fiends to the point of feud with God.[31]

The image of the bracelet-adorned bride of God can be explained in patristic terms: on the tropological or moral level of allegory, she symbolizes the soul of man wed to the bridegroom Christ.[32] On the allegorical level, relating to the life of Christ, the "nuptial chamber" becomes Mary's womb, through which Christ will pass.[33] On the anagogical level, Mary as Virgin Spouse becomes a type of the Church itself. Ambrose remarks that "It is well that Mary was married, but virgin; because she is a type of the Church, which is immaculate, but married. The Virgin has conceived us of the Spirit, the Virgin has delivered us without pangs."[34] As the Church, she gave man spiritual life, just as Eve first gave man natural life through the propagation of the human race and was thus named by Adam "Life."[35]

Mary's anagogical significance as Ecclesia deepens the meaning of the epithet "bracelet-adorned queen" if in Poem Nine she is understood as playing an Anglo-Saxon heroic role in confronting the Devil, chief enemy of the Church. Ambrose depicts Mary as *miles Christi*, heroically treading upon the head of the serpent in fulfillment of the promise to Eve:

> We can understand through the woman in this place the Blessed Mary, because she is Mother of the Church, and is daughter of the Church because she is the greatest member of the Church. The dragon therefore stood before the woman, so that when she gave birth to the Son he might devour him: because at the beginning of Christ's birth the dragon had wanted to kill him through Herod his minister. He stands also before the woman, that is, the Church, in order to destroy through persuasion to evil those whom through baptism she begets for God.[36]

Such martial energy will serve as a model for the militant female saints and warriors who aid God in the Anglo-Saxon religious epics *Juliana*, *Judith*, and *Elene*.

Later in Poem 9 (27–73), the poet moves backward from the New Testament image of Mary as Bride of Christ, Ecclesia, to her Old Testament prefiguration as the Door or Gate through which the Messiah would enter prophesized by Isaiah. In lines 27–53, when Isaiah relates that he was taken where he could see all of life, he reveals that he saw "A great door, entirely bound, decorated with treasure, surrounded by wonderchains" ("Eal wæs gebunden / deoran since duru ormæte,/wunderclommum bewriþen," 34b–36a). When he imagines that no one will ever be able to open that door, the angel of God replies that God Himself will pass through to visit earth, but that the door will close again thereafter (43–51). In lines 54–73, the poet addresses Mary as that gate: "Þu eart þæt wealldor" (54a) through which the Lord passed and afterwards which the Lord of angels locked. Thus the poet in this second part of the lyric (lines 54–73) unifies the entire poem through the figure of the virgin queen as "wealldor," now and forever, by linking the New Testament vision of the peace-weaving "bracelet-adorned bride" from lines 1–26 and the Old Testament vision of the "adorned gate" from lines 27–53. Indeed, because her intercession between man and God enables man to reach heaven (lines 68–73), the poet requests vigorous and bold "peace-weaving" from this heavenly queen: "Intercede for us now with bold words" ("Geþinga us nu þristum wordum," 68).

In this passage, the poet draws on ideas from several Church Fathers who understood Mary as a symbolic Gate, among them Saint Ephrem, Saint Epiphenius, Saint Jerome, and Saint Ambrose. Glosses on Canticles 4:12, "My sister, my spouse, is a garden enclosed," and on Ezechiel 44:1–3, and on 11, 2, either praised Mary as the Gate of Life, or else praised the Gate itself as a metaphor for her perpetual virginity. The closest in spirit to Poem 9 is Saint Ambrose's allegorical comments on Ezechiel 11:2:

> The prophet [Ezechiel] says that he witnessed the building of a city on a very high mountain (Ezechiel 11:2ff), whose gates signified many things; one nevertheless is described as closed. . . . What is this gate except Mary, and closed, because a virgin? Mary then is the gate through which Christ entered into this world, when he was shed forth by virginal birth, and the birth did not unbind the barricade of virginity. . . . And now we can demonstrate that each man has a gate whereby Christ enters, as it is written: "Lift up your gates, O ye princes, and be ye lifted up, O eternal gates, and the King of Glory enter in" (Psalm 23, 7). How much more therefore was there a gate in Mary, in whom Christ sat, and from whom he exited? . . . A closed gate is virginity: you are an enclosed garden, O virgin. . . . A closed gate you are, virgin. Let no one open the gate, which once for ever the Holy and True has shut, "He who holds the key of David, who opens and no one shuts; who shuts and no one opens."[37]

The similarities between Ambrose's gloss and Poem 9 consist of the parallel image of Mary as the Gate, and of the idea that each man possesses a gate through which Christ must enter.

Mary does not reappear until the last and twelfth poem, "Eala hwæt, þæt is wræclic wrixl" (or "O admirabile commercium" in Latin), "O that is a marvelous change," when Christ joins her to represent the fruits of a marriage of heaven and earth in a final apotheosis. The High Lord of the Heavens ("heofona heahfrea," 9a) "brought help / to man's kind through his mother's womb" ("helpe gefremede / monna cynne þurh his modor hrif," 9b–10). But such help did not come through the ordinary means of seed: "nor through seed of man on earth came the Wielder of Victory" ("ne þurh *sæd* se cwom   sigores agend / monnes ofer moldan," 5–6a). Nevertheless, the image of the heavenly seed invokes planting and fertility, and indeed the poem concludes the Advent Sequence with the perpetual promise of Christ's love in *eðle,* or native land (21a, *lond,* 22b) of the living. Certainly Christ through the Virgin Mother brought the grace of Heaven to earth to link two realms. And Mary comes to represent the role of earth in accepting the seed of God in heaven (4–6), almost akin to the pagan image of Mother Earth: "Erce, Erce, Erce, eorþan modor" is celebrated in the Charm for Unfruitful Land, in which the Evangelists and Christ and Mary are invoked in order to raise the crops.[38] Of course Mary was conventionally associated with the earthly flowering rod of Jesse even if not with Mother Earth, but additionally Saint John Chrysostom also regarded the Virgin as prefigured in the virgin earth of Eden:

> The word Eden signifies virgin land. Now such was that region in which God planted paradise. . . . Now this virgin (earth) is a type of the Virgin. For as that land, without having received any seed, blossomed forth for us paradise; so too Mary, without having conceived of man, blossomed forth for us Christ.[39]

It is an appropriate metaphor and idea with which to end *Christ I,* because it connects the origins of mankind (in the phrase "mankind's mild Creator," "moncynnes milde scyppend," 2), to the ultimate ideal end of all men, in that "world without end" (24b) in which Christ will dwell perpetually. In Christ's beginning—in the womb of his mother—exists his own end, and the end of all men. What remains clear in this last lyric is the necessary role of the Virgin in completing this "marvelous change in the life of men" (1). Although she is named only as the Virgin, *fæmne* (3a), and seems to lose all personality and human identity in this final lyric, in actuality the poet has returned us to her original role as *fæmne* in the second lyric when she first appeared as the young girl chosen by God. The anonymity of the initial human image merges here with the more abstract and symbolic anonymity of the final cosmic image of the Virgin as Mother Earth, or at least the earthly principle conjoined with the heavenly principle.

The sequence, in short, is unified through a circularity dependent not only on Christ's Advent and promise of Eternal Life but also on the perpetual virginity of his mother, from young girl to symbolic principle. The antiphon *O* thus guides the creative principle responsible for the structural unity of the entire sequence, the reiterated *Eala* in Anglo-Saxon making concrete the predominant figure. The duality of that *Eala/O* reinforces the combination of Anglo-Saxon social images of the Virgin and Latinate and patristic religious images throughout the sequence. A similar wedding of the concretely heroic and the abstractly allegorical occurs in three Anglo-Saxon religious epics, *Juliana, Judith,* and *Elene,* whose female heroes are modeled upon the Virgin, as we shall see in the next chapter.

3

Brave Judith, Juliana, and Elene

Allegorical Figures of the Soul, Christ, and the Church

T HE SECOND BIBLICAL MODEL for Anglo-Saxon women—in addition to the Virgin—was the Vulgate Judith, responsible for decapitating Holofernes and leading her Hebrew tribe to victory over the Assyrians. Although the actual Anglo-Saxon adaptation exists only as a fragment of the original, it has been seen as having a unity of its own as a "religious lay" similar to the secular lays of the *Finnsburg Fragment* or the *Battle of Maldon*. Most likely it was a much longer poem resembling *Juliana* and *Elene*, the only two religious epics with women saints as their subjects.[1] And, indeed, these three religious epics bear other affinities, despite the tenth-century date of *Judith* and the ninth-century date of *Juliana* and *Elene*,[2] the latter two identified as Cynewulf's from their runic signatures. For example, Alfred S. Cook has noted that the phraseology of the three is linked and related in particular to *Andreas*, *Genesis A*, the *Battle of Maldon*, and *Beowulf*.[3] Further, all three illustrate women of military sanctity: B. J. Timmer has noted that "*Judith* belongs to the type of poetry to which *Juliana* and *Elene* belong, the religious epic describing the deeds of a fighting saint."[4] Why would their poets have selected fighting women saints as the subjects of religious epics?

Several reasons emerge: first, and most generally, when the Anglo-Saxons converted to Christianity, they inherited a spiritual heroic past contained within the lives of the various apostles, martyrs, and confessors. These lives were bolstered by missionaries, relics, church dedications, and, especially in the seventh century, through manuscripts of saints' lives sent from Rome.[5] Apparently most of the extant saints' lives in Anglo-Latin or Anglo-Saxon derived from the seventh and eighth centuries in Northumbria and then Mercia, where they were disseminated before an

A choir of saints, among them the Virgin Mary, Saint Aetheldryth, and Mary Magdalene, all bearing crowns and haloes. That three of the virgins carry books reinforces their signification as wise and may also have suggested an identification with Ecclesia as teacher. Tenth century, from *The Benedictional of St. Ethelwold,* Additional MS 49598, fol. 1b. Photo permission of the British Library, London.

audience of monks and nuns partly for entertainment and partly for instruction. Most importantly, there appeared some chauvinism in the pride with which English saints were lauded in these centuries, saints such as Oswald and Cuthbert, King Edmund, Aetheldryth of Ely, and her sister Seaxburh, in that local recognition of a saint at that time did not require papal canonization.[6] As to why these three women in particular received extended treatment in religious heroic poems, the question is more difficult to answer. The passion of Juliana was a relatively popular story, even though she was not very famous and "had no connection with England."[7] Further, what relation does the story of Juliana bear to that of Judith, who was not a saint at all, much less a Christian, and to Elene, whose poem really focuses on the *inventio crucis* and not on her martial exploits? Yet all three share important similarities: first, an emphasis on chastity; second, an emphasis on martial spirit conceived as a spiritual weapon against vices, the Devil, or Synagogue and the heathen; and third, a particularly English bond in that all manifest topical historical or political significance in relation to the defense of the nation or the newly established English Church. All three similarities are in some way connected with Aldhelm's *De virginitate,* written in A.D. 680.

The general emphasis on chastity in Anglo-Saxon England seems to have derived from the patristic contrast between Eve and the Virgin as two women similar initially in their virginity but dissimilar in their obedience (or lack of it) to God. Where Eve failed, bringing death into the world, the Virgin succeeded, bringing life into the world through her Son, by whom, according to Saint Jerome, she reinstituted the gift of virginity to women, and who created a new family for Himself in his chaste followers Judith, Aman, James, and John.[8] While the lives of the virgin martyrs praised virginity in moral and doctrinal treatises,[9] virginity (or at least chastity) also stamped the contemplative life for more conventional monks and nuns. Saint Jerome also notes that the Virgin Christ and the Virgin Mary epitomized *virginitatis principia,* models for the virginal or chaste Apostles, bishops, priests, deacons,[10] and later, monks and nuns. Thus, it was appropriate that many of the Church Fathers had written treatises on virginity—Tertullian, Cyprian, Jerome, Ambrose, and Augustine; poetic versions also existed by Alcimus Avitus and Venantius Fortunatus. Most importantly for our three religious epics, Aldhelm's long prose and verse treatise in Latin on the virtues of virginity entitled *De virginitate* indicated a familiarity with the treatises of Cyprian, Jerome, Ambrose, and Augustine while it diverged from most of the others.[11] In this treatise written for the abbess Hildelith and the nuns of Barking and known to Bede, who also wrote a *Martyrology,* Aldhelm provides two clues as to why Judith, Juliana, and Elene were chosen as subjects of religious epics.

The first clue derives from the special conditions of late seventh-century England and thus illustrates one way in which his treatise on virginity differs from those of the Church Fathers. The Church Fathers categorized three grades of chastity—virginity, widowhood, and conjugality—but Aldhelm substitutes chastity *(castitas)* for widowhood, primarily because so many women of that time had left marriages for monastic life. He declares,

> Moreover, the catholic Church accepts a three-fold distinction of the human race, which increases orthodox faith, as it is described by an angelic narrative in a certain volume, how 'virginity', 'chastity' and 'conjugality' differ the one from the other in three ranks. . . . From the evidence of this distinction, it is permissible to deduce or conjecture what virginity is, which unharmed by any carnal defilement continues pure out of the spontaneous desire for celibacy; (and) chastity on the other hand which, having been assigned to marital contracts, has scorned the commerce of matrimony for the sake of the heavenly kingdom; or conjugality which, for propagating the progeny of posterity and for the sake of procreating children, is bound by the legal ties of marriage.[12]

It is interesting to note that Juliana, Judith, and Elene seem to reflect these three categories of virginity. Juliana, who refuses to marry Heliseus, maintains her virginity *(virginitas);* Judith, a widow in the Vulgate and in Aldhelm's account of her exploits, is praised especially for her chastity *(castitas);* and Elene, finally, mother of Constantine the Great, represents abstinence within marriage *(iugalitas)*, although in reality she was divorced at the time of her quest.

Another way in which all three heroines are related—their militancy—also derives from Aldhelm's possible influence, although as we have mentioned spiritual heroism in general was inherited from the lives of the saints after the conversion of the Anglo-Saxons. Aldhelm changed his sources (the Church Fathers) additionally by appending to his list of female virgins a list of male virgins, possibly because Barking was a double house.[13] A kind of rationale for virginity in both sexes is provided by the martial image of the virgins as warriors of Christ intent on savaging the eight chief sins and the Devil. This imagery drawn from Ephesians 6 may have attracted an Anglo-Saxon audience to whom martial exploits were common. Aldhelm first characterizes the virgins of Christ as types of the soul battling vices with the breastplate of virginity and the shield of modesty:

> Virgins of Christ and raw recruits of the Church must therefore fight
> with muscular energy against the horrendous monster of Pride and at
> the same time against those seven wild beasts of the virulent vices,
> who with rabid molars and venomous bicuspids strive to mangle
> violently whoever is unarmed and despoiled of the breastplate of
> virginity and stripped of the shield of modesty.[14]

Next, the weapons change to the armament of the virtues in general used by the warriors of Christ:

> . . . and they must struggle zealously with the arrows of spiritual
> armament and the iron-tipped spears of the virtues as if against the
> most ferocious armies of barbarians, who do not desist from battering
> repeatedly the shield-wall of the young soldiers of Christ with the
> catapult of perverse deceit. In no way let us sloppily offer to these
> savage enemies the backs of our shoulder-blades in place of shield-
> bosses, after the fashion of timid soldiers effeminately fearing the
> horror of war and the battle-calls of the trumpeter!

Finally, the members of this "monastic army" use the sword of the Word, the breast-plate of faith, and a secure shield to defend the Church against spiritual wickedness promoted by the greater powers of darkness, the "dominion of the Leviathan":

> Rather, as combatants in the monastic army, boldly offering our
> foreheads armed with the banner of the Cross among the ranks of our
> competitors, and carrying tightly the warlike instruments of arma-
> ment—which the distinguished warrior [St. Paul] enumerates, that is
> to say, the sword of the Holy Word and the impenetrable breast-plate
> of faith (Eph. VI.17)—and protected by the secure shield against the
> thousand harmful tricks of spiritual wickedness, we shall then
> blessedly rejoice in the heavenly kingdom, revelling in celestial glory
> (and) ready to receive the due triumph of victory from Christ our
> paymaster—if we now fight strenuously in the forefront of the battle
> as rulers of the world or as warriors of the Lord, steadfastly struggling
> with steadfast foes, against the dominion of Leviathan and the powers
> of darkness.

Judith, Juliana, and *Elene* demonstrate similar kinds of allegorical battling. *Judith* seems to portray all three types in the same contest—the chaste soul or *anima* battling the lechery of Olofernes (Holofernes), the virtuous warrior of God or *miles Dei* modeled on Christ opposing the viciousness of the tyrant and evil associated with the Devil, and finally, a prefiguration of the Church or Ecclesia triumphing over Synagogue and paganism.[15] *Juliana,* the most conventional of the Cynewulfian poems, demonstrates the soul battling the wrath and lechery of Heliseus and the wrath of her father Affricanus as well as the *miles Christi* opposing a very literal Devil and also the powers of the Christian Church triumphing over paganism, as both Heliseus and Affricanus remain pagan.[16] Finally, unlike the others, *Elene,* the most famous and interesting signed Cynewulfian poem, does not show her as a type of the soul battling a particular vice, although certainly Constantine her son battles with pride and despair on the night before certain defeat in battle when he witnesses the vision of the cross; instead, when she fights against the Old Man Judas, literally and spiritually, she comes to fulfill the image of Ecclesia thwarting the unconverted Jews, or Synagogue.[17] These three levels of allegory were defined by Origen in the early Greek patristic commentaries as the moral or tropological, the allegorical, and the anagogical levels, their currency strong in the medieval period as late as the fourteenth century and Dante's Letter to Can Grande.[18]

The final way in which all three figures are linked actually stems from the last of the three allegorical levels mentioned above. If it may be proclaimed that all three, Judith, Juliana, and Elene, came to be depicted as types of the Church, or Ecclesia, confronting Synagogue, or the heathen, then why and how? The contrast between Synagogue and Ecclesia was widespread in the Middle Ages beginning with the Church Fathers and literary and theological writings down to the sixteenth century.[19] Often this contrast was expressed through the conflict between the Jews and Christians: because they resisted the Christian sacrament of baptism, the Jews were portrayed iconographically as blind, and so too Synagogue appeared either blind or blindfolded. Further, etymologically Synagogue was linked with cattle, from *congregatio,* as opposed to Ecclesia, or *convocatio;* plastic arts depicted her with an ass, a broken spear, a blindfold, and tables of the law. Synagogue was frequently shown as a concubine (Hagar) contrasted with the Church (Sarah), as the False Pretender contrasted with the True Bride, or as an adulterous matron contrasted with her daughter Ecclesia.[20] A more specific explanation of the contrast can be applied to our three tales through Aldhelm's story of Judith in *De virginitate.* Judith is first described as chaste: "Flowering like a bright lily in her devout chastity and hiding from the public gaze she lived a pure life in an upstairs solar."[21] Her Ecclesia-like chastity and her use of physical charms to overthrow Holofernes distinguishes her from the adulterous and stubborn woman of Proverbs 7:23, whom Aldhelm identified as Synagogue,

> that stubborn and insolent woman in Proverbs who foreshadows the figure of the Synagogue, who promised that her own husband would (only) return when the moon was full (and who), in the trappings of a harlot and with alluring luxury, is described as having enticed a foolish young man and, when she had deceived him with the fraudulent delights of her promises, destroyed him pitiably, so that (it was) truly like an ox led to the slaughter, enchained by the wantonness of his own blind desire (that) he entered the vile brothel of this whore without fear.[22]

Implicitly, then, Judith prefigures the Church, an idea which may have influenced the *Judith*-poet's later depiction of her and possibly also the two Cynewulfian poems, *Juliana* and *Elene*. The link may have occurred through Bede, who supposedly knew Aldhelm's tract, who also wrote a life of Juliana in his *Martyrology* in addition to the *History of the English Church and People*, and who very likely influenced Cynewulf. In addition, *Juliana* takes place at the same time as *Elene*, a work with specifically English and national ties that may have prompted the depictions of the two saints not only as figures of Ecclesia but in especial of the *English* Church.

That is, *Juliana* takes place sometime during the reign of Maximian in A.D. 308–14, when he was fighting Constantine, his son-in-law. When Juliana is asked by the senator and prefect of Nicodemia, Heliseus, to marry him, she insists on his prior conversion to Christianity; his refusal and her continuing abstinence leads to her torture and death (between A.D. 305 and 311).

Maximian, persecutor of the Christians, provides a bond between *Juliana* and *Elene*: father-in-law of Constantius Chlorus, he adopted him as caesar in 292 and gave him the government of Gaul. However, Constantius Chlorus, or Constantius I, married Saint Elene (Helena), British-born mother of Constantine the Great, although he divorced her when he became caesar. Not only did Constantius I become emperor of the West after Maximian's (and Diocletian's) abdication in 305, he also died at Eboracum (York), and his son Constantine the Great who was Roman Emperor 306–337 was proclaimed caesar at York in 306. *Elene* takes place in 312, when Constantine first received the vision of the Cross on the eve before he faced Maxentius for the last of three times, and later, in its second and longer part, in 325, when his mother Elene built the Church of the Holy Sepulcher and Church of the Nativity in Jerusalem. Together, the two tales of *Juliana* and *Elene* suggest the roots of the founding of the English Church in these two women saints who lived at the same time (Elene died in 330). Just as Juliana resists and triumphs over her pagan adversaries who represent a threat to Christianity in general, Elene, as a type of Ecclesia, confronts and triumphs over Synagogue as represented by 3000 Jews initially and by Judas finally. Her British ties implicitly anglicize not only this confrontation but also the finding of the True Cross and even Constantine's conversion to Christianity.

I

Aldhelm includes Judith as one of the Virgins primarily because he identifies chastity within widowhood as the second grade of virginity; he also presents her as vanquishing Holofernes through her physical charm and beauty:

> Judith, the daughter of Merari, scorned the flattering allurements of suitors after the death of Manasses, taking up the weeds of widowhood and rejecting a wedding dress. . . . (And) when in company of her hand-maiden she undertook to overthrow the dreadful leader of the Assyrians, who had terrified the quaking world with his innumerable thousands of soldiers glorying in the cavalry and infantry, she did not believe he could be deceived in any other way, nor think that he could be killed otherwise, than by ensnaring him by means of the innate beauty of her face and also by her bodily adornment . . . . You see, it is not by my assertion but by the statement of Scripture that the adornment of women is called the depredation of men! But, because she is known to have done this during the close siege of Bethulia, grieving for her kinsfolk with the affection of compassion and not through any disaffection from chastity, for that reason, having kept the honour of her modesty intact, she brought back a renowned trophy to her fearful fellow-citizens and a distinguished triumph for (these) timid townsfolk—in the form of the tyrant's head and its canopy.[23]

The tenth-century *Judith* uses the Aldhelm-emphasis on her "virginity" and her beauty to transform her into a type of virginity battling with lechery in the figure of Olofernes, indeed, virtue battling with vice, and the Aldhelm-contrast between Judith and the stubborn woman of Proverbs as a type of Synagogue to transform her into a type of Ecclesia.

Other critics have interpreted the *Judith*-poet's lack of stress on her widowhood as political or social in motivation—either because the chief audience of the poem would have included influential wives and not widows in Anglo-Saxon households responsible for protecting the kingdom from the Danes, or because an audience of widows listening to a story about a militant widow would have shamed the men also listening into defensive action against the Danes.[24] But it is not that the *Judith*-poet deemphasizes her widowhood; in fact he stresses her virginity. "Virgin" or "maiden" is a word used to describe her throughout the poem (*mægð*; 35a, 78a, 135a, 145a, 165a, 254b, 260a, 334a; *meowle*, 56b, 261a), often accompanied by the adjectives "blessed," "bright," "holy," "triumphant," "wise," and frequently coupled with "of the Creator" or "the Lord." The reason for this emphasis stems from the poet's intention to contrast her virgin beauty as a type of chastity with the lechery of Olofernes. Indeed, Olofernes "intended to infect the bright lady with defilement and with sin" ("þohte ða beorhtan idese / mid widle and mid womme besmitan," 58b–9a). Her bright beauty throughout the poem resembles that of Mary in *Christ I* and that of the bright and shining Eve and Lucifer in *Genesis B*, whose gleaming beauty, like virginity itself, suggested precious treasure. Judith is described as a beautiful lady "shining like an elf" ("ides ælfscinu," 14a), as well as a bright virgin ("þa torhtan mægð," 43a,/ "seo beorhte mægð," 254b) and a bright lady ("beorhtan idese," 58b, 340b). The contamination of this purity is attempted by the drunken Olofernes, who fortunately loses consciousness and thereby gives Judith the opportunity to decapitate him. Throughout he is described as particularly lecherous—the lascivious one ("galferhð," 62a), the impure one ("se unsyfra," 76b, and "womfull," 77a); and the lecher, terrible and fierce ("se galmoda, / egesfull ond afor," 256b–57a). The beauty which Aldhelm's Judith deliberately uses to captivate and destroy Holofernes here becomes a sign of the virginity which the lecherous Anglo-Saxon Olofernes seeks to contaminate and destroy but which, instead, like the breastplate of virginity and shield of modesty belonging to the Aldhelm soldier of Christ, overcomes the vicious tyrant instead.

Indeed, the *Judith*-poet deliberately employs Anglo-Saxon heroic imagery and diction to cast their confrontation as an encounter between the soldier of God and her assailant.[25] Judith anachronistically appears as an aristocratic Anglo-Saxon lady, "adorned with armlets, with rings adorned" ("beagum gehlæste, / hringum gehrodene," 36b–37a, and "beahhrodene," 138b); a gold-adorned ("golde gefrætewod," 171b) lady with braided-locks ("wundenlocc," 77b and 103b). But she also is charac-

terized like the heroic Virgin who stamps upon the Devil—she is coura-
geous ("ellenrof," 109a and 146a), brave ("ellenþriste," 133b), bold-hearted
("collenferhðe," 134b), triumphant ("eadhreðige," 135a; "modigre," 334a).
Her assailant corresponds to the bad king and tyrant; he is the terrible
lord of earls ("egesful eorla dryhten," 21a), stern-hearted ("se stiðmoda,"
25a), the cruel lord of men ("þearlmod ðeoden gumena," 66a), a treaty-
breaker ("ðone wærlogan," 71b), a hateful tyrant ("laðne leodhatan," 72a),
a murderer ("þysne morðres bryttan," 90a), a severe lord of men
("þearlmod þeoden gumena," 91a). Most importantly, she wields a sword
to decapitate him in a warlike action more common to the battlefield than
the boudoir.

In addition to this moral or tropological level on which the battle
between the two takes place, there also exists an allegorical and anagogical
level of allegory. Judith exemplifies the soldier of Christ (one from Aldhelm's "monastic armies") who opposes a figure epitomizing at first other
vices beyond lechery but finally epitomizing sheer evil, the Devil himself.
Olofernes is proud and drunken ("modig and medugal," 26a) and an
arrogant giver of treasure ("swiðmod sinces brytta," 30a), adding pride,
gluttony, and avarice to his sins. In his wickedness, indeed, he almost
assumes a diabolical character: he is the wicked one ("se inwidda," 28a,
"ðaes unlædan," 102a), hateful to the Savior ("nergende lað," 45b), the evil
one ("se bealofulla," 48b), the diabolical one ("se deofulcunda," 61b), the
baleful one ("bealofull," 63a, 100b, 248a), the terrible one ("þone atolan,"
75a). Part of his evil derives from his paganism, against which the Church
might be expected to fight. He is the heathen man ("þone hæðenan
mannan," 98b), the heathen dog ("þone hæðenan hund," 110a), the most
hated heathen warrior ("ðæs laðestan / hæðenes heaðorinces,"
178b-79a). Judith, in contrast, representing the Church whose wisdom
and clear vision antithetizes the blindness of Synagogue (perhaps signified
here by Olofernes' drunken stupor and his decapitation), is described
continually as prudent, or prudent in thought ("ferhðgleawe," 41a; "gleaw
on geðonce," 13b), a wise lady, maiden, virgin, woman ("ða snoteran
idese," 55a; "seo snotere mægð," 125a; "searoðoncol mægð," 145a;
"gleawhydig wif," 148a; "seo gleawe," 171a). These three levels of allegory
are also delineated in *Juliana.*

II

Juliana, which is contained in the *Exeter Book* following *The Phoenix* and
preceding *The Wanderer,*[26] is based on a Latin prose *Vita* included in the

Acta sanctorum for February 16, the date on which her martyrdom was celebrated. Recent critical studies have attempted to demonstrate *Juliana*'s artistry by explaining the significance of Cynewulf's changes and additions to the original text. [27] This brief analysis of the moral, allegorical, and anagogical levels in the poem will assume its artistry without duplicating this procedure. The moral or tropological level is primarily developed in its first section, to line 236, during which Juliana resists both Heliseus' offer of marriage and her father's arguments in support of the union by demanding his prior conversion to Christianity. The allegorical level is primarily developed after she is cast into prison when, as a saint and *miles Christi*, she battles the Devil in a heavily heroic passage (to line 557). The anagogical level is primarily developed after she is released from prison: as an Ecclesia-figure, she delivers a homily, before she is beheaded, on the need for protecting the house of the soul (to the end, line 731). Unlike *Judith*, the poem distributes the three levels among three different sections to underscore its structural as well as thematic unity.

Like Judith, Juliana represents a virgin whose radiant beauty symbolically reflects her chastity. She is termed a maiden (*fæmne*, 27a, 32a, 40b, 59b; or *mægð*, 568a, 608a), "clean and chosen" ("clæne ond gecorene," 613a), and "without sin" ("synna lease," 614a). Further, she "desired earnestly that she would hold her maidenhood cleanly because of Christ's love of each man" ("hogde georne / þaet hire mægðhad mana gehwylces / fore Cristes lufan   clæne geheolde," 29b-31). Her beauty (*wlite*, 163a) causes the old warriors of the *duguð* to marvel; even her *brydguma* Heliseus (165) greets her as the light of the sun ("sunnan scima," 166b) and acknowledges her radiance ("glæm," 167b), the blossom of her youth ("geoguðhades blæd," 168b). The light and shining quality of her beauty, illustrating the purity of her virginity, links her with that of the chaste Judith, the Virgin Mary, and the unfallen Lucifer and Eve.

Heliseus, in contrast, the noble, powerful heathen who wishes to marry her, is described initially as "firendædum fah," stained with sinful deeds (59a, 571a; also "se synscaþa," 671b). The moral epithets used to describe him stress especially his wrath (*yrre*, 58b, 90b, 582b), perhaps because he is brutal ("hreoh," 61a) and irrational ("hygeblind," 61a), a sin shared by her father Affricanus when she refuses to marry Heliseus. Affricanus is determined and angry ("anræd ond yreþweorg," 90a), furious, raging, wroth, terrible, and savage ("ellenwod, /yrre ond repe,   frecne ond ferðgrim," 140-1a). The wrath of both increases as her resistance grows: parleying together, they are identified as "sick with sins" ("synnum seoce," 65a), almost as if their anger resembled a disease; but both are also heathen ("hæðne," 64b), perhaps intended as an explanation for the disease. Certainly Heliseus' anger, after Affricanus delivers her for punishment and torture, develops from a more fierce mood ("frecne mode," 184b) into a cruelty (he is "gealgmod guma," a cruel-minded man, 531a) that progresses to the ordering of various horrid deaths from which she is saved miraculously. His "loss of his head" through anger and irrationality ironically contrasts with her final peaceful and even joyous acceptance of her beheading.

Olofernes' lechery in *Judith* comes to signify Sin generally, as does the anger of Heliseus in *Juliana*. And in both cases, the spiritual contest between the adversaries is depicted imagistically or symbolically as a martial contest: the symbolism of Judith's knife-wielding is replaced here by imagery drawn from the Germanic *comitatus*[28] to depict the men of Heliseus as warriors. Later, in the prison, the symbolism is replaced by the allegorical contest between Juliana as *miles Christi* and the demon. When she has defeated him, in his confession he reveals that a stalwart and heroic soul (her mirror image) resists his attacks. Indeed, the poem even begins like the heroic epic *Beowulf* with the formulaic "Hwæt! We ðæt hyrdon hæleð eahtian," "We have heard heroes declare." The epic struggle pits the cruel king Maximian ("arleas cyning," 4a) against the Christians (God's warriors, "godes cempan," 17a) whom he persecutes by destroying their churches and setting up false idols. Other images describe as Germanic retainers the men of Heliseus who wait when Africanus enters to speak with him: the "warriors leaned their spears together," "hy togædre garas hlændon, / hildeþremman," 63–64a. Heliseus himself regards her recalcitrance as the stimulus for epic contest and responds by speaking "boast words" drawn from the epic ("beotwordum," 185a) in front of the people. The poet here terms him a warrior (*se hererinc*, 189a)) and depicts him as fantasizing that he has already won the battle: "This is the supremacy (*ealdordom*) of our battle seized at the beginning" (190–1a). But the fearless ("seo unforhte," 147a, 209b) and mild-minded virgin ("milde modsefan," 235a) retainer-like merely leans on her faith in God, the strong "Guardian of heaven, the mild Protector, the Lord of hosts" ("heofonrices weard, / mildne mundboran, mægna waldend," 212b–13).

Within the prison into which she is cast in the middle section of the poem, the martial contest between Christ and the Devil is duplicated between Juliana and a demon. Even the temptation of Christ is repeated: this "prisoner of Hell" ("helle hæftling," 246b) tempts her to avoid cruel torments by capitulation and acceptance of the false gods, a counsel made more inviting by the assertion that he is God's angel and a servant sent of high to help her. The suspicious Juliana perceives he may be a monster-hero ("se aglæca," 268b) and an enemy of glory ("wuldres wiþerbreca," 269a), so girds the loins of her soul ("She makes fast her soul with firmness in her innocence," "Ongan þa fæstlice ferð staþelian, / geong gron-dorleas," 270-1a), and calls on God as the protector of men ("beorna hleo," 272a) to reveal the identity of this angel. When a heavenly voice tells her to seize him and make him utter the truth, her superior spiritual (as well as physical) strength results in a confession wrung from the demon that is missing in the damaged Old English text but available in the original Latin: the demon, responsible for the mistakes of Adam, Eve, Cain, Judas, Herod, Simon, Nero, Aegeas, has been sent by the king of hell-dwellers ("hellwarena cyning," 322a) to mislead men by deceit. Yet he is motivated by fear of his cruel tyrant: Satan, the terrible warrior, is not gentle to them if they have not done evil, "Ne biþ us frea milde, / egesful ealdor, gif we yfles noht / gedon habbaþ," 328b-30a. Satan even sends his þegnas (333a) throughout the world to persecute erring demons.

Within the contest between the holy Juliana and the enemy of the soul ("sawla feond," 348a), a second confession truly betrays his cruel master by explaining how sin enters the heart of the righteous through vices, cruel thoughts, delusions, and deceptions. These vices and decep-tions so sweeten the pleasures of sin and wicked affections that the Christian ceases to pray, begins to love vices, and becomes afraid. Only the *miles Dei,* or *metodnes cempa* (383b), can resist. This mirror reflection of the role played by Juliana is here guided by the martial imagery of Ephesians 6[29] also found in Aldhelm's *De virginitate:*

> If I encounter any valiant
> brave warrior of the Lord
> opposing the arrow-force, he will not far thence
> flee from the battle, but he will raise the buckler
> against (me),
> wise-minded, the holy shield,
> the spiritural war-armor, he will not abandon God.
>
> (Gif ic ænige ellenrofne
> gemete modigne metodnes cempan
> wið flanþræce, nele feor þonan
> bugan from beaduwe, ac he bord ongean
> hefeð hygesnottor, haligne scyld
> gæstlic guðreaf, nele gode swican. 382–87)

Skulking away to bemoan his failure in the contest, the demon seeks a less-valiant warrior whom he can hinder in battle. This envisaged warrior is here described less as a warrior than as a fortress under seige:

                            I open the gate of the wall
through assault;   when the tower is pierced through,
the entrance opened,   then I first will send
to him through   a flight of arrows
into the mind   bitter thoughts,
through deceit   of the heart,
so that he himself   thinks it better
to perform sins,   the lusts of the body,
instead of the love of God.

                            (Ic þæs wealles geat
ontyne þurh teonan;   bið se torr þyrel,
ingong geopenad,   þonne ic ærest him
þurh eargfare   in onsende
in breostsefan   bitre geþoncas
þurh mislice   modes willan,
þæt him sylfum   selle þynceð
leahtras to fremman   ofer lof godes,
lices lustas. 401b–409a)

The demon's confession of his methods demonstrates the superiority of Juliana's martial skill and her spiritual faith in *wuldorcyning* (King of Heaven, 428a)—but in addition he asks explicitly how she, among all women, could thus become daring through deep thought, bold in combat ("hu þu gedyrstig   þurh deop gehygd / wurde þus wigþrist   ofer eall wifa cyn," 431–2), so that she could bind him in fetters. The question surely remains rhetorical, as he himself has already explained how the strong Christian can resist him through faith in God. Indeed, he repeats the expected answer, contrasting her faith in the *wuldorcyning* (428a) with his own service to the *hellwarena cyning* (437a).

    In the third section of the poem (559–end), the demon repeats his praise of her as an exceptional lady unlike any other he has ever encountered by way of reminder that she now assumes a larger allegorical role, as Ecclesia. Not only a saint or holy one (*halge, halig, seo halie*, 533a, 536a, 567b), she becomes a queen whom the demon addresses as "My lady" ("hlæfdige min," 539b), almost as if he had pledged his service to her. His admiration of her seems unqualified:

                                  I know in truth
that I have neither before   nor after encountered
a woman like you   in the worldly kingdom,
neither one bolder of thought   nor one more thwart-timbered
of the race of maidens.

(Ic to soþe wat
þæt ic ær ne sið ænig ne mette
in woruldrice wife þe gelic,
þristran geþohtes ne þweorhtimbran
mægþa cynnes. 547b–51a)

This exceptional maiden delivers a homily to the people before she is beheaded as if indeed she represents Ecclesia. Instructing the people to "Remember the joy of the warriors and the glory of heaven" ("Gemunað wigena wyn ond wuldres þrym," 641), presumably a joy and glory derived from spiritual and figurative contest, she then warns against vice and advocates the construction of a strong-walled house to protect them against sin. Her education during her own spiritual contest with the devil (who had confessed responsibility for the fall of Adam and Eve and many other historical figures) has provided her with the means for the Church and its members to withstand further attacks: the fortified house may signify the armed soul derived from the image of the fortress in the demon's confession, or it may signify Holy Church, like Unite in *Piers Plowman*. This house she urges upon them as a solution contrasts with the pagan hall of Heliseus the *hlaford* (681a) and his band of *þegnas* (683a) in Hell, a house they discover after they are killed on the "swan road" (675a):

> Nor needed then the thanes in that dark home,
> the bank of companions in that low den,
> from the chieftain to expect
> possession of allotted riches, that they in the wine-hall
> above the beer-seat might receive rings,
> appled gold.

> (Ne þorftan þa þegnas in þam þystran ham,
> seo geneatscolu in þam neolan scræfe,
> to þam frumgare feohgesteahda
> witedra wenan, þæt hy in winsele
> ofer beorsetle beagas þegon,
> æpplede gold. 683–88a)

Although Juliana does not appear at all in the fourth part of the poem, that is, in Cynewulf's epilogue,[30] nevertheless the three levels of her allegorical significance explain aspects of Cynewulf's final appeal to this saint. First, he appeals to Juliana for help because two comrades dearest of all, a married pair, divide or separate him ("þonne me gedælað deorast ealra, / sibbe toslitað sinhiwan tu," 697–98). The two com-

rades represent his soul and his body, which must separate because of the
need for the dead man's soul after death to seek out another dwelling
commensurate with his deeds during life: "My soul must (go) from the
body on a journey, I know not myself whither, the yard unknown" ("Min
sceal of lice / sawul on siðfæt,   nat ic sylfa hwider, / eardes uncyðgu,"
699b–701a). Finally, he imagines sinful men as sheep who must await their
final judgment, a vision which prompts him to request mercy by calling
on Juliana. The image of soul and body as a united or married pair
reminds the reader of the prospective union between Juliana and Heliseus
which is forestalled by her chaste and Christian objection to his sinful
heathenness. That tropological conflict in the main poem led to the
allegorical contest in the prison between the *miles Christi* Juliana and the
demon, and then to the anagogical image of Ecclesia attempting to protect
the people in the Afterlife by counsel delivered in this world; the order in
the epilogue, however, is changed to tropological, anagogical, and only
then allegorical. Cynewulf for the second level imagines sinful men as
sheep who must await the final judgment, a vision imbued with anagogy;
this vision prompts him to request mercy from the highest King through
the intercession of his *miles Christi* Juliana, who has in this poem already
proved her martial and spiritual skill in allegorical contest with the
demon. It is appropriate that this allegorical image of Juliana as intercessor ends Cynewulf's epilogue because the primary focus in the poem
has fallen upon that middle section in which she duplicates the harrowing
of Hell performed by Christ. Ultimately she becomes a means of intercession between quarreling body and soul, between this world and the next,
and between man and God. Once again a chaste saint comes to resemble
the ultimate and perfect model of the Virgin Mary.

III

Elene is contained in the Vercelli Book, the last poem in a series which
includes *Andreas, Fates of the Apostles, Address of the Soul to the Body,
Falsehood of Men,* and *Dream of the Rood.* The chief sources of the poem
were probably a Latin version of a legend Syriac in origin, the *Vita
Quiriaci,* and also the *Inventio sancta crucis.* The legend of the discovery
of the cross is ceremoniously linked with Saint Helena in that her feast-
day actually is celebrated as the Feast of the Invention of the Cross, on 3
May, a feast derived from France but established in England before the
close of the eighth century.[31] One of the major critical problems concerning *Elene* not only involves an analysis of the significance of

Cynewulf's changes in his sources but also a justification of the three- (or four-) part structure of the poem. Elene plays an important role only in the longest, and second, part.[32]

A militant queen described as a *guðcwen* (254a, 331a) or *sigecwen* (260a, 997a)[33] rather than a virgin like Judith or Juliana, Elene in her role as the mother of Constantine who finds the True Cross actually unites the three seemingly unconnected portions of the poem. In the first part she represents the literal mother of Constantine; in the second, the spiritual mother of the "Old Man" Judas; and in the third, which is the epilogue of Cynewulf, the mother-muse of this literally "old" man. Her role in the first part seems somewhat oblique, in that she does not appear at all during Constantine's battle with his despair on the eve of imminent and disastrous battle with the Huns, Hrethgoths, Franks and Hugas. However, her presence is manifested figuratively in three senses—through the vision of the True Cross which aids her son in overcoming his despair, through the angel accompanying it, and through her willingness to accept the quest of the True Cross granted her by Constantine. Further, in the second part in her battle with the 3000 Jews that culminates in the dialogue with the lone Judas, she becomes Ecclesia battling with Synagogue. And in an echo of the first part, in the third part Cynewulf battles himself as an old man, discovering relief through the work of art *Elene* and the victory-queen's signal role. In this poem the tropological and anagogical levels of allegory flower. The first and third parts represent what might be viewed as the tropological (horizontal) beam of the Cross juxtaposed with the anagogical (vertical) stem.

The image of battling is made explicit in the first part (1–211) through Constantine's war against the Germanic tribes, which mirrors his internal war within himself against despair. Thus Germanic epithets like *hild-fruma*, battle-prince (10a, 101a), *se leodhwata*, people-protector (11a), *lindgeborga*, shield-valiant (11b), and *guðweard gumena*, a battle-guard of men (14a), remind the reader that this Roman is being depicted as a Germanic chieftain to underscore the heroic nature of the spiritual quest he will initiate. Similarly, the proverbial Anglo-Saxon beasts of battle howl and scream before his battle-fray (28b–29a, 52b–53). And after the vision of the True Cross, which indicates he will overcome the enemy with its aid, he pledges himself to God's service, *godes þeowdom* (201b), like a Christian retainer or Germanic *miles Christi*. Interestingly enough, the angelic messenger who appears before the vision as an emissary is described as a "lovely peace-weaver," *fæle friðowebba* (88a), in a striking echo of the image conventionally used in Anglo-Saxon poetry to describe the role of the queen of the tribe. One reason for the use of the kenning may lie in Elene's analogous role, as a queen who weaves peace between her tribe and God by triumphing over the Jews in her wisdom and thus discovering the True Cross.

That her role remains heroic as well as Christian is clarified not only by the epithets *guðcwen* (battle-queen) and *sigecwen* (victory-queen) but also by the much-vaunted description of her sea-voyage which occurs at the beginning (237–47) of the long mid-section of *Elene* (212–1235). The poet seems anxious to ally the Germanic heroic imagery of the first part with this longer second part and thereby link Constantine with his mother Elene. In the lengthy description of the high ship foaming over the sea, the "wave-floater" breaking over the seaway under its swelling sails, the poet intrudes to note that "I have not heard before nor after of a lady leading a fairer troop   on the ocean stream, on the sea-street," "Ne hyrde ic sið ne ær / on egstreame   idese lædan, / on merestræte,   mægen fægerre" (240b–42), perhaps to counterpoint how unusual it is to find a woman at all leading a troop across the sea. That her quest mirrors Beowulf's chosen quest to help Hygelac and the persecuted Geats is also emphasized by the similar diction used in *Beowulf* (210–24) to describe the advent of his "foamy-necked ship." Thus she is identified upon her arrival at the lands of the Greeks as "the warlike queen with her band of men," "sio guðcwen   gumena þreate" (254), and her nobles wear Anglo-Saxon armor consisting of woven corselet, sword, shining armor, and helmets (256ff). Truly this unconventional woman is rightly called "bold in thought," *þriste on geþance* (267a).

In her "battle" with Judas, which climaxes her confrontations first with 3000 of those gathered to counsel her on the law of Moses, then with the 1000 scholars most learned in the Hebraic tradition, and finally with the 500 wisest of the wise, she clearly represents Ecclesia, Mother of the Church, just as Judas represents Synagogue. Her role as educator involves converting the Old Man into a New Man through dialogue and punishment. This Old Man is revealed during their "battle" as cunning and bound to the senses and the letter. When she asks him to declare the location of the burial-place of the Cross, providing him with a choice of life or death as incentive, he murkily replies with an ironic parable that depicts him as a man in the wilderness, "meadless and meatless," who is offered a loaf of bread or a stone and who would be crazy to take the stone for food when he could have the bread. His parable suggests that he resembles Christ in the wilderness, but unlike Christ, who resisted the temptation of the flesh, he succumbs to a salvation as literal and physical as that promised by bread to stave off hunger. When she presses him further, promising him victory in heaven for a truthful answer, he replies that he does not know the whereabouts of the Cross because too much time has elapsed. Yet she points out that the historians can record the even more antique heroic deeds of the Trojans and number the men dead from the slaughter. As historians of death rather than life, they ally with the letter, with battles leading to death rather than life: "You set down in writing the graves under the stony slopes, and the place as well, and the number of years" ("Ge þa byrgenna / under stanhleoðum, ond þa stowe swa some, / ond þa wintergerim on gewritu setton," 652b–54). Judas can admit only that those deeds were recorded when fresh, but he knows nothing of the burial place of the Cross. Her punishment for his obstinate literalism, his "oldness," is the starvation and hunger of which he spoke parabolically before. She wishes him to understand that the hunger of the spirit is greater than that of the flesh.

The New Man Judas emerges to help Elene find the Cross and convert to Christianity after seven days in the dry cistern. As the True Cross is revealed miraculously by the return to life of a dead youth, so Judas is similarly returned to "Life" as Cyriacus, which according to Cynewulf means "the Savior's faith." He becomes a representative of Elene-as-Ecclesia after he is baptized, educated by the bishop of Rome, Eusebius, in order to be placed in the priesthood as bishop, and then left to preside over Jerusalem as a Christian authority and healer of the sick. The conflict between Judas and Elene, or Synagogue and Ecclesia, has been annealed by the peace and love with which the quest ends— witnessed between the Jews and Christians left to live together amicably. Elene herself teaches both groups the meaning of love and peace before she departs and sends on to her formerly warlike son, on the advice of a wise man, the nails of the Cross, to be made into a bit for the steed of the noblest king on earth. The martial imagery used in the prophet's description of the bridle's purpose must derive from the same kind of spiritual contest as that drawn between Ecclesia and Synagogue, but here broadened to include the test between the *miles Christi* and the forces of evil, because it is peace and not war that dominates the end of the poem. The prophet declares,

                                                          That to many
            throughout the world   will become known,
            when in battle with it   he can overcome
            each enemy,   when brave men
            on two sides   seek battle,
            the foes,   where they on account of it win victory,
            foe against foe.   He shall possess success in war,
            victory in battle,   and everywhere peace,
            peace in fight,   he who before leads
            the bridle on a white (horse),   when the brave ones

to the battle,   those proven men,
bear shield and spear,   This shall be for all
against warriors   an unconquered
weapon in battle.

                     (Þæt manigum sceall
geond middangeard   mære weorðan,
þonne æt sæcce mid þy   oferswiðan mæge
feonda gehwylcne,   þonne fyrdhwate
on twa healfe   tohtan secaþ,
sweordgeniðlan,   þaer hie ymb sige winnað,
wrað wið wraðum.   He ah æt wigge sped,
sigor æt sæcce,   ond sybbe gehwær,
æt gefeohte frið,   se ðe foran lædeð
bridels on blancan,   þonne beadurofe
æt garþræce,   guman gecoste,
berað bord ond ord.   Þis bið beorna gehwam
wið æglæce   unoferswiðed
wæpen æt wigge. 1175b–88a)

Just as Judas is transformed into his opposite, Cyriacus (these transformed doubles parallel the earlier doubles of the unconverted and
converted Constantine, and Cyriacus himself is a spiritual twin of Judas'
martyred Christian brother Stephen), so in the epilogue Cynewulf is
transformed from an old man—also an allegorical Old Man (*frod*, 1236a)—
into a "new." As the old man who longs for revelation, he suffers from an
anguish akin to that suffered spiritually by Constantine early in the poem
and physically by Judas in the second part. Wracked with old age and
despair, Cynewulf is granted consolation by art, or the Word, specifically
as represented by the poem *Elene*.

                        I was stained by deeds,
fettered by sins,   tortured by sorrows,
bound by bitterness,   burdened by troubles,
before he granted lore to me,   in a bright manner
help to the old one,   the glorious gift
the mighty King measured out   and poured out into (my) mind,
the clear light revealed,   extended by times,
unbound my body,   unlocked my soul,
opened the art of poetry.

                    (Ic wæs weorcum fah,
synnum asæled,   sorgum gewæled,
bitrum gebunden,   bisgum beþrungen,

ær me lare onlag   þurh leohtne had
gamelum to geoce,   gife unscynde
mægencyning amæt   ond on gemynd begeat,
torht ontynde,   tidum gerymde,
bancofan onband,   breostlocan onwand,
leoðucraeft onleac. 1242b–50a)

Conversion in the two earlier parts becomes analogous to the art of
poetry in this third—the efficacy of the Word paralleled to the word.
Aged, ready to depart this world, in the anguish of the night Cynewulf has
"woven with word-craft   and collected wonders," or "wordcræftum
wæf   ond wundrum læs" (1237). The image of the artist Cynewulf weaving here recalls the angelic peace-weaver who similarly appeared before
Constantine in his night of anguish to save him from despair, and of course
the conventional Anglo-Saxon image of the woman as peace-weaver between two tribes—in a sense, Elene who brings peace and love to the
previously bellicose Christians and Jews remaining behind in Jerusalem.
The artist Cynewulf rescues himself through the writing of *Elene* to play a
role similar to that of the angel and to Elene—or one might say that Elene
herself inspired Cynewulf out of his anguish just as the angel inspired
Constantine. Thus he looks back on the old world—here viewed as
pagan—which the new world symbolized by the radiant Cross will redeem. That old and pagan world is envisioned in an *ubi sunt* passage
studded with runes signifying Cynewulf's name. It depicts the "old man,"
of which Cynewulf, Constantine, and Judas are types, as a Germanic man
always in sorrow, although he has received appled gold in the mead-hall
("þeah he in medohealle   maðmas þege, / æplede gold" 1258–59a), se-
cretly in anguish even though his horse has run proudly mounted with
adornments along the mile-paths (1259b–63a). The pleasures of the old
way, the old world, do not suffice, so Cynewulf laments the passing of
youth and the advent of age, but age here surely seen in spiritual terms
rather than literal and chronological ones: "youth has passed, the old
pride," "geoguð is gecyrred, / ald onmedla" (1264b–65a). The gleam of
youth was ours before, "wæs geara / geogoðhades glæm" (1265b–66a). We
are all either Constantines or Judases, old men who must be renewed
through the Cross and aided by the discoverer of the Cross, Elene as
individual soul and Ecclesia.

The Cross would have remained buried without Elene, just as
Constantine would have stayed immersed in his dark despair without the
angel who "discovered" his Cross and just as Judas would have remained
imprisoned within the cistern—in his oldness, his Hebraic faith—without
Elene, who discovered Cyriacus buried within him. The poem is in-

tended to be read as a palimpsest; when this happens, the visions of Elene as the *guðcwen, sigecwen,* intersect, one merging with the other, and the angel, Elene, and the artist Cynewulf intersect—as peace-weavers.

In these three religious epics, women saints and biblical heroes function martially on three allegorical levels as types of the Virgin. Tropologically, they represent the chaste soul; allegorically, they represent the *miles Christi,* that is, a type of Christ; anagogically, they represent the church militant, Eccelesia as hero. They thus provide models for Anglo-Saxon women who themselves strove to be chaste, holy—and heroic. We turn now to exceptional women of the period, saints, abbesses, and queens.

4

The Saint, the Abbess, the Chaste Queen

Wise, Holy, and Heroic

ANGLO-SAXON WOMEN who aspired to imitate the Virgin Mary (or her biblical and hagiographical types, Judith, Juliana, and Elene) usually became abbesses and more rarely saints. Even more rarely, they remained queens whose singular chastity, wisdom, and sanctity so dissociated them from their sex that they could function politically and socially more actively than their less chaste counterparts. Indeed, queens without the "armor" of spirituality and chastity who behaved unconventionally—that is, who attempted to rule or take over a kingdom—were usually castigated as lascivious, immoral, and even diabolic. To find out why, we shall examine in this chapter on the one hand hagiographical and legendary materials and on the other legal and historical documents.

By practicing chastity, a woman relinquishes that which makes her female—she becomes, according to Saint Jerome, a virago. Female sexuality inhibited an active social and political role for women because of the religious view that woman was naturally passionate and the cause of man's Fall. Only when masculine support was obtained either through a literal male intermediary or more figuratively through the masculine trait of reason (or through God's help) was a woman permitted to govern men and control wealth. The saints' lives of this period corroborate this idea by describing women saints of heroic chastity and spirituality, a handful of whom literally don masculine disguise to hide a female form—and presumably "female" desire. Similarly, when queens attained a reputation for chastity and sanctity, or when they became abbesses, which marked their intentions as socially or spiritually acceptable, their political power within the community increased.

Antithetically, when queens ruled singly or attempted to rule over

Saint Ætheldryth as a type of the Virgin Mary (note that she carries
the Virgin's flower, the lily): "Imago Sanctae Aetheldrythae Ab-
batissae ac Perpetuae Virginis," "The Image of St. Ætheldryth abbess
and perpetual virgin." Tenth century, from *The Benedictional of St.
Ethelwold*. Additional MS 49598, fol. 9ov. Photo permission of the
British Library, London.

their husbands without these qualities of chastity and sanctity, they were depicted especially in legendary accounts as highly incontinent and immoral creatures whose excessive sexuality, when linked with warlike or masculine behavior, became a metaphor for unnatural and heathen or devilish proclivities. Such behavior is depicted in marked contrast to that of Anglo-Saxon women in historical sources, wherein generally they occupy a passive and peacemaking role within marriage and the nation; only by working through a male agent or relative were they allowed to control lands or money, or to express a greater power than normal.

In tracing the stages in this argument, we shall look first at the saints' lives, chiefly the Old English *Martyrology* and Ælfric's *Lives of Saints*, then at the history of abbesses, as detailed in Bede's *History of the English Church and People*, next at historical and legendary accounts of Anglo-Saxon queens, in the Anglo-Saxon *Chronicles* and in William of Malmesbury's *Chronicle of the Kings of England*, and finally at historical and legendary evidence of both placid and errant queens in wills, writs, chronicles, and other documents.

I

Judith, Juliana, and Elene in their heroic chastity resemble the late antique and Anglo-Saxon lives of women saints described in the *Old English Martyrology* (ca. A.D. 850), and Ælfric's *Lives of Saints* (ca. 994–early 11th century). While many of these saints are not Anglo-Saxon and while their lives are translated into Old English from the Latin, nevertheless their popularity argues at least for strength of interest in them in this period: these women behave heroically by refusing to succumb to natural sexual desires conventionally associated with the female, because of their spiritual weapon of faith in God. As such they emulate the biblical and patristic models provided by the Virgin Mary, Judith, Juliana, and Elene. Although a group of twenty-two lives merely describes briefly the life, miracles, or faith of the female saint,[1] a second group of thirty-four lives portrays this *miles Christi* as abjuring all contact either physical or spiritual with a usually lecherous and pagan assailant. Six of these lives concern a queen or wife who remains chaste within marriage, either miraculously or voluntarily, and in addition a few of these convert their husbands or assailants to the Christian faith.[2] Twenty of these lives concern virgin martyrs who cling to their chastity and faith despite torture and even murder.[3] Finally, eight lives present women saints withstanding sexual assault by dressing, looking, and behaving like men.

In the twenty lives of the virgin martyrs, the description of the torture often veils with obvious sexual symbolism the act of intercourse. Thus, when Saint Lucia in the *Martyrology* resists the advances of the pagan Paschasius, he condemns her to be "defiled" *(bysmrian)* in a whorehouse as punishment; she retorts, "To me the intercourse with thy slave is not more pleasant than if an adder would hurt me" (p. 218, "'nis me þynes weales hæmed næfre þe leofre me nædre toslyte'"). And when the naked Saint Lucia must be tortured, she is finally wounded in the stomach with an obviously phallic sword (p. 218). The virgin martyr becomes a type of the feminine soul joined with Christ to become a *miles Christi*. She spurns sexual contact with men because in a sense she enjoys a spiritual bond with the Perfect Man. Such love between the female soul and Christ is anticipated in the Canticum Canticorum as a celebration of the wedding of the Sponsa and Sponsus, symbolically the Church and Christ, which provides an analogous basis for the holy sacrament of marriage. Such imagery had been established by Greek patristic writers from Methodius to John Climachus and by the Church Fathers Gregory and Augustine, who transmitted it to the Anglo-Saxon and Celtic Churches.[4] Eighth-century writers were familiar with the image of the Heavenly Bride, as in *Blickling Homily* "Annunciatio S. Mariae," and Bede in his *History of the English Church and People* describes royal English daughters being sent to monasteries in France and Gaul, chiefly those of Brie, Chelles, and Andely, to learn and to be bound to the "heavenly bridegroom," "to læranne 7 to geþeodenne þæm heofonlican brydguman" (3.8; see also 3.24).[5] Later, Aelfric identifies the love of Solomon and Sheba as a type of love between Christ and the Church, in "On the Dedication of a Church,"[6] and portrays Christ as a pure Bridegroom who speaks "in the midnight of deep ignorance" in "On the Nativity of the Holy Virgins."[7] He demonstrates the more erotic form of this image in his *Life* of the virgin Saint Agnes, who admits that

> When I love Him,   I am wholly pure;
> when I touch Him,   I am unstained,
> when I receive Him,   I am still virgin,
> and there, in the bridal,   no child lacketh.

> (Þonne ic hine lufige   ic beo eallunga clæne.
> Þonne Ic hine hreppe   ic beo unwemme.
> ðonne Ic hine under-fó   ic beo mæden forð.
> and þær bærn ne ateoriað   on ðam bryd-lace. I, 172)

Appropriately, then, the threat of seduction of the virgin martyr symbolically represents the Devil's adulterous assault on the feminine soul.

For this reason, when Saint Eulalia turns thirteen in the *Martyrology*, Datianus the reeve arrives in town attempting to "*seduce* the Christian men by force from the Christian faith" ("crystene men to nydanne fram Crystes geleafan," my trans., p. 216). But Saint Eulalia and not "Christian men" is subjected to rape, mutilation, and torture (p. 216).

In the remaining eight lives, women saints adopt specifically masculine dress and behavior as a weapon against sexual or spiritual assault in addition to a more figurative spiritual reliance on God as champion of the soul. Six women saints cut off their hair and don masculine garb which allows them to become monks or abbots (Eufemia, Perpetua, Thecla, Pelagia, Eugenia, and Eufrasia).[8] Only two women saints employ the strength of a female animal (she-bear, lioness) to conquer and eventually to convert a pagan male opponent (Columba and Daria).[9] But in a sense all these feminine saints protect themselves from literal or figurative penetration by the Devil when they assume the "armor" of God—masculine *geþohte*, determination, thought, or reason. Just as a woman successfully frustrates and even converts her would-be seducer by appearing and behaving like a man, so also the feminine soul overcomes the Devil by behaving like the masculine part of the soul, reason. The rational soul, or the spirit, is equated with Adam and the concupiscent soul, or the body, with Eve, in illustration of the normal Anglo-Saxon sexual differentiation of epistemological faculties in Bede's quoting of Pope Gregory in his *Letter to Archbishop Augustine*, found in the *History of the English Church and People:*

> For every sin is fulfilled in three ways, namely, first through suggestion, and through delight, and through consent. Suggestion is of the devil, delight of the body, consent of the spirit. For the accursed spirit suggested the first sin through the serpent, and Eve then, as it were the body, took delight, and Adam then, as it were the spirit, consented: then was the sin fulfilled.

> (Forþon þrim gemetum bið gefylled ghwilc syn, þaet is, ærest þurh scynnesse, [ond] þurh lustfullnesse, [ond] þurh geðafunge. Seo scynis bið þurh deoful, seo lustfulnes bið þurh lichoman, seo geðafung þurh gast. Forðon þa ærestan synne se weriga gast scyde þurh þa næddran, ond Euae þa swa swa lichoma wæs lustfulliende, ond Adam heo þonne swa swa gast geþafode: ða wæs seo synn gefylled. 1.27, p. 88)[10]

In the saint's life, the role behavior is reversed: a lusting man pursues and attempts to seduce a feminine *spiritus* or *anima*. Such a desire on the part of a woman to function as a determinedly rational and even heroic man is voiced by Saint Perpetua in the *Martyrology* when she dreams that she has actually become a man, fighting valiantly with a sword and overcoming "the devil and the heathen persecutors with *manly determination*" ("heo mid *werlice geþohte* deofol oferswiðe ond þa hæðnan ehteras," p. 36).

What is clear from these accounts is a patristic identification of the sexes with complementary traits—the masculine with reason and determination, leading to an active and heroic social and political role, and the feminine with passion and passivity, leading to a reduction of political activity unless a queen dissociated from her sex by maintaining exceptional chastity and spirituality, like the woman saint. This interpretation applies also to the strong abbesses of the period, who were similarly chaste and spiritual.

II

Strong queens and leaders manifested a sanctity and chastity that were responsible for the respect they earned within their communities; they can be found in Bede's *History of the English Church and People* (completed A.D. 731) in three roughly chronological groups of exemplary seventh-century women differentiated by their relationships with men, or what might be termed degrees of chastity and sanctity.

The first group consists of secular women who either maintained the practice of Christianity while married to a heathen king or who actually converted a husband, often as a condition of marriage. Examples include Byrhte of the Franks, married to Aethelbehrt; Aethelbeorg, daughter of Aethelbehrt of Kent, married to Eadwine of Northumbria; and Ealhflæd, or Alchfled, daughter of Oswiu of Northumbria, married to Peada, King of the Middle Angles and son of Penda.[11]

A second group consists of lone queens who became strong abbesses but who displayed consistent continence and exemplary Christianity during their transformation from secular to ecclesiastical rulers. Etheldreda or Aetheldryth, daughter of Anna, king of the East Angles, first married Tondberht, prince of the South Gyrwas, but as he died soon after the marriage she then married Ecgfrith. After thirteen years she still remained a virgin, even though Bishop Wilferth had been promised land and money if he could convince her to share Ecgfrith's bed. Because Aetheldryth wished to serve Christ in a monastery, Ecgfrith permitted her to leave. She later became an abbess in the Ely district where she founded a monastery of virgins dedicated to God and became a spiritual mother to many both by her example and her admonitions. After her death, her body did not decay, a fact discovered sixteen years later when the coffin was transferred to the Church, which indicated "that she remained inviolate from man's touch" ("þaet heo from werlicre hrinenesse ungewemmed awundade," 4.19). She is the only English saint mentioned in Aelfric's tenth-century *Lives,* and as an English saint was as popular in England as Saint Brigit was in Ireland, presumably because of her likeness to the Virgin Mary.[12]

A third group, the largest, focuses on kings' daughters who were consecrated to the Lord at an early age and who subsequently attained leadership positions in the monasteries, usually because of their wisdom, sanctity, and chastity. Such strong abbesses included Sæthryth, daughter of the wife of Anna, king of the East Angles, and Aethelberg, the king's own daughter by birth, both of whom became abbesses at the French monastery of Brie despite their foreign birth. Aethelberg's remarkable virginity or *clænisse* was responsible for a miraculous lack of physical decay seven years after her death, made apparent when her coffin was moved to a consecrated church from the unfinished church at her monastery that she had dedicated to the apostles (3.8). Another example, Aelfflæd, daughter of Oswiu, was promised to God as a virgin because of Oswiu's victory over Penda, king of Mercia. She entered Hartlepool and then Streoneshealh, or Whitby, where she functioned first as a pupil and novice, later as a *magister* and *lareow* (teacher) until the age of fifty-nine, "when this blessed virgin passed to the embrace and espousals of the heavenly bridegroom" ("þa heo to clypnesse [ond] to gemungum þæs heofonlican brydguman eadig fæmne ineode," 3.24). Aethelburg, a strong and pious abbess of Barking in the late seventh century, was similarly regarded as "the pious mother of God's congregation" ("seo arfæste modor Gode þære leofan gesomnunge") and the "well-beloved of God" ("Gode seo leofe") about whom other sisters in her abbey had visions before her death and who inspired various sisters to speechlessness, paralysis, and early deaths (4.9). However, the most important example of a strong abbess in this group, and in her worldly career as influential in England as was Aethelryth in her otherworldly sanctity, is Hild, abbess in 680 of the double monastery at Whitby. Daughter of the nephew of King Eadwine, called Hereric, she went into exile for God at the Chelles monastery in France for a year, followed by a year of English conventual discipline, and then became abbess at Hartlepool. This monastery had been built by Hegiu, said to be the first Northumbrian woman to become a nun, and left to Hild's rule when Hegiu built another monastery in Tadcaster. Hild was notable not only for her sanctity but also and especially "for her prudence and wisdom and love for the divine services" ("for hire snytro [ond] wiisdome [ond] for lufe þæs godcundan þeowdomes," 4.23), for

which Bishop Aidan and many other godly men visited her. At Whitby
she constructed another monastery, where "She was of such great prudence and wisdom, that not only ordinary men came there about their
business, but even kings and princes often sought counsel and wisdom
from her, and there readily found it" ("Ond heo swa swiðe leornunge
godcundra gewreota [ond] soðfæstnisse weorcum hire underþeodde dyde
to bigongenne, þætte þær eaðelice monige meahton beon gemette þa þe
to ciriclicum hade, þæt is to wigbedes þegnunge, geþungne wæron,"
4.23). Five bishops studied the Scriptures under her in preparation for
the altar—Bose, Etla, Oftfor, John, and Wilferth. No other abbess exemplifies wisdom and learned counsel quite like Hild. Again, her continence and sanctity may have seemed to the Anglo-Saxons "more than
female spirit."

III

As we have seen, strong and successful Anglo-Saxon queens who were not
abbesses are rare; when they appear in the chronicles and legendary
histories, however, in their chastity and sanctity they resemble their
ecclesiastical and hagiographical counterparts. The strong but unsuccessful queens, accordingly, suffer from a reputation of being immoral and
even heathen.

In the chronicles, only four women played active roles—founding,
building, demolishing, or obtaining control of monasteries and towns.[13]
Seaxburh ruled the West Saxons for a year in 672 after her husband's
death; next, Cuthburh founded a monastery at Wimborne in 718; her
sister-in-law, Queen Aethelburh, demolished Taunton, built by her husband Ine in 722; finally, Aethelflæd, sister of Eadward and "lady" of the
Mercians, between 912 and 918 built boroughs at Scergeat, Bridgnorth,
Tamworth, and Stafford, and obtained control of Derby and Leicester. Of
the four, only Seaxburh and Aethelburh were queens.

When these same four Anglo-Saxon women reappear in William of
Malmesbury's twelfth-century Welsh-Norman legendary (and therefore
not altogether trustworthy) *Chronicle of the Kings of England*, it becomes
clearer why they established monasteries or boroughs so easily. These
women all shared a single characteristic: they manifested great religious
devotion, often which involved the practice of continence either within a
religious community or even within marriage. Thus Cuthburh, after
reading Aldhelm's tracts on virginity, separated from Aelfred, King of
Northumbria, and thereafter led a life devoted to God.[14] Aethelburh or

Ethelburg, her sister-in-law, gained influence through her strong religious beliefs: after converting King Ine to her view of earth's corruptibility, she "soothes his sorrows, serves as his example, helps in his salvation" (in Rome Ine grows old in private, his hair shorn and body modestly garbed; "nec deerat tanti dux foemina facti; quae cum antea virum ad hoc audendum incitasset, tunc moerentem verbis lenire, labantem exemplis erigere, prorsus quod ad salutem ejus spectaret, nihil dimitteret").[15] Æthelflæd, who built or controlled six different boroughs although merely a sister of a king and not a queen, became influential and respected probably because she abstained from sexual contact after the birth of her first child.[16] Finally, Seaxburh, ruling for a year after her husband's death, awed her enemies: "in short, she conducted all things in such a manner, that no difference was discernible except that of her sex. But *breathing more than female spirit,* she died, having scarcely reigned a year" ("She levied new forces, preserved the old in their duty; ruled her subjects with moderation, and overawed her enemies," "prorsus omnia facere, ut nihil praeter sexum discerneres: *veruntamen plus quam foemineos animos anhelantem vita destituit, annua vix potestate perfunctam*").[17] What of queens who "breathed *only* female spirit"? If they remained passive peacemakers, they were accepted by society; if they attempted to gain sovereignty in a kingdom without manifesting chastity and sanctity, they were accused of lechery and immorality—even of ties with the Devil.

IV

The social ideal of woman enunciated in the Old English *Maxims I,* as we have seen, marks her as the peaceful and peace-making complement of the warring male.[18] Thus when Anglo-Saxon documents mention women, and such mentions occur infrequently, those women are introduced in passive roles which underscore their subordinate relationships. Identified mostly in terms of a relationship with a male parent, brother, or husband by means of a phrase such as "daughter of," "sister of," "wife of," and rarely by the title of queen or abbess,[19] such women received mention in the chronicles at the time of marriage or separation, but mention in the passive role of being "taken" in marriage by a husband or "given" in marriage by father[20]; for singular chastity or continence within marriage, or for general sanctity[21]; at the time of death[22]; and at the time of abduction, capture, or murder—for example, when the Southumbrians slew Æthelred's queen Osthryth in 697, or when the English captured

Hæsten's wife and two sons only to release them later, or when the female
Aelfwin, daughter of the powerful Aethelflæd who had ruled after her
husband's death and had reconquered areas previously taken by the
Danes, in 917 "was deprived of all authority in Mercia and taken into
Wessex,"[23] presumably by her uncle. Such dangerous royal daughters
were often sent to obscure convents or married to foreign princes to check
possible claims to the throne by a potential son through whom she might
attempt to rule.

More exceptionally in the chronicles but more frequently in the
charters and writs, noble women appear in active roles wherein they
inherit or bequeath land, testify to others' ownership of land or establish
claims of their own, or wherein they build monasteries, administer as
abbesses, or rule as ladies or as queens. Single women in the wills from
the mid-tenth century to the Norman conquest bequeathed substantial
estates and landholdings as well as jewelry, cups, offering cloths, inden-
tured servants, horses and stock, shields and spears, and even clothing;
among the most substantial bequests were those of Wynflæd (ca. 950) and
Aelfflæd (ca. 1002).[25] However, the control of such property was only
granted to a widow. While married, a woman remained a passive partici-
pant and legal dependent of her husband. A minor woman either came
under the protection of her father, or, if a religious, her abbess and bishop.
Thus relatively few women actually received land charters themselves,
and those who did achieved greater independence than those who did
not, increasing the inequality of women to each other.

Whatever the woman's status, married or widowed, religious or
laywoman, she required male support both legally and physically to
protect her possessions.[26] When women involved themselves in land-
disputes or litigation, they relied upon a man's help; if violence was
perpetrated, a man was usually responsible. For example, Byrhtric,
kinsman of a widow whose lands had been claimed by others, urged her to
take possession of the disputed lands "through violence" ("on reaflace").[27]
And when a woman wished to disown an heir or to change the terms of her
will, her representative generally was male. When Eânwen disowned her
son Eadwine by bequeathing all of her property to her kinswoman
Leoflæd before 1036, the kinswoman's husband Thurkil White aptly conveyed Eânwen's intentions.[28] Further, when a woman wrote a charter
herself, she identified herself in terms of a relationship with a man rather
than in terms of her political role. A king would have begun in Latin with a
preface invoking God the Father as King over all kings analogous to the
English king who reigned over all of the English nation.[29] In contrast, a
woman began in Anglo-Saxon by stating her claim directly after she had
identified her position in terms of the reign of a husband or son: "Eadgið

se hlauedi   Eadwardes kinges lefe," Eadgith wrote, establishing herself as a "lady" and a "relict" or widow of Eadward.[30]

Other noble Anglo-Saxon women mentioned in William of Malmesbury's twelfth-century *Chronicle of the Kings of England* pursued an active political role without the support of a male relative, friend, or champion—except that their intrigues against a king and other ruses designed to gain sovereignty over a kingdom were interpreted as markedly unnatural and immoral. As adversaries they manifested incontinence and paganism which linked them with the Devil. For example, Peada's wife hastened his death through her intrigues, cutting short the "joyful prospects" of his conversion to Christianity.[31] Two more examples of infamous women were both related to Offa. First, his granddaughter Quendrida killed her brother Saint Kenelm while she was supposedly educating him: "But she, *falsely entertaining hopes of the kingdom for herself*, gave her little brother in charge to a servant of her household, with an order to despatch him" (italics added, pp. 238–9) ("Sed illa, *falso sibi regnum praesagiens*, fraterculum tollendum e medio satelliti qui alumpnus erat commendavit").[32] This evil woman was appropriately punished by having her eyes torn from their sockets as she read the Psalms backwards. Second, Offa the Mercian's daughter Eadburga became queen of the West Saxons by marrying Bertric, after which, jealous of anyone seeking her husband's favor, she tried to manipulate the courtiers and gain power for herself. Indeed, she "used to persuade him, a tender-hearted man, as they report, to the destruction of the innocent, and would herself take off by poison those against whom her accusations failed."[33] After she accidentally killed the king himself with her poison, she was driven from the kingdom and placed in a monastery; later she was expelled because of her incontinence. Her cruelty and power-seeking compelled the West Saxons to refuse the king's consort the title of queen and the seat next to the king until Aethelwulf fifty years later granted these privileges to his *foreign* wife, Judith—inciting his son to overthrow him and marry his stepmother Judith himself.[34]

The foreign nationality of Judith encouraged William of Malmesbury to identify her apparent intrigue against Aethelwulf as immoral. Such interesting logic can perhaps be explained by a metaphor used in a passage from Asser's ninth-century *De rebus gestis Aelfredi* that describes pagans who "fled like women" ("muliebriter fugam arripiunt") when Aethelwulf and his Christian men "manfully withstood them" in battle ("viriliter obviaverunt").[35]

The value of bravery for the Anglo-Saxons is naturally associated with masculine and Christian heroes; cowardice as non-heroic behavior is manifested by women and pagans. Similarly, Saxo Grammaticus' twelfth-century *History of the Danes* describes Zealanders who thought "it shameful to obey the rule of a woman" ("femineis parere legibus probrosum rati").[36] They appealed to Ole "not to suffer men that had been used to serve under a famous king to be kept under a woman's yoke" (p. 319, "Olonem accedunt, postulantes, ne clarissimi regis milicie assuetos muliebri iugo obnoxios haberi pateretur," 8.264). Ole subsequently forced the ruling woman, Hetha, to relinquish her rule over all regions except Jutland, which he made into a tributary state "so as not to allow a woman the free control of a kingdom" (p. 319, "ne femine liberum regni usum tribueret," 8. 265).

Even women agreed they should forego sovereignty over men. Gorm's wife, Thyra, daughter of the English king Aethelred, felt honored to permit her two sons to displace her as heirs to her father's kingdom. The English king acted prudently, "for he knew that it beseemed men to enjoy the sovereignty rather than women, and considered that he ought to separate the lot of his *unwarlike* daughter from that of her *valiant* sons" (p. 388; "quoniam aliquanto speciosius mares quam feminas regni usum decere nouerat, *imbellis* filie ac *fortissimorum* nepotum condicionem separandam existimans," 9.320, italics added).

These unconventional Anglo-Saxon queens and abbesses have illustrated a remarkable consistency in relation to our argument that chastity, wisdom, and sanctity permitted women to play an active role both socially and politically. The stories we have used—a mixture of historical document and literary work—have also demonstrated a confluence between fact and fiction. Literature verges into history, history or document borrows from legend, and legendary chronicle mixes both. This interweaving also occurs with biblical history and Anglo-Saxon literature. Anglo-Saxon women who usurp sovereignty, who behave in an unfeminine fashion, also have a biblical counterpart—Eve. Throughout the literature of the period, unconventional queens of all types find themselves allied with Eve both implicitly and explicitly, as we shall see.

5

Eve in *Genesis B*

Anti-Type of the Peace-Weaver and the Virgin Mary

A NGLO-SAXON WOMAN'S ideal secular role as peace-weaver or peace
pledge was analogous to the Virgin's role as intermediary between
man and God; in addition, the Virgin perfected all the secular roles
available to women—maiden, wife, mother, virago. The virgin Juliana,
the widow Judith, and the chaste mother Elene represent attempts to
imitate these individual roles of Mary. Abbesses and queens of the period
could thus adapt their behavior to that glorified and sanctified in the
religious literature.

For queens who did not remain chaste and acquiescent, there was a
different model, one also found in the Bible—Eve. She was the exemplar
for the disobedient wife, the uninformed virgin bride, and her behavior,
of which the Anglo-Saxons disapproved, would thus be portrayed as an
inversion of the role of the peace-weaver through an arrogation of the
heroic role of the retainer. This biblical model in the Anglo-Saxon translation of *Genesis B* provides an explicit anti-type of the Virgin that would be
used for comparison with other failed women—in the elegies spoken by
female narrators and in the epic *Beowulf*.

In *Genesis B* the concept of Eve's disobedience to God because of
her seduction by an angelic Tempter governs the poet's portrayal of her in
both theological and social terms, and thus can be used to resolve the
problem of her innocence or guilt, which has been probed rather exten-
sively by critics of the poem. The problem derives from the poet's explanation for the temptation of Eve in that she had a "mind weaker" (*wacran
hige*, 590b) than that of Adam; does this mean that she was unfairly
deceived and thus blameless; that she was not innocent but nevertheless
not guilty of vanity and pride; that Adam was more at fault than Eve; or

þeron þam lupum com··

A line drawing of Eve and Adam being tempted by an angelic
Tempter. Early eleventh-century illustration for *Genesis B*. MS
Junius XI, fol. 28. Photo permission of the Bodleian Library, Oxford.

that the Tempter was primarily culpable?[1] One clue to the poet's intentions may exist in the contrast by Saint Irenaeus between the disobedience of Eve as a *virgin* and the obedience of Mary as *Virgin:* "For as Eve
was seduced by an angel's words so as to shun God, after she had
transgressed His word, so Mary also by an angel's word had the glad
tidings given her, that she might bear God, obeying his word . . . a
virgin's disobedience is saved by a Virgin's obedience."[2] This very virginity, according to one patristic commentator, was responsible for her
weaker nature, perhaps because of her innocence, and the angel's decision
to "seduce" her: Saint Cyril of Jerusalem comments on Genesis 3:12, 13
that Satan "did not dare to approach the man because of his strength, but

addressed himself to the woman as the weaker, whilst she was still a virgin."[3]

In this chapter, I shall argue, first, that this virginity not only explains the phrase "wacran hige," which many critics have regarded as a pejorative description of Eve's intelligence,[4] but that it also explains, through implicit patristic notions of the parallels between Eva and Ave, previously unexplained segments of the poem dealing with the prelapsarian (and Eve-like, original) beauty of Satan, of the Tree of Life, and of the vision of creation granted to her by the Tempter. In addition, I shall argue that one reason for the parallel between Satan and Eve derives from the Germanic tradition: Satan, during his Fall and later temptation of Eve, is also depicted as a disloyal retainer in counterpoint to Eve as peaceweaver. The angel tempts her with appeals to her future role as peaceweaver and mother, and, given her "wacran hige," she succumbs, believing it her duty to fulfill those roles and protect the peace between Adam and the Lord. Thirdly, I shall argue that the consequences of the Fall explicitly stress Eve's role as weaver, if not peace-weaver, a particularly attractive image to an Anglo-Saxon audience. Thus the poem boasts two levels, biblical and Germanic, which interlace with each another throughout.

I

Although Eve is not termed a virgin by the Anglo-Saxon poet, she is described as a *bryd, wif,* and *ides* in images that suggest light, brightness, shining, beauty, and purity. "Þas bryd" (line 526b) is a "wlitesciene wif" (527a), "the brightly beautiful woman," or the most beautiful woman, "wifa wlitegost" (lines 627a, 822a). *Wlite* means "beauty" but can also mean "glory" or "ornament" and according to Bosworth-Toller is used to refer to the brightness of gems, flowers, the sun and the soul as well as to physical beauty. *Scine* (or *sciene, scene, sceone, scione, scyne*) is the word most often used to describe her, which means beautiful, bright, fair, but which also connoted clarity, glittering, shining, and sheen, as in the case of stars, the sun, and jewels, according to the citations in Bosworth-Toller. She is "shaped fair," or "formed bright" ("sceone gesceapene," 549a), the most shining of ladies, "idesa scenost" (626b, 704b, 821b). Eve's beauty resembles treasure and precious objects; its shining splendor kin to that of stars and sun resembles the glory of the initial creation by God. Indeed, three other figures or symbols in the poem are described similarly, probably in order to link them with the virgin bride Eve as equally "shining" in beauty—unfallen, prelapsarian, perfect. These three foils include the unfallen Lucifer, the Tree of Life, and the vision of creation granted to Eve.

First, Lucifer before his fall is termed white (radiant), beautiful, shining. God made him

> so white [radiant],
> so beautiful was his form in heaven   that came to him from the lord
>   of the band,
> like he was to the lights of the stars.

> (swa hwitne geworhtne,
> swa wynlic wæs his wæstm on heofonum   þæt him com from
>   weroda drihtne,
> gelic wæs he þam leohtum steorrum. 254b–6a)

"Hwit" as "white" or "shining" is also used of a helmet in *Beowulf* (1448), of stone, and the white of an egg; *hwitan* means "to polish." Together these significations suggest the brightness of silver treasure and light and link Lucifer with Eve. Indeed, because he is conscious of his great beauty of form (he is also mightier in thought and in strength than the other angels, that is, made "swa swiðne geworhtne, / swa mihtigne on his modgeþohte," 252b–53a), he becomes very aroused and proud, admitting in words similar to those describing Eve that his body is light and shining, white and hue-bright: "cwæð þæt his lic wære   leoht and scene, / hwit and hiowbeorht" (265–66a). As the most shining of the angels ("engla scynost," 338b) and the whitest in heaven ("hwitost on heofne," 339a), he appropriately falls to his dark opposite—"swart hell" ("þære sweartan helle," 345b) in a low deep bottomless place to contrast with his original supernal radiance and light.

His prelapsarian state is reflected also in the bright and shining Tree of Life just as his fallen state in hell is reflected in the dark Tree of Death. In the description of the two trees the word *se wæstm*, "form," "result," or "growth," but also, more literally, "fruit," echoes the same word used previously to describe the beauty of Satan's form ("fruit") given to him by the lord of the hosts; the words *scene* (shining), *wynlic* (pleasing) and *wlitig* (beautiful) echo the descriptions of both Satan and Eve. Of the two trees,

> The form was not the same!
> The other was so pleasing,   beautiful and shining,
> lithe and praiseworthy,   that was the Beam of Life.

(Næs se wæstm gelic!
Oðer wæs swa wynlic,   wlitig and scene,
liðe and lofsum,   þæt wæs lifes beam. 466b–68)

He who eats of this tree lives forever in gladness, without old age or illness, with honors or favor (*hyldo,* 474a) of the heavenly king in high heaven. But the Tree of Death was "entirely swart, dim and dark; that was the Beam of Death, which bore much bitterness" ("Þonne wæs se oðer   eallenga sweart, / dim and þystre;   þæt wæs deaðes beam, / se bær bitres fela," 477–79a). The consequences of eating this fruit parallel the consequences of the fall of Lucifer—old age, misery, darkness, death, hell, fire.

This addition of the unattractive Tree of Death to the Old Saxon original may have been prompted by the rather conventional contrast of the Tree of Knowledge of Good and Evil and the "tree" of Christ's crucifixion, behind which of course looms the contrast between Eve and Mary. Saint Ambrose remarks in his Sermon 45, "De primo Adam et secundo," that

> Eve made us to be damned by an apple of the tree, Mary absolved us by the gift of the tree: because Christ also hung upon the tree, as if fruit.
>
> As if therefore we died through a tree, so through a tree we are brought to life. A tree manifested to us our nakedness, a tree dressed us with leaves of indulgence: a tree stimulated the heat of sins; a tree of knowledge prepared us with clothes for the cold after the dispossession: a tree begot thorns and briars, a tree of knowledge hope and salvation.
>
> (Eva nos damnari fecit per arboris pomum, Maria absolvit per arboris donum; quia et Christus in ligno pependit, ut fructus.
>
> Igitur sicut per arborem mortui, ita per arborem vivificati. Arbor nobis nuditatem ostendit, arbor indulgentiae foliis vestivit: arbor peccatorum incussit ardorem; refrigerium delictorum vestibus praeparavit arbor scientiae: arbor spinas et tribulos genuit, spem et salutem arbor scientiae peperit.)[5]

The truer "fruit" is that of Christ and not mere formal beauty seen as an end in itself, especially by Lucifer.

The third parallel exists in the vision of creation granted to Eve by the Tempter to share with Adam; it suggests the purity and brilliance of the original creation while it also extends the earlier "two visions" of the unfallen Lucifer and Eve. To Eve it appeared that heaven and earth had become *hwitre*, whiter (603a), and all the world *wlitigre*, more beautiful, more shining (604a), two words used to describe Lucifer, the Tree of Life, and herself in their pristine original beauty. In another sense the vision represents "treasure" which she receives in response to her "obedience." But there exist other parallels. Here too the word *wæstm* (form, result, fruit) recurs to link all three passages. The messenger has first reminded Eve of her new fallen power or "fruit":

> You can now see yourself, as I need not say to you
> Eve the good, that to you is unlike
> the beauty and *forms* [*fruits*].
>
> ("þu meaht nu þe self geseon, swa ic hit þe secgan ne þearf,
> Eue seo gode, þæt þe is ungelic
> wlite and wæstmas." 611–13a)

Then he points out the splendor of the heavenly vision which so parallels her own and Lucifer's original beauty: "Nu scineð þe leoht fore / glædlic ongean þæt ic from gode brohte / hwit of heofonum" (614–16a; "Now shines the light before you gladly that I from heaven brought, / white from the heavens"). The previous contrast between the light and dark of Lucifer's two states and the two trees reappears here in the vision from heaven and the "fruits" or "consequences" of the fall of Adam and Eve. After the fall, Adam "received from the woman hell and a journey from this world [death], though it was not called so, but it must have the name of fruit (*ofetes*)," "He æt þam wife onfeng / helle and hinnsið, þeah hit nære haten swa, / ac hit ofetes noman agan sceolde," 717b–19). That is, all created things as well as consequences of actions are not only formed from the results of growth, but are also fruits, as symbolized by the fruit of the two Trees and in this case the "fruit" of the fall of Adam and Eve, hell and death.

II

These parallels and contrasts derive from the poet's desire to render the concept of disobedience by Satan and especially Eve through the contemporary guise of Anglo-Saxon social roles. The Anglo-Saxon emphasis on Eve's characterization and role in the poem concurs with what has been found to be one of the major differences between *Genesis B* and its sources—that is, the conception of Satan as a proud, defiant, Germanic warrior.[6] If Adam fails as retainer to the Lord, then Satan too serves as a foil for his failure. And if Eve oversteps the bounds of the Anglo-Saxon peace-weaver, then, because the role of peace-weaver was not alone responsible for social order, Eve's sin of disobedience cannot be regarded as more heinous than that of her lord Adam. Nevertheless, the poet wishes his audience to understand that all three figures are related by their disobedience, an idea concretized through the similar contrasts between white and shining and dark and infernal imagery and diction describing each.

Satan exemplifies the retainer who forsakes loyalty to his lord out of a desire to pursue his own interests, perhaps the most despicable crime possible in the *comitatus*. Many of the Germanic images in the description of Satan and his actions have already been noted by scholars of the poem[7]: God is a chieftain ("drihten," ruler, 299a; "hearra," lord, 358b; "drihtna drihten," ruler of rulers, 637a; "waldend," leader, 673a) whose throne ("stol," 281b) this proud king ("se ofermoda cyning," 338a) desires in order to rule over brave warriors ("rofe rincas," 286a) who have betrayed their service ("þegnscipe," 326b) to their rightful lord. Further, and rather ironically, he invokes the loyalty of his own comrades in his attempt to overthrow first the Lord and later Adam and Eve. In the first situation he demands to know

> Why must I after his favor seek,
> bow before him with such homage?   I can be God as he can.
> Stand by me strong companions,   who will not fail me in the strife;
> bold-spirited heroes.   They have chosen me for lord,
> brave warriors;   with such can one consider a plan,
> implement it with such companions in war.   They are my zealous
>   friends,
> loyal in their minds.   I can be their lord,
> rule in this kingdom.

> (Hwy sceal ic æfter his hyldo ðeowian,
> bugan him swilces geongordomes?   Ic mæg wesan god swa he.
> Bigstandað me strange geneatas,   þa ne willað me æt þam striðe
>   geswican,
> hæleþas heardmode.   Hie habbað me to hearran gecorene,
> rofe rincas;   mid swilcum mæg man ræd geþencean,
> fon mid swilcum folcgesteallan.   Frynd synd hie mine georne,
> holde on hyra hygesceaftum.   Ic mæg hyra hearra wesan,
> rædan on þis rice. 282b–89a)

In the second instance, he asks for a follower's loyal service: to fly out of
the prison of hell and to tempt Adam and Eve as repayment for his gifts of
treasures in the past (409–20). The Tempter who volunteers for the mission then proceeds to arm himself in a passage with epic echoes, but
Anglo-Saxon heroic diction:

> Began then to prepare himself   the enemy of God,
> ready in his trappings   (he had a faithless spirit),
> a helm that makes the wearer invisible he set upon his head and
>   bound it full hard,
> fastened it with clips.
>
> (Angan hine þa gyrwan   godes andsaca,
> fus on frætwum,   [hæfde fæcne hyge],
> hæleðhelm on heafod asette   and þone ful hearde geband,
> spenn mid spangum. 442–45a)

This Tempter performs his service faithfully and imagines his lord will be
pleased.

His temptation of Adam in some ways resembles Lucifer's arguments to convince himself of the value of overthrowing God's throne, but
it differs in that the Tempter requests obedience and service from this
"retainer" of God rather than usurpation of a throne. Certainly it invites a
normally loyal retainer to prove his *comitatus* virtues once again. First,
the Tempter suggests that, after eating the fruit, he will become more
glorious (*mara*, 501b)—in his strength (*abal*), skill (*cræft*, 500b) and mind
(*modsefa*, 501a)—and his body (*lichoma*, 502a) lighter (*leohtra*, 502b) and
more radiant (*scenran*, 503a). Here is a miniature parody of the self-
conscious narcissistic motivations of Satan and the "shining" diction used
to describe them. Second, the Tempter stresses the duty of service in
return for the *hyldo* (504b–6, Germanic favor, Christian grace) of the
heavenly king through the use of the word *læstan* (509a, 517b, "to serve or
follow") with its similar dual connotations. But in a higher form of obedience to his lord, the retainer Adam spurns the Tempter's bidding,
because God has previously warned him never to eat of the fruit of the
Tree of Death and because he is confused and uncertain about the angel's
words and non-angelic appearance. It is only then that the Tempter turns
to Eve, for whom God had shaped a "weaker mind" ("hæfde hire wacran
hige / metod gemearcod," 590b–1a). In accord with the Anglo-Saxon
context outlined above, this "weaker mind" must be read not only as a

virgin mind but as the mind of the peace-weaver, who occupied a less aggressive and warlike role than that of the lord.

The basis of the Tempter's appeal to Eve is revealed in his opening arguments, one addressed to the future mother whose primary concern centers on the birth of healthy children and one to the peace-weaver whose primary concern involves the establishment of peace between two different tribes or members of a single tribe. He argues first that she should now obey God by eating the fruit to prevent future injuries to their offspring: "he said that the greatest of injuries to all of their offspring afterwards would exist in the world" if she would not eat ("cwæð þæt sceaðena mæst / eallum heora eaforum   æfter siððan / wurde on worulde," 549b–51a). Second, in a much longer speech (551–87), he argues that she should protect Adam from God's wrath and even earn God's favor by convincing him to eat of the fruit, too. He stresses initially the necessity to reduce enmity between Adam and the Lord, enmity which will surely ensue if he does not obey:

> "I know that mighty God at you two
> will be angered,   when I Him this message
> say myself,   when I from this journey come
> over a long way,   that you two do not perform well
> each command   as He from the east hither
> at this time sends."

> ("Ic wat, inc waldend god
> abolgen wyrð,   swa ic him þisne bodscipe
> selfa secge,   þonne ic of þys siðe cume
> ofer langne weg,   þæt git ne læstan wel
> hwilc ærende swa   he easten hider
> on þysne sið sendeð." 551b–56a)

The use of the word *læstan* in 554b (and again in 572a) signifies "performance" or "doing service" with heroic connotations, as it is used of Beowulf in line 2663 and also of Grendel's body in line 812 when, like a retainer to a lord, it fails to "serve" him. Specifically God will be angry at their failure to perform the kind of service expected from retainers. The Tempter then appeals to Eve's emotional investment in the role of peace-weaver as a way of ameliorating the hostility that may exist between God and his retainer Adam: "Think in your heart that you can ward off punishment from you both, as I will show you" ("Gehyge on þinum breostum   þæt þu inc bam twam meaht / wite bewarigan,   swa ic þe wisie," 562–63). The means to

the achievement of this peace, and even to the favor *(hyldo)* of her Lord
(557), exists in the apple which she must eat. The word *hyldo* recurs
throughout the various temptations and manifests the double levels so
important to an understanding of the poem, as "grace" in the Christian
sense, "favor" in the Germanic sense.[8] Further, the Tempter stresses the
strife between Adam and the Lord to remind Eve of the need for her
peacemaking abilities. He declares, "If you say to him truly what precept
you yourself have in your breast, that you the bidding of God perform by
teaching, he will forsake the *hostile strife*" ("Gif þu him to soðe
sægst   hwylce þu selfa hæfst / bisne on breostum,   þæs þu gebod godes /
lare læstes,   he þone laðan strið / . . . an forlæteð," 570–73). "Strið"
appears only in *Genesis B,* according to Bosworth-Toller, in three instances: first, in line 284 when Satan mentions his warriors loyal to him in
the strife or battle between himself and God; second, here, when the
Tempter mentions the enmity between Adam and Eve and God; and
third, in line 663 when the Tempter advises Adam to forego the strife
between Adam and Eve and God. In return for the service of Eve as a
peace-weaver, the Tempter will conceal from God Adam's insults concerning his non-angelic appearance and thus reinforce her peacemaking
efforts. His argument concludes with another appeal to her pride as "the
best of women," "idesa seo betste" (578), implicitly demanding her coop-
eration *as* a woman.

Because she is a woman whose chief work in the Anglo-Saxon sense
is peace making and not warfare, she succumbs to his wiles. At this point
the poet reminds the audience of her "weaker mind": "the thought of the
worm began to surge   (God had marked for her a *weaker mind*), so that
she began to turn her mind toward that teaching" ("weallan wyrmes
geþeaht,   [hæfde hire *wacran hige* / metod gemearcod],   þæt heo hire
mod ongan / lætan æfter þam larum," 590–92). The use of the word
wacran in other contexts indicates it can in one sense denote "more
yielding" or "more pliant," or in another, "more wanting in courage, or
mental or moral strength," as in manly strength. Wulfstan, for example, in
"De fide catholica," condemns the weak Christian man who cannot think
as he has been formed to think ("Wac bið þæt geðanc on cristenum men,
gif he ne cann understandan þurh rihtne geleafan þæne þe hine gescop"[9]).
Thus Eve fails here not because she is unintelligent or inferior to Adam
but because she has not been trained to resist, to fight, to remain strong
against an adversary, and because this "best of women" in an Anglo-Saxon
society would have been trained instead to concede, to ameliorate, and to
harmonize.

After Eve eats the fruit, she turns to convince Adam to do the same
through two main arguments related to the Germanic *comitatus* roles of

the Tempter and herself. The first centers on her belief in the "loyal intent" ("holdne hyge," 654) of the Tempter, who has himself declared his long service to God ("herran minum, / drihtne selfum," 586b–87a) through his loyal mind ("þurh holdne hyge," 586a) as a *þegn* (the verb *þegnode,* 585b), and thus has convinced Eve by his use of these heroic words of his efficacy and sincerity as a retainer. She also believes him to be a true angel of God because she would not have received the heavenly vision of light if he had not been an angel. But her second argument is more important to her: she is anxious to reduce the enmity (*wiðermedo,* 660b) between them and the Lord, and like a faithful peace-weaver urges her husband to eat the fruit because she wishes to win for them His favor (*hyldo,* 659b):

> "His *favor* is for us better
> to be winning   than his enmity.
> If you today spoke   harms to him,
> he will nevertheless forgive it   if we two to him homage
> will perform.   What for you must such hateful strife
> against the messenger of your lord do?   To us is his *favor* needful;
> he can for us carry tidings   to the ruler,
> the king of heaven."

> ("His *hyldo* is unc betere
> to gewinnanne   þonne his wiðermedo.
> Gif þu him heodæg wuht   hearmes gespræce,
> he forgifð hit þeah,   gif wit him geongordom
> læstan willað.   Hwæt scal þe swa laðlic strið
> wið þines hearran bodan?   Unc is his *hyldo* þearf;
> he mæg unc ærendian   to þam alwaldan,
> heofoncyninge." 659b–66a)

The words she uses mirror her consciousness of the *comitatus* roles they play. The contrast between feud (*wiðermedo,* 660b; *laðlic strið,* 663b) and favor (*hyldo,* 659b, 664b) is made more profound by the use of *comitatus* words like *geongordom* (homage, 662b), *læstan* (to perform or serve, 663a), and *hearran* (664a) and *heofoncyninge* (666a), for the "ruler" and "heavenly king."

The poet exonerates Eve, to a certain extent, because she faithfully pursues her role as peace-weaver. "She did it nevertheless through *loyal mind;* she did not know that there so many harms must follow, sinful woes" ("Heo dyde hit þeah þurh *holdne hyge,*   nyste þæt þær hearma swa fela, / fyrenearfeða,   fylgean sceolde," 708–709). The fact of her partial innocence

as a peace-weaver is confirmed by the statement that she would not have
sought such a peace if she had known such enmity and misery would
ensue. However, the same phrase, "þurh holdne hyge," is also used by
the Tempter to assure Eve that he serves God "through loyal mind" (586a),
and again when he grants her the vision to convince her of "his loyal
mind" (654a). It is the retainer and not the peace-weaver who usually
serves his lord "þurh holdne hyge." But perhaps that *is* the poet's point: in
making decisions for both her lord and herself, even if a decision to make
peace, Eve has arrogated for the peace-weaver the duties of the retainer.
Thus the poet adds, "she thought that she had worked the *hyldo* of the
heavenly king with these words" ("ac wende þæt heo *hyldo*   heofoncyninges / worhte mid þam wordum" 712–13a), as if she were the retainer
seeking favor and not a peace-weaver attempting peace. The poet's second
point is that in serving Adam loyally she has unfortunately ignored the
higher obligation of every human soul first to serve the Lord loyally. Her
excessive preoccupation with her lord and husband is revealed by the use
of her *comitatus* address to "frea min" (655a) and "wine min" (823b).

    After Adam eats the fruit, the consequences of their actions are
made clear to them in both *comitatus* and patristic terms. Suddenly, they
become aware that they have earned not the favor of God but his hate
(*hete*, 768a) and his feud (*nið*, 768b). Eve mourns that she has failed as a
peace-weaver and lost the favor of God: "The woman mourned, sad in
heart (she had lost the favor of God, / his counsel)," "Þaet wif gnornode, /
hof hreowigmod,   (hæfde hyldo godes, / lare forlætan)" (770b–72a). Adam
blames Eve, regrets ever seeing her, and mourns the loss of God's favor:
"So now I can regret / that I ever saw you with my eyes" ("Swa me nu
hreowan mæg / æfre to aldre   þæt ic þe minum eagum geseah," 819–20);
and "Now I have forfeited my lord's favor" ("nu ic mines þeodnes hafa /
hyldo forworhte," 836b–37a). The difference in their reactions to the Fall
is interesting, largely because Adam appears to deny responsibility for his
own fault and Eve clearly accepts it. Adam's regret that he has ever seen
Eve "with his eyes" is not, however, merely a crude attempt to forego
responsibility. As the white, shining, gleaming epitome of female beauty,
the virgin bride has represented to him a silver-like treasure for which he
has demonstrated an inordinate *comitatus* fondness. Consequently, he has
relinquished his duty as retainer to the Lord to her. Thus blaming his eyes
for originally seeing (and coveting) her virgin beauty represents another
way of pinpointing his blame not only as uxoriousness but also as avarice,
or concupiscence of the eyes. Eve similarly acknowledges her guilt in the
failure of her emotions, specifically her anxiety for peace and her rather
excessively maternal love and concern for Adam: "Nevertheless it can be

no worse for you / in your mind to sorrow   than it does for me in my heart" ("hit þe þeah wyrs ne mæg / on þinum hyge hreowan   þonne hit me æt heortan deð," 825b–26).

III

The consequences of their actions are also clarified for them in a vision of the future whose significance can be explained through patristic commentators and Anglo-Saxon metaphors. Adam becomes aware of hunger, thirst, and especially nakedness, the latter which leaves them without protection from the elements. Much of his complaint derives from his fears about the wind, frost, rain, and extreme heat—metynomies for the four seasons—that will affect them adversely in their nakedness:

> "How shall we now live   or exist in this land,
> if the wind comes here,   or from the west or east,
> south or north?   If a cloud rises up,
> comes a shower of hail,   driving from heaven,
> fares the frost in our midst,   which is cold to men.
> For a while from the heavens   heat shines,
> glitters this bright sun,   and we here bare stand,
> unguarded by clothes.   We do not have above us an umbrella [*lit.*
>   protection],
> against storms,   nor a whit of *sceatt* [penny]
> marked out for food,   for toward us mighty God,
> the Ruler, is wrath-minded."

> ("Hu sculon wit nu libban   oððe on þys lande wesan,
> gif her wind cymð,   westan oððe eastan,
> suðan oððe norðan?   Gesweorc up færeð,
> cymeð hægles scur   hefone getenge,
> færeð forst on gemang,   se byð fyrnum ceald.
> Hwilum of heofnum   hate scineð,
> blicð þeos beorhte sunne,   and wit her baru standað,
> unwered wædo.   Nys unc wuht beforan
> to scursceade,   ne sceattes wiht
> to mete gemearcod,   ac unc is mihtig god,
> waldend wraðmod." 805–15a)

After confessing their shame and contrition, they seek out the "protection of this forest" ("þisses holtes hleo," 840a) because "we can no longer be thus bare together" ("Ac wit þus baru ne magon   bu tu ætsomne / wesan," 838–39a). The emphasis on the need for shelter and clothing culminates in the image of their covering their bodies with leaves and foliage, for they had no weeds ("Þa hie heora lichoman   leafum beþeahton, / weredon mid ðy wealde,   wæda ne hæfdon," 845–46).

Interestingly enough, several patristic commentators regarded Eve as appropriately responsible for devising clothing from leaves as a punishment for her sin in making them both aware of their nakedness. Saint Epiphanius in *Haerarchia* 78, n. 19, glosses the ancient Greek rendering of Job 38, 36 (which differs from the Vulgate), *Who hath given to woman wisdom, or knowledge of weaving,* by contrasting the clothing woven by Eve with the garment of immortality created out of the Lamb by the Virgin Mary.

> Since, on the one hand, the first wise Eve devised material garments for Adam, whom she had made to be naked—for to her was given this toil. And because through her it was that the nakedness was discovered, to her it was given to clothe that body thus exposed to visible nakedness. But to Mary was it given by God to bear for us a lamb and sheep, that out of the glory of that same lamb and sheep might be wrought for us, as from a fleece, in wisdom through its virtue, a garment of immortality.[10]

The "wise Eve" who assumed too much responsibility in dealing with the Tempter is here given a different kind of responsibility, that, for an Anglo-Saxon society, would seem fitting, given Eve's (and woman's) role as a peace-weaver. Thus the punishment fits the crime. Although the *Genesis B* poet does not remind his audience of this role explicitly, and although he may not have been aware of, much less have understood, the Greek text of Saint Epiphanius (even with the possible influence of the Hibernian scholars of the seventh and eighth centuries, those who knew some Greek), nevertheless he does implicitly emphasize the clothing, or lack of clothing, of the pair in the above long passage, and throughout the poem his selection of details seems to rely on some awareness of the Ave-Eva contrasts cited by the commentators. Indeed, there exists one other image of Mary herself as part of a divine weaving metaphor that relates both to the patristic role of Eve as weaver and the Anglo-Saxon Eve of *Genesis B* as peace-weaver. Saint Proclus, in his *Oratio* 1: *Laudatio in sanctissimam Dei genitricem Mariam,* describes the Incarnation allegorically through images of the loom, weaver, wool, woof, and weaving-shuttle, with the Virgin as the woof:

the awful loom of the Incarnation, wherein in ineffable manner that garment of union was wrought of which the Holy Ghost is weaver; the overshadowing Power from on high, weaveress; the old fleece of Adam, the wool; the most pure flesh of the Virgin, the woof; the immense grace of her who bore the Artificer, the weaving-shuttle— the Word, in fine, coming gently in from on high at the hearing of the ear.[11]

Implicitly, then, the *Genesis B* poet ends his poem with a note of optimism through the clothing of Adam and Eve: this first and postlapsarian weaving by Eve in the midst of shame, fear, confusion, and the darkness of the future will be glorified by the later heavenly weaving of the Holy Ghost through the Virgin Mary, bringing with it the promise of redemption and recovery of Paradise. Interlaced with this biblical image of clothing and weaving is the Germanic *comitatus* image of the peace-weaver who has failed but who will continue in succeeding centuries to toil for peace between family members and between tribes, weaving through words and offspring what the First Peace-weaver attempted through her disobedient eating of the fruit and her later weaving of leaves into suitable covering for the pair. Leaving these dual levels—biblical and Germanic—of *Genesis B* and the appropriately dual images of Eve as a type of the Virgin Mary and as peace-weaver, we turn now to the images of Eve in the woman narrators of the elegies and Grendel's Mother in the epic *Beowulf*.

6

The Errant Woman as *Scop* in *Wulf and Eadwacer* and *The Wife's Lament*

T HE EARLIEST EDITOR of *Wulf and Eadwacer* excused his inability to translate the poem with these words: "Of this I make no sense."[1] An enigma, it thus resembles another Old English elegy, *The Wife's Lament*, with its description of the puzzling and unexplained details of the narrator's life. Both of these poems, written in the late ninth or early tenth century, are commonly believed to be narrated by women, although—in accord with their generally elliptical natures—there exists one school of critics that believes their speakers are male.[2] While only one critic has hazarded this view of *Wulf and Eadwacer*, others, beginning with Benjamin Thorpe in his 1842 edition and continuing to the present, have argued that the feminine forms in the first two lines of *The Wife's Lament*, forms such as *geomorre* (line 1) and *minre sylfre* (line 2), are merely scribal errors.[3] In support of this view, it should be noted that it is unusual to find love poetry in English spoken by women[4] at this relatively early date, late ninth or tenth century.

Nevertheless, this study will argue that these puzzling poems were indeed narrated by women *personae*, if not actually written by them (a point which cannot be proven), and that the authors of these elegies portrayed these *personae* as *scopas* who have inverted feminine social roles. The contrast between their perspective as mock *scopas* can best be seen when these two poems are examined in the light of poems by, or about, *scopas* themselves, *Widsith* and *Deor*.

The metaphor of the *scop* is chiefly conveyed through the use of the word *giedd* or *gidd* to describe what the narrator is reciting. Generally, the word *gidd* describes a metrical composition usually true and sad recited by the *scop* in a heroic setting or by some wise man at another

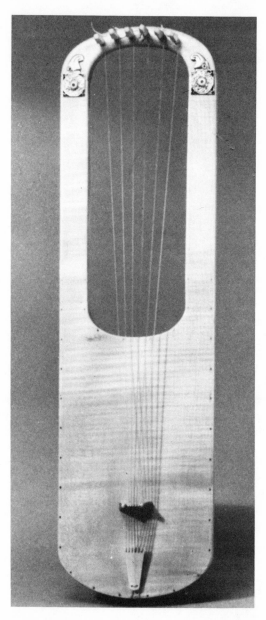

The scop's lyre, reconstructed from the Sutton Hoo ship–burial fragments. Photo reproduced by permission of the Trustees of the British Museum.

ceremonial occasion. It can as well connote the prophetic and enigmatic. In *The Lament* the wife employs the word *giedd* to describe her own story, which involves her experiences with her lover or husband: "I this *giedd* will recite about me full sad, about the journey of my self" ("Ic þis giedd wrece   bi me ful geomorre,/ minre sylfre sið," 1–2a). In *Wulf and Ead-wacer*, the speaker concludes by apparently describing her relationship with her lover or husband as a *giedd:* "One easily slits what was never united, our *giedd* together" ("þæt mon eaþe tosliteð   þætte næfre gesom-nad wæs,/ uncer giedd geador," 18–19).

The use of the word in these two poems startles because of its contextual incongruity—both poems have natural exterior rather than civilized interior settings—and both have female narrators. In both poems we shall find that the narrator imagines herself in the ironic role of *scop* singing a *giedd* and her lover in the role of lord, to lament his unconven-tional and even unheroic treatment of her. In each case the use of the image of the *scop* or retainer to the lord masks the failure, possibly involuntary, of a feminine social role. To illustrate this thesis, we shall look first at the word *giedd* and its Old English usages, and then compare these elegies with *Widsith* and *Deor*, which explicitly define the role of the artist, to discover how these *scopas* have inverted conventional female roles. The woman *persona*, we shall find, adopts the guise of a *scop* to dramatize her "wanderings" and to castigate and chastise her ungenerous and unsupportive "lord." Understanding these two cryptic poems in this way depends by necessity on conjecture—as do all interpretations of their meaning.

I

According to the twenty-six instances listed by Bosworth-Toller, the *giedd* may be designated as a formal metrical song conveying *sentence*, often heavily rhetorical[5]; the didactic material often refers to history and legend or proverbs and gnomic wisdom.[6] The *giedd* is usually recited at a banquet, funeral, or some other ceremonial occasion; the term also refers to other kinds of ceremonial songs, particularly funeral laments.[7] How-ever, most instances present the word *giedd* within a specifically heroic and secular context wherein a *scop*, or someone playing that role, appears, and many of these derive from the heroic poem *par excellence, Beowulf.*[8] The speakers are almost always male, and they perform either the role of a *scop* or the role of a wise man with knowledge of the art of song,[9] with two exceptions—Hildeburh lamenting for her son and brother at the funeral pyre in *Beowulf* and the narrator reciting his experiences in *The Seafarer*. But even in these instances Hildeburh mourns at a public ceremony, whereas the Seafarer represents a man whose harsh experiences have increased his wisdom. Only in the two poems in question, *The Wife's Lament* and *Wulf and Eadwacer*, is the *giedd* rehearsed by a woman in an isolated and private situation, that is, outside any public formal occasion.

Wulf and Eadwacer, in its artfulness and riddle-like character, resembles a *giedd* and may be linked not only with the riddles but also with *Deor*, the other poem spoken by a *scop*. Certainly the former poem, with its normal use of alliteration to bind together the two halves of each line, and its abnormal use of a refrain to bind together the parts of the first half, suggests the nature of a *giedd* as an artful, bound creation (only two poems, this elegy and *Deor*, manifest such refrains in Old English poetry[10]; moreover, in its riddle-like character and form,[11] it also resembles a *giedd*.

In addition, *Wulf and Eadwacer*, *Deor*, the riddles, and even *The Wife's Lament* may all be linked, in form or theme, through their enigmatic and riddle-like character. In the manuscript *Wulf and Eadwacer* immediately follows *Deor*, after which appear the first fifty-nine riddles and *The Wife's Lament*. Certainly *The Wife's Lament* and *Wulf and Eadwacer* are thematically linked as well, and in addition *Wulf and Eadwacer* bears strong affinities to *Deor*, partly in terms of its similar use of heroic and legendary materials from the Volsung and Odoacer legends, which makes it seem to be a response to the situation of Deor in loving the woman of *Wulf and Eadwacer*.[12] But also the two lyrics *Deor* and *Wulf and Eadwacer* are linked in part thematically and imagistically through the lament of the *scop* Deor. How exactly was the role of the *scop* defined in Anglo-Saxon England?[13]

The characterization of the *scop*—as a wise and skillful man who may travel frequently but who must always profess loyalty to his current lord through praise—has been defined in two Old English poems and in passages throughout *Beowulf*. In this heroic epic, the *scop* remains a thane of the king (*cyninges þegn*, 867b), largely because of his obligation to sing of the fame of Hrothgar, promote his glory, and hence manifest loyalty. Further, this *scop* is described as *guma gilphlæden*, a man boast-laden or glory-laden, presumably because his mind is heavy with heroic deeds; certainly he possesses an excellent memory ("mindful of songs, he who a great many of old traditions, a large number remembered," 868b–70a, "gidda gemyndig, / sē ðe ealfela ealdgesegena / worn gemunde") and thus functions as well as a historian for the tribe. One of his talents involves "varying his words"—*wordum wrixlan* (874a)—probably in part because he must again tell of Beowulf's undertaking and has told many times of Sigemund and the dragon.

Similarly, Widsith, in the poem of the same name in *The Exeter Book*, is a minstrel rich in words, boasting an extensive vocabulary described as a "wordhoard" that he "unlocks as he speaks" ("wordhord onleac," 1). This particular minstrel, unlike Hrothgar's, must travel frequently, cut off from kinsmen, serving far and wide: "Thus I went forth through many strange lands, through wide ground. Good and evil there I endured deprived of kinsmen, far from my kinsmen; I served far and wide" ("Swa ic geondferde fela fremdra londa / geond ginne grund. Godes ond yfles / þær ic cunnade cnosle bidæled, / freomægum feor folgade wide," 50–53). For this reason he has good cause to sing, to praise nobles—he has a vested interest in pleasing the gold-giver, not only for gold, food, shelter, but also for saving his own skin.

For this minstrel Widsith very clearly praises three groups in the three parts of his poem: first, all the lords he has known, in lines 10–56; second, all the tribes he has known, in lines 57–108, and finally all the good and wise companions he has known, in lines 109–30. He reminds his audience, at the end of each catalogue of names, of the powerful role of the *scop* as voice of praise or blame. At the end of the first part he declares, "Therefore I can sing and say a spell; recite before the band in the mead hall how to me the noble ones were generous in their liberality" ("Forþon ic mæg singan ond secgan spell, / mænan fore mengo in meoduhealle / hu me cynegode cystum dohten," 54–56). This leads to the praise of tribes in the second section, after which he binds this second catalogue with the first by focusing on the single victorious lord to whom Scilling and he sing their songs: "Then Scilling and I together with clear voice before our victory-lord raised the song" ("Ðonne wit Scilling sciran reorde / for uncrum sigedryhtne song ahofan," 103–104). The link with the last section that praises good companions is found in the mention of Scilling, another *scop*. Widsith concludes that the minstrel and the king are made for one another because the former needs gold and protection and the latter needs glory for his valor:

> Thus wandering they travel in creation
> the gleemen of men through many lands,
> utter need, speak thank-words,
> ever south or north they meet a certain one
> prudent in songs, not niggardly in gifts,
> who before the duguth wishes to exalt his glory,
> to perform heroic deeds, until all has passed,

light and life together;   he works praise,
has under the heavens   the highest glory.

(Swa scriþende   gesceapum hweorfað
gleomen gumena   geond grunda fela,
þearfe secgað,   þoncword sprecaþ,
simle suð oþþe norð   sumne gemetað
gydda gleawne,   geofum unhneawne,
se þe fore duguþe wile   dom aræran,
eorlscipe æfnan,   oþþæt eal scæceð
leoht ond lif somod;   lof se gewyrceð,
         hafað under heofonum   heahfæstne dom. 135–43.)

The awful predicament of a *scop* supplanted in his lord's favor by another is illustrated in *Deor*, the other, later poem dealing with the plight of a poet whose land-right has been given to Heorrenda. Being indeed a wise as well as a word-ready man, Deor provides Boethian consolation for himself—all that has passed away, so may this.

In the two poems in question, *Wulf and Eadwacer* and *The Wife's Lament*, both speakers adopt the role and diction of the *scop* as enunciated in the poem *Widsith* and these other passages. Both have suffered from feuds and missing kinsmen, both travel (in one sense or another, literally or mentally), both share the isolation of the *scop*, and both long for a good and wise lord. However, neither receives food, treasure, or even praise for her endeavors, and what she sings would not please her lord. Instead, her songs convey hallucination, isolation, nothingness, privation, suffering, and bitterness, without the optimism of a Deor or the ability to place suffering within a historical context of the suffering of others. And both, as we have suggested earlier, assume the masculine and somewhat heroic posture of the *scop*, especially the Wife in *The Wife's Lament*, less so the speaker in *Wulf and Eadwacer*, whom we shall discuss first.

II

In *Wulf and Eadwacer*, although the woman speaker resembles the wandering Widsith in the mental journeys she makes, her fantasies resemble those of the Wife, and the image of the *giedd*, or "song" used to describe her relationship with Wulf as one easily "slit," derives from *Deor* and from other poetic images of women which she inverts in her poem. A woman who has had too much time to think, she describes herself as a psychological traveler: "Of my Wulf I suffered in wide-wandering tracks (of my mind)" ("Wulfes ic mines widlastum wenum dogode," 9), particularly when it was rainy weather and she sat tearful, and when the "bold-in-battle man" (Eadwacer) wrapped his arms around her ("þonne hit wæs renig weder ond ic reotugu sæt, /þonne mec se beaducafa bogum bilegde," 10–11). Apparently, in a conscious effort to separate mind from body or to divorce herself from reality, either when it rains and she cannot leave or when Eadwacer makes love to her, she flees psychologically from the spiritual imprisonment imposed by Eadwacer, through thoughts of her real lover (or husband?), Wulf. This solution may indeed represent "wish-fulfillment," a hallucination that will bring her joy,[14] but it also reflects her repugnance for Eadwacer, her guilt over experiencing physical joy in his lovemaking (12), and her anger for not being rescued by Wulf (expressed in lines 13–15 when she mentions that what made her sick were thoughts of Wulf, as well as his "seldomcomings, a mourning mind, and not at all lack of food," "wena me þine / seoce gedydon, þine seldcymas, / murnende mod, nales meteliste").

What is interesting in this poem is the woman's awareness of her lover's failure to fulfill the role of lord in relation to her apparent role as *scop* (or retainer). At the very beginning of the poem, she bitterly and ironically laments his inability to protect the tribe to which he is bound by her apparent marriage to him. Normally the gold-giver was responsible for protecting his tribe and giving them gold for valor in battle, just as the queen or pledge-of-peace was responsible for uniting two tribes in peace and promoting harmony within the tribe, as we have previously seen in *Maxims* I, 83–5. Thus, King Beowulf must attempt to protect his nation against the dragon (and the Swedes), just as Wealhtheow functions as *friðusibb folca* (2017) or peace pledge between the Danes and Helmings, Hildeburh between the Danes and Frisians, and Freawaru between the Danes and Heathobards, each uniting the blood of two tribes through her children. But, in the vexed passage at the beginning of *Wulf and Eadwacer,* the narrator suggests that Wulf has not protected their tribes: "To my people it is as if one might give to them *service,*" *lac,* a word with multiple meaning ("Leodum is minum swylce him mon *lac* gife," 1). In the heroic sense, the word "service" suggests that Wulf might rescue them by coming with a troop to do battle. Indeed, she adds in line 2 (and again in line 7), "They will receive him if he comes in a troop," "willað hy hine aþecgan, gif he on þreat cymeð," an ironic reference to her tribe imagined as receiving him happily, in line 2, and to the dominant but cruel tribe of which Eadwacer is apparently a member imagined as battling with him relatively fiercely, in line 7 ("Sindon wælreowe weras þær on ige," 6). She concludes that this is not likely, in the refrain of

"Ungelic is us": the first mention of the refrain (in line 3) is intended for
her and her own tribe, the second mention of the refrain (in line 8) for
Wulf and for her as separated leaders of separated tribes.

The emphasis on the separation of the king and queen (or man and
woman) reinforces the narrator's failure as a peace pledge that normally
unites rather than divides. She despairs of the possibility of rescue because Wulf remains on one island and she on another, with that island fast
and surrounded by a fen ("Wulf is on iege,   ic on oþerre. / Fæst is þæt
eglond,   fenne biworpen," 4–5). In addition to focusing on that separation which belies and undercuts her role as peace pledge, she also longs
for battle and she seems darkly joyful that her child (whether Wulf's or
Eadwacer's), whom she regards as a "miserable whelp," has been borne to
the woods by the wolf (or Wulf). She addresses Eadwacer, "Gehyrest þu,
Eadwacer?   Uncerne earne hwelp / bireð wulf to wuda" (16–17). Whether
dead, or alive and suffering privation, the child hardly seems the hope of
nations, and the triumphant and vengeful cry of his mother destroys any
sense that she is a peace pledge (indeed, her pledge—the child—is
missing). It also darkens the maxim that "Tu beoð gemæccan; / sceal wif
ond wer   in woruld cennan / bearn mid gebyrdum," "Two are consorts; / a
woman and a man   must into the world bring forth / a child through
birth" (*Maxims* I, 23–5).

This concept of the woman narrator as a peace pledge whose social
role has been inverted and of her lover as a failed lord who cannot, for
whatever reason, afford to her, to their child, and to her tribe the protection and wise guidance that he should, remains crucial to understanding
her transformation into a *scop* who will describe their relationship as a
giedd in the puzzling last two lines: "Þæt mon eaþe tosliteð   þætte næfre
gesomnad wæs, / uncer giedd geador" (18–19), "That one easily slits
which was never bound, / our song together." The line couples a double
metaphor, that of binding or uniting with slitting, and that of the relationship as a *giedd* or song, at first glance an incongruous mixture of
metaphors. The use of the word *tosliteð*, however, in addition to biblical
echoes also invokes the implicit notion of woman as a peace-weaver, a
word used to describe Ealhhild in *Widsith* (6a) and Thryth or Mod-Thryth
in *Beowulf* (1942a). The *Beowulf*-poet is certainly conscious of the denota-
tions of the word, for he depicts Thryth not as the *pacis textris* and
conciliatrix into which the word is translated in Latin (according to Grein
in Bosworth-Toller), but as what her name implies, Strength or Mind-
Strength, who in her pride uses the sword to shear (*scyran*, 1939b) the
"hand-woven deadly bonds" of life for any suitor caught staring at her regal
beauty ("wælbende . . . / handegewriþene," 1936a–7a). That which the
narrator of *Wulf and Eadwacer* should unite is the two of them and their

two tribes through her role as peace pledge; but for whatever reason, she has not—their geographical separation, their possible lack of marriage, the weakness of Wulf, the loss of the child. Thus the relationship has been "easily slit," torn, divided, in a metaphor which directly inverts that normally characterizing the role of woman. Note that the poem symbolizes this slit in two singular and ruptured half lines, line 17 ("bireð wulf to wuda"), and line 19, the last line, "uncer giedd geador." As a result, she now seeks to repair the rip in this song, the *giedd* which becomes the woven fabric of the relationship she longs to have in reality but cannot have except in art—the little poem that will immortalize the lovers' union. In this sense the unsuccessful peace-weaver desperately retains her social function by subliminating the real-life relationship through the bound and crafty art of the *scop*. It is perhaps no accident that the loom and the lyre were closely linked by ancient writers because of their similarity, and, as we have already seen, that the "singing" made by the sound of the shuttle or warp-threads might be likened to the singing of the *scop*. The Anglo-Saxons were familiar with advanced methods of weaving (involving the shuttle, the shedding operation, and the toothed batten) as evidenced in three Old English loom riddles (nos. 35, 56, and 70),[15] songs themselves performed perhaps by a bard in the mead-hall. In short, it is perhaps no accident that the failed peace-weaver here becomes more successful as a singer of peace.

The image of the binding art of the *scop*—expressed in *Wulf and Eadwacer* through the image of the *giedd*—echoes that of the *scop* in *Deor*. In both cases, out of something "slit" or destroyed an artist reconstructs a bound and harmonious artifact. In *Deor*, the tyrant Nithhad first hamstrings Weland, "be wurman" or hindrances, after which he lays fetters of "supple-sinew-bonds" ("Swoncre seonobende," 6) on him, but the vengeful artist Weland constructs jewelry out of the bones of the raped Beadohild's brothers and through her produces a son, Widia, to avenge him.[16] Just so, the woman here constructs a poem out of her "slit" bonds with Wulf, that caused by the forced adultery with Eadwacer. She also resembles the moaning Mæthhild of the third stanza who suffers so from love of Geat that either she cannot sleep or that she dies. And Eadwacer the "Property-Watcher" who imprisons her resembles the tyrant Nithhad in the first stanza, as well as the tyrants Theodoric and Eormanric in the fourth and fifth stanzas. Finally, the woman of *Wulf and Eadwacer* finds consolation in her art—in the small tapestry into which she has woven the union of Wulf and herself—whereas Deor, whose place was taken by Heorrenda the "leoðcræftig monn" ("the man skilled in song," 40), finds consolation in the Boethian idea that all things of this world pass: "þæs ofereode, þisses swa mæg."

These two resolutions are very different: the woman remains too aware of how all things pass and fears the emphemerality of her earlier happiness with Wulf, therefore seeking a permanence through song (and the song *is* all that remains of that union). Deor wishes only for this painful situation to pass and forces his thoughts to control his sorrowing emotion:

> If a man sits full of sorrow,   deprived of joys,
> he can then think   that throughout this world
> the wise Lord   frequently changes,
> to many an earl   shows grace,
> assured glory,   to some a portion of misery.
>
> (Siteð *sorgcearig*,   sælum bidæled, . . .
> Mæg þonne *geþencan*,   þæt geond þas woruld
> witig dryhten   wendeþ geneahhe,
> eorle monegum   are gesceawað,
> wislicne blæd,   sumum weana dæl. 28, 31–4, emphasis added)

In contrast, woman in *Deor*—at least Beadohild—cannot "boldly think" what to do ("ne meahte / þriste geþencan," 11b–12a), nor can the woman of *Wulf and Eadwacer*, who makes herself sick suffering excessive feelings of sorrow, anger, guilt. Thus she laments bitterly, whereas the wise poet Deor moralizes.

III

In *The Wife's Lament*, the speaker casts herself in the role of *scop* in order to recite her own experiences in a *giedd* and thereby help to distance herself from her pain. The poem is divided into three major parts[17] prefaced by a statement of her purpose in lines 1–5. The first part (lines 6–26) details her *past* when her lord left the country, when she tried to find another lord to serve abroad, and when the kinsmen of the previous lord plotted against her. The second part (lines 27–41) describes the *present*—her incarceration in a cave as the result of the plotting (possibly because of her adultery).[18] The third part (lines 42–53) functions as her fantasy for the *future:* it constitutes a curse on the young man responsible for her plight.

Throughout this poem, I would surmise that the narrator deliberately represses her female qualities and instead views herself in masculine terms, terms which suggest the relationship between a *scop* or retainer and a lord. First, the narrator frequently refers to the man she loves as would a *scop* or retainer his lord—*hlaford* (6 and 15), *frea* (33), *leodfruma* (8), and the more innocuous *freond* (47).[19] Further, the diction throughout the poem portrays them both as occupying heroic and masculine roles. For example, these lovers had "boasted" (*beotedan*, 21)—a word often used in an epic and heroic sense—that they would never be parted except by death (22–25a). And after her lord parted from her, she regarded herself (perhaps figuratively) as a *wineleas wræcca*, a lordless exile (line 10) who endured exile-journeys (*wræsiþas*, 5 and 38) in order to seek the service of another lord, as might a *scop* or retainer ("ic me feran gewat   folgað secan," 9).

The description of the relationship between a man and woman in Germanic heroic terms is not altogether unusual for Anglo-Saxon poetry, however. In *Genesis B*, Eve functions like a retainer to her lord Adam, but she oversteps her role in attempting to serve God directly rather than permitting Adam to do so. She addresses Adam as "my lord" or "my friend" (*frea min*, 655a; *wine min*, 824b),[20] and persuades him "through her loyal mind" ("þurh holdne hyge," 708a) to eat the fruit, just as the Tempter tells her he serves God "through loyal mind" (586a and 654a). The Tempter gains his real lord Satan's "favor" (726b) through this same loyal mind, that is, by tempting Adam and Eve, just as Eve's decision to eat was prompted by the desire for the "favor" (*hyldo*, 567b) of the Lord, and because she wishes to "serve" Him (*læstan*, 554b, 572a, and 576a, a word with Germanic heroic connotations also used in *Beowulf* in 2663b). Later she realizes she has forsaken the *hyldo*[21] or favor of the Lord (771b) as does Adam (837a). Eve in particular suffers from the desire to serve the Lord as she should serve Adam, but demonstrated in the manner of a retainer to his lord, through masculine heroic service. This desire underscores the social as well as spiritual nature of her Fall.

In *The Wife's Lament*, the woman, like Eve, both fails to serve her lord well—in the masculine heroic sense—and fails as a peace-weaver. That the social reality of the woman's failure is mirrored in the metaphor of the retainer's failure is demonstrated by the use of the technical word for feud, *fæhðu*: "I must far or near / with my much loved one   feud endure" ("Sceal ic feor ge neah / mines felaleofan   fæhðu dreogan," 25b–26). Although this term supposedly can refer only to a state of feud between two men or tribes and cannot refer to hostility between husband and wife,[22] the same word is also used by the *Beowulf*-poet for the vendetta between Grendel's Mother and Hrothgar because of the death of her son ("fæhðe," line 1340b; also "gyrnwræce," 2118a); she wishes to "avenge the death of her son" ("sunu dēoð wrecan," 1278b). Similarly, Eve in *Genesis B* urges Adam to perform the task set out by the Tempter so that the "hostile strife"—"þone laðan strið," 572b—between them and the Lord will cease, the word *strið* appearing only in *Genesis B* but linked in connotation with the *fæhðu* between the Wife and her lord. After the deed is performed, she fears the enmity of the Lord ("heofoncyninges nið," 768b). Both Eve because of her pride and Grendel's Mother because of her monstrosity fail as "peace-weavers," like the Wife of *The Lament* who fails because of external factors. The appearance of the term in *The Lament* suggests that the poet wishes to regard the narrator as so acutely conscious of her social failure as a conventional peace pledge that she must resort to heroic diction to define her present socially anomalous position. But the metaphor works as well to express her psychological position: she uses the word *begeat* to explain how she was seized after her lord's departure (32b) and also to express how she can never find rest for her mind-sorrow or all the longings which have similarly "seized" her (*begeat*, 41b), the same word used again to end the mid-section of her poem, on the present. Finally, her bitterness over her lord's departure and her friends lying in their beds while she has to sit at daybreak for the summer-long day weeping over her "exile-journeys" appears either aristocratically feminine or possibly merely jejune.

In addition to creating a portrait of herself as a masculine *scop* or retainer to the lord of her lover, the speaker of *The Lament* also imagines her present habitation as a mock ring-hall wherein all seems gloomy and dark instead of bright and joyful. She calls the earth-cavern in a grove of trees[23] an old *eorðsele*, or earth-hall (29a), a compound reminiscent of the ironic hall-compounds used by the *Beowulf*-poet to describe both Heorot at the time of Grendel's visit (*gūðsele*, battle-hall, 443a) and the abode of Grendel's Mother (also *gūðsele*, 2139a; *nīðsele*, battle-hall, 1513a), who represents an ironic queen in the second half of her section of the poem when she "entertains" her "hall-guest" (*selegyst*, 1545a, and *gist*, 1522b) by battling with him.[24] The Wife also sings her song in her hall as the mock-*scop* Grendel sings in Heorot: those near the wall heard his weeping, "the enemy of God   singing a terrible song, / a song of defeat" ("gryreleoð galan   Godes andsacan, / sigeleasne sang," 786–87a).[25] The Wife's song of defeat is sung alone, however, within a "hall" that she imagines from the actual earth-cave, dunes, valleys, and briar-covered "turrets" and "dwellings" she thinks she sees:

> Old is this earthhall,   I am wholly seized with longing,
> the valleys are dim,   the dunes raised aloft,
> the bitter burg-towns,   with briars overgrown
> a dwelling joyless.
>
> (Eald is þes eorðsele,   eal ic eom oflongad,
> sindon dena dimme,   duna uphea,

bitre burgtunas, brerum beweaxne
wic wynne leas. 29–32a)

Finally, in the third part of her poem she curses the man who has imprisoned her in this earth-hall in contradistinction to a male *scop*, who would ideally praise the gold-giver and victorious lord rewarding him in the mead-hall for such praise—or more bitterly, like the *scop* in *Deor*, who curses his former lord. Because she fears no further enmity, she remains free to curse this lord who has abandoned her. She hopes first that he will suffer within his heart, even if he seems tranquil or happy on the surface, and thus have to derive all his joy from himself:

> Ever may the young man be sad-minded,
> hard the thought of his heart, likewise must have
> a blithe demeanor, also care in his breast,
> affliction of sorrows, be from himself consequent
> all his worldly joy, be fully banished
> in a distant land. (42–47)

Her specific fantasy of an appropriate punishment for her lord mirrors her actual incarceration in the earth-hall and contrasts with her desire to be present in the mead-hall. She imagines this lord in a distant land sitting under rocky slopes, chilled by storm, weary-minded, water flowing in the dreary hall ("wætre beflowen / on dreorsele," 49b–50a), although it is not clear whether this "dreary hall" is a ruin or a watery cave or—as one critic would have it—a boat.[26] This *dreorsele* will parallel her *eorðsele*: if he occupies a similar joyless dwelling perhaps he will remember too often a happier dwelling ("he gemon to oft / wynlicran wic," 51b–52a). The poem ends miserably—her own misery, and his, imagined—with the lines, "woe be for him who must / from longing for the beloved abide" ("Wa bið þam þe sceal / of langoþe leofes abidan," 52b–53).

The narrators of *Wulf and Eadwacer* and *The Wife's Lament* are depicted as expressing extreme intense emotion. The speaker of the former verges on schizophrenia, divorcing her mind from her body, because of the intolerable situation she finds herself in—making love to her captor while she thinks of her lover (or husband):

> Wulf, my Wulf, thoughts of you
> made me sick, your seldom-comings,
> a mourning mind, not at all food-lack.

(Wulf, min Wulf,   wena me þine
seoce gedydon,   þine seldcymas,
murnende mod,   nales meteliste. 13–15).

In *The Wife's Lament*, the speaker similarly reveals unrestrained emotion, "excited feelings" indicative of an asyndetic and not a logical sequence of thought. For example, line 24 lacks metrical form and line 42 uses involved constructions.[27] In addition, the Wife confesses, "therefore I can never / of my mind-sorrow   find rest, / nor of all the longings   which in this life have conquered me" ("forþon ic æfre ne mæg / þære mod-ceare   minre gerestan, / ne ealles þæs longaþes   þe mec on þissum life begeat," 39b–41). This last line is hypermetrical, emphasizing through its length how she has been conquered by longing.

Such excessive emotion to an ecclesiastical Anglo-Saxon audience may well have been interpreted as bordering on pride. But the wives of *Wulf and Eadwacer* and *The Lament* also complain of lords who have disappeared and treated them unbecomingly. Like the classical archetype of Penelope seated at her loom, unweaving at night what she has woven by day to prevent a remarriage with one of her suitors, these women narrators are depicted as turning to art, becoming *scopas* who channel their turbulent emotions into peaceful, harmonious, and rational symbols of the social reality they desire. Fantasy is thus transmuted, for good or for ill, into a kind of reality, if only an artistic one, and the forces of isolation, suffering, privation, loss, and even death—nothingness—are therefore, even if only temporarily, forestalled.

7

Grendel's Mother as Epic Anti-Type of the Virgin and Queen

HROUGHOUT THE EPIC *Beowulf,* Grendel's mother, rather oddly, is
described in human and social terms, and through words like *wīf* and
ides normally reserved for human women. She has the form of a woman
(*idese onlīcnes,* 1351)[1] and is weaker than a man (1282ff) and more cow-
ardly, for she flees in fear for her life when discovered in Heorot (1292–3).
She is specifically called a *wīf unhȳre* (2120b), a "monstrous woman," and
an *ides āglǣcwīf* (1259a), a "lady monster-woman." *Ides,* as we have seen
in other literary works and as it is also used in *Beowulf,*[2] normally denotes
"lady" and connotes either a queen or a woman of high social rank. But
unlike most queens, Grendel's Mother fights her own battles, an activity
that, as we have seen in *Maxims* I, 83–5, was normally practiced only by
the Anglo-Saxon lord.[3]

As if to stress her inversion of the Anglo-Saxon ideal of woman, the
poet labels her domain a "battle-hall" (*nīðsele,* 1513a; *gūðsele,* 2139a).[4] In
addition, he occasionally uses a masculine pronoun in referring to her
(*sē þe* instead of *seō þe* in 1260a, 1497b; *hē* instead of *hēo* in 1392b, 1394b;[5]
such a change in pronoun occurs elsewhere in the poem only in reference
to abstract feminine nouns used as personifications and to concrete feminine nouns used as synecdoches), and he applies epithets to her that are
usually applied to male figures: warrior, *sinnige secg,* in 1379a; destroyer,
mihtig mānscaða, in 1339a; and [male] guardian, *gryrelīcne grundhyrde,*
in 2136. Indeed in the phrase *ides āglǣcwīf,* applied to Grendel's mother
as a "lady monster-woman," the phrase *āglǣa* not only means "monster,"
as it does when directed at Grendel (159a, 425a, 433b, 556a, 592a, 646b,
732a, 739a, 816a, 989b, 1000b, 1269a) or the water monsters (1512a), but
also "fierce combatant" or "strong adversary," as when directed at Sige-

Reconstruction of a warrior's helmet, from the Sutton Hoo ship burial. Photo reproduced by permission of the Trustees of the British Museum.

mund in line 893 and at Beowulf and the dragon in line 2592a.[6] Such a woman might be wretched or monstrous to an Anglo-Saxon audience because she blurs the sexual and social categories of roles. For example she arrogates to herself the masculine role of the warrior or lord.

This inversion of the Anglo-Saxon image of woman as peacemaker is congruent with recent interpretations of the other two monsters in the epic. Grendel and the dragon have been interpreted recently as monstrous projections of flaws in Germanic civilization, portrayed by the poet as "Negative Men."[7] Grendel is introduced as a mock "hall-retainer" (*healðegn* 142a; *renweard*, 770a) who envies the men of Heorot their joy of community; he subsequently attacks the hall in a raid that is described through the parodic hall ceremonies of feasting, ale-drinking, gift-receiving, and singing.[8] The dragon is introduced as a mock "gold-king" or *hordweard* (2293b, 2302b, 2554b, 2593a), who avariciously guards his barrow or "ring-hall" (*hringsele*, 3053a),[9] and attacks Beowulf's kingdom after he discovers the loss of a single cup. The envy of the evil hall-retainer and the avarice of the evil gold-king antithesize the Germanic *comitatus* ideal first enunciated in Tacitus' *Germania* and pervading heroic and elegiac Anglo-Saxon literature: the *comitatus'* well-being depended upon the retainer's valor in battle and loyalty to his lord and the lord's protection and treasure-giving in return.[10]

Grendel's Mother differs from Grendel and the dragon in that she is used as a parodic inversion both of the Anglo-Saxon queen and mother,[11] the ideal of which was embodied in the Virgin Mary. That is, the word *ides* in Latin and Old English glosses is paired with *virgo* to suggest maidenhood, as when *on idesan* equals *in virgunculam*.[12] (It is interesting to note that Grendel's *father* never appears.) In addition, as if the poet wished to stress her maternal role, she is characterized usually as Grendel's *modor* or kinswoman (*māge*, 1391), the former a word almost exclusively reserved for her, although other mothers appear in the poem.[13] Her vengefulness as a mother invites implicit comparison with the love and mercy of the Virgin Mother.

These two roles, while related, are linked to her two appearances in the poem, one at Heorot, one at her mere. That is, her episode is appropriately divided into two parts, like her monstrous but human nature and her female but male behavior, which illustrate the two roles, that of the mother or kinswoman and that of the queen or lady, that she inverts. The poet constantly highlights the unnatural behavior of Grendel's dam by contrasting it with feminine ideals.

Thus the episode involving Grendel's mother is not structurally and thematically extraneous, a blot on the unity of the epic, as it so often has been termed,[14] but a vital part of the parody of social roles embodied in the three monsters. Despite its brevity in comparison to the episodes of Grendel (1100–1200 lines, from 86 to 1250) or the dragon (1000 lines, from 2200 to 3182),[15] her section of roughly 500 lines (from 1251 to 1784) is more than a "transition between two great crises."[16] Indeed, as we shall see, her episode should be lengthened to a thousand lines (from 1251 to 2199) so as to include Hrothgar's sermon and Hygelac's court celebration, in that the idea she represents dominates these events both literally and symbolically as do Grendel and the dragon the events in their sections. We turn first to an examination of the female ideal in *Beowulf*, then to a detailed analysis of the episode involving Grendel's mother and its two parts, and finally to some conclusions regarding the way in which her episode is key to the structural unity of the entire epic.

I

The role of woman in *Beowulf*, as in Anglo-Saxon society, primarily depends upon peace making, either biologically through her marital ties with foreign kings as a peace pledge or mother of sons, or socially and psychologically as a cup-passing and peace-weaving queen within a hall. The *Beowulf*-poet takes care to remind us of this role: Wealhtheow becomes a peace pledge or *friðusibb folca* (2017) to unite the Danes and Helmings; Hildeburh similarly unites the Danes and Frisians through her marriage; and Freawaru at least intends to pledge peace between the Danes and Heathobards.

In addition, woman functions domestically within the nation as a cup-passer during hall festivities of peace *(freoþo)* and joy *(drēam)* after battle or contest. The mead-sharing ritual and the cup-passer herself come to symbolize peace-weaving and peace because they strengthen the societal and familial bonds between lord and retainers. First, the literal action of the *freoðuwebbe* (peace-weaver, 1942) as she passes the cup from warrior to warrior weaves an invisible web of peace: the order in which each man is served, according to his social position, reveals each man's dependence upon and responsibility toward another. For example, after Wealhtheow gives the cup to Hrothgar she bids him to be joyful at drinking as well as loving to his people (615ff). Then she offers it to the *duguð* (old retainers), then to the *geoguð* (young retainers), and finally to the guest Beowulf. Second, her peace-weaving also takes a verbal form: her speeches accompanying the mead-sharing stress the peace and joy contingent upon the fulfillment of each man's duty to his nation. At the joyous celebration after Grendel's defeat Wealhtheow concludes her speeches with a tribute to the harmony of the present moment by reminding her tribe of its cause, that is, adherence to the *comitatus* ethic. Each man remains true to the other; each is loyal to the king; the nation is ready and alert; the drinking warriors attend to the ale-dispenser herself (1228–31). Yet minutes before she attempted to forestall future danger to her family and nation by preventive peace-weaving: she advised Hrothgar to leave his kingdom to his sons, and then, as if sensing the future, she reminded Hrothulf, his nephew, of his obligations to those sons (obligations he will later deny). Third, the peace-weaver herself emblematizes peace, for she appears in the poem with her mead-vessel only after a contest has been concluded. Thus, Wealhtheow enters the hall only after the contest between Unferth and Beowulf (612); she does not appear again until after Beowulf has overcome Grendel, when the more elaborate feasting invites the peace-making speeches mentioned above. After Grendel's mother is defeated, the poet preserves the integrity of the pattern of feminine cup-passing after masculine contest by describing the homecoming banquet at Hygelac's court, where Hygd conveys the mead-vessel. This structural pattern to which we shall return simultaneously weaves together the Danish part of the poem with its Geatish part.

Most of the other female characters figure as well in this middle section so that the female monster's adventures are framed by descriptions of other women for ironic contrast. The role of mother highlights the first half of the middle section with the *scop*'s mention of Hildeburh (1071ff) and the entrance of Wealhtheow, both of whom preface the first appearance of Grendel's dam (1258) in her role as avenging mother. Then the introduction of Hygd, Thryth, and Freawaru after the female monster's death (1590) stresses the role of queen as peace-weaver and cup-passer to preface Beowulf's final narration of the female monster's downfall (2143). The actual adventures of Grendel's mother cluster then at the center of the middle section of the poem.

II

In the first part of the female monster's section, the idea is stressed that a kinswoman or mother must passively accept and not actively avenge the loss of her son. The story of the mother Hildeburh is recited by the *scop* early on the evening Grendel's Mother will visit Heorot. The lay ends at line 1159; Grendel's Mother enters the poem a mere hundred lines later when she attacks the Danish hall, as the Frisian contingent attacked the hall lodging Hildeburh's Danish brother in the *Finnsburg Fragment*. The

Beowulf-poet alters the focus of the fragment: he stresses the consequences of the surprise attack rather than the attack itself in order to reveal Hildeburh's maternal reactions to them.

Hildeburh is unjustly (*unsynnum*, 1072b) deprived of her Danish brother and Finnish son, but all she does, this sad woman (*geōmuru ides*, 1075b) is to mourn her loss with dirges and stoically place her son on the pyre. In fact, she can do nothing, caught in the very web she has woven as peace pledge: her husband's men have killed her brother, her brother's men have killed her son. Later the Danish Hengest will avenge the feud with her husband Finn, whether she approves or not, by overwhelming the Frisians and returning Hildeburh to her original tribe. The point remains: the peace pledge must accept a passive role precisely because the ties she knots bind *her*—she *is* the knot, the pledge of peace. Her fate interlaces with that of her husband and brothers through her role as a mother bearing a son: thus Hildeburh appropriately mourns the loss of her symbolic tie at the pyre, the failure of her self as peace pledge, the loss of her identity. Like Hildeburh, Grendel's dam will also lose her son and thus her identity as mother. However, she has never had an identity as peace pledge to lose since she was never a wife.

As if reminded of her own role as mother by hearing of Hildeburh's plight, Wealhtheow demonstrates her maternal concern in an address to Hrothgar immediately after the *scop* sings this lay. In it she first alludes to Hrothgar's adoption of Beowulf as a son: apparently troubled by this, she insists that Hrothgar leave his kingdom only to his actual kinsmen or descendants when he dies (1178–79). Then she urges her foster "son" Hrothulf (actually a nephew) to remember his obligations to them so that he will "repay our sons with liberality" (1184–85). Finally, she moves to the mead-bench where the adopted Beowulf sits, rather symbolically, next to her sons Hrethric and Hrothmund (1188–91). The *past* helplessness of the first mother, Hildeburh, to requite the death of her son counterpoints the anxiously maternal Wealhtheow's attempts to weave the ties of kinship and obligation, thereby forestalling *future* danger to her sons. Later that night, Grendel's Mother, intent on avenging the loss of her son in the *present*, attacks Heorot, her masculine aggression contrasting with the feminine passivity of both Hildeburh and Wealhtheow. Indeed, she resembles a grieving human mother: like Hildeburh she is guiltless and *galgmōd* ("gloomy-minded," possibly "gallows-minded," 1277a); her journey to Heorot must be sorrowful (1278) for she "remembered her misery" (1259b). But a woman's role as peace pledge was reserved for her husband, not for her son, according to the Danish history of Saxo Grammaticus.[17] Perhaps for this reason Grendel's Mother is presented as husbandless and son-obsessed to suggest to an Anglo-Saxon audience the incestuous dangers inherent in woman's function as *friðusibb*.

However, her attempts to avenge her son's death could be justified if she were human and male, for no *wergild* has been offered to her by the homicide Beowulf.[18] The role of the masculine avenger is emphasized throughout the passage (1255–78) in defining her motivation to attack: she performs the role of avenger (*wrecend*, 1256b) "to avenge the death of her son" (1278b). Whatever her maternal feelings, she actually fulfills the duty of the kinsman. Unlike Hildeburh, she cannot wait for a Hengest to resolve the feud in some way; unlike Freawaru, she cannot act as a peace pledge to settle the feud. Tribeless, not kinless, forced to rely on her own might, she seizes and kills Æschere, Hrothgar's most beloved retainer, in an appropriate retribution for the loss of her own most beloved "retainer" and "lord"—her son. She thus implicitly parodies the Virgin in response to the loss of her son.

The monstrosity of her action is at first not evident. Hrothgar suspects she has carried the "feud" too far (1339–40). And from the Danish and human point of view she possesses no legal right to exact compensation for her kinsman's loss because Grendel is himself a homicide. However, Beowulf later implies that the two feuds must remain separate, as she desires her own "revenge for injury" (*gyrnwracu*, 2118a). Perhaps he is thinking of her as a retainer duty-bound to avenge the death of his lord, regardless of the acts he has committed. If so, then she behaves monstrously in only one way. It is monstrous for a mother to "avenge" her son (2121) as if she were a retainer, he were her lord, and avenging more important than peace making. An analogy conveying her effect on the men in Heorot when she first appears suggests how unusual are her actions in human terms. Her horror "is as much less as is the skill (strength) of maidens, the war-horror of a woman, in comparison to a (weaponed) man, when the bound sword shears the one standing opposite" ("Wæs se gryre læssa/ efne swā micle,   swā bið mægþa cræft, / wīggryre wīfes   be wæpnedmen, / þonne heoru bunden. . . . andweard scireð," 1282–87). In their eyes recognizably female, she threatens them physically less than her son. But because female "peacemakers" do not wage war, the analogy implies, by litotes, that her unnatural behavior seems *more* horrible. If we compare her vendetta to the Virgin's forgiveness, it becomes even more monstrous.

In the second part of her adventure, Grendel's Mother no longer behaves solely as an avenging monster, antitype of Hildeburh and Wealhtheow, who are both through marriage "visitors" to the hall like Grendel and his dam. Such hall-visitors contrast with the hall-rulers of this second part: the *merewīf* as queen or guardian (*grundhyrde*, 2136b) protects her "battle-hall," the cave-like lair, from the visiting hero like the regal dragon guarding his ring-hall, and like King Beowulf his kingdom, in the last section of the poem. Accordingly, the stress on the relationship between mother and son delineated in the first part of her adventure changes to a stress on the relationship between host and guest.

As a tribeless queen or lady *(ides āglǣcwīf)* she rudely receives her "hall-guest" Beowulf (*selegyst*, 1545a, *gist*, 1522b) by "embracing" him and then "repaying him" for his valor not with treasure but with "grim grips" ("Hēo him eft hraþe   andlēan forgeald/grimman grāpum," 1541–2) just as the dragon will "entertain" him in the future.[19] Indeed, the parody of the hall-ceremony of treasure-giving is complete when a *"scop"* (Beowulf's sword, acting as bard) sings a fierce "war song" off the side of her head ("hire on hafelan   hringmǣl āgēl/ grǣdig gūðlēoð," 1521–22a). It is interesting to note that this "hall-celebration" of the mock peace-weaver to welcome her valorous guest Beowulf following her attack on Heorot and her curiously listless "contest" with Æschere duplicates the pattern of mead-sharing ceremonies involving peacemakers which follow masculine contests throughout the poem.

It is also interesting to note that the contest between this apparently lordless "queen" and her "guest" contrasts in its mock-sensual embracing and grasping with the other two major battles of the hero—the briefly described arm-wrestling between Grendel and Beowulf and the conventional sword-wielding of Beowulf against the fire-breathing dragon. Indeed, before Beowulf arrives at the "battle-hall," Hrothgar introduces the question of how Grendel was begotten when the king of the Danes admits that they do not know of a father (1355), or of possible additional progeny in addition to Grendel, apparently engendered incestually upon Grendel's Mother by her own son (1356–57). The mystery of his begetting and conception hints at a possible parody of the conception and birth of Christ. While Hrothgar's ostensible point is to warn Beowulf of additional monsters lurking nearby, it serves as well to remind the reader that Grendel's mother has a monstrous or sexual nature very different from that of a civilized *ides*. For, during the passage describing their battle, the poet exploits the basic resemblance between sexual intercourse and battle to emphasize the inversion of the feminine role of the queen or hall-ruler by Grendel's Mother. This is achieved in three steps: first, the emphasis upon clutching, grasping, and embracing while they fight; second, the contest for a dominant position astride the other; and third, the use of fingers, knife, or sword to penetrate clothing or the body, the latter always accompanied by the implied figurative kinship between the sword and the phallus and between decapitation and castration. The personal and physical nature of the battle symbolizes her monstrosity as mock-peace-weaver as effectively as Grendel's arm-wrestling and the dragon's sword-battle symbolizes theirs as mock-retainer and mock-lord.

She welcomes him to the *mere* with an almost fatal embrace similar to the "embrace" (*fæðm*, 2128) to which Æschere has succumbed. She "grasped then towards him" (1501a), seizing him with "horrible grips" (1502a) envisioned earlier by the hero as a "battle grip" (1446a) and a "malicious grasp" (1447a). Second, inside the "castle" (*hof*, 1507b) where she has transported him, each grapples for a superior position over the other. After his sword fails him, for example, he "grasped her by the shoulder," hurling her to the ground. The poet, conscious of the monster's sex and Beowulf's definitely unchivalrous behavior, drily protests that in this case "the lord of the Battle-Geats did not at all lament the hostile act" (1537–38). Then, as "reward" for his valor, this lady "repaid" him with the treasure of her "grimman grāpum," forcing him to stumble and fall (1541–44), after which she climbs, rather ludicrously, on top of her "hall-guest" (*selegyst*, 1545a), intent on stabbing him and thereby (again) avenging her only offspring (1546–47). Third, the battle culminates in very suggestive swordplay, and wordplay too. Earlier her "hostile fingers" (1505b) tried to "penetrate" ("ðurhfōn," 1504b) his locked coat-of-mail; now she tries unsuccessfully to pierce the woven breast-net with her knife. Previously Beowulf discovered his own weapon was impotent against the charm or spell of the "sword-greedy" woman (*heorogīfre*, 1498a), who collects the swords of giants. Now the "sword-grim" hero substitutes one of these swords, an appropriate tool to quell such a woman. The "sword entirely penetrated [ðurhwōd] the doomed-to-die body" (1567b–68a). After this final "embrace" of the "grasping" of her neck, the "sweord wæs swātig, secg weorce gefeh" ("the sword was sweaty, the warrior rejoiced in the work," 1569). The alliteration links *sweord* and *secg*, to identify the bloody sword with the rejoicing, laboring "man-sword" (*secg*); the "battle" appropriately evokes erotic undertones. The equation of the sword and warrior, with the subsequent sexual connotations, resembles the synecdoche controlling Riddle Twenty, "The Sword," in which the sword becomes a retainer who serves his lord through celibacy, foregoing the "joy-game" of marriage and the "treasure" of children, and whose only unpleasant battle occurs with a woman, because he must overcome her desire while she voices her terror, claps her hands, rebukes him with words, and cries out "ungod."[20] Similarly, in *Beowulf*, once the sword finally penetrates the body, its blade miraculously melts—like ice into water—either from the poison of Grendel's blood or of his mother's, the poem does not specify which (1608). And even the *mere* itself, in whose stirred-up and bloody waters sea monsters lurk and the strange battle-hall remains hidden, and the approach to which occurs only through winding passageways, slopes, and paths, symbolically projects the mystery and danger of female sexuality run rampant.

Such erotic overtones in descriptions of battles between a male and female adversary are not especially common in Anglo-Saxon literature but can be found, in sadomasochistic form, as we have seen, in various saints' lives in the *Old English Martyrology* (ca. 850) and in Aelfric's *Lives of Saints* (ca. 994–early eleventh century),[21] and in another epic poem, *Judith*, contained in the same manuscript as *Beowulf*.[22] In Ms. Cotton Vitellius A.xv, this fragmentary epic portrays similar sexual overtones in Judith's "battle" with Holofernes. As in *Beowulf* a warrior battles a monster: the blessed maiden grapples with the "drunken vicious monster" (*se inwidda*, 28a) Holofernes. However, the sexual role behavior of *Beowulf* occurs in reverse in *Judith*: Holofernes parallels Grendel's dam, but whereas the *wif* is aggressive and sword-greedy, Holofernes seems slightly effete (his bed enclosed by gold curtains, for example) and impotent from mead-drinking: "The lord fell, the powerful one so drunken, in the middle of his bed, as if he knew no reason in his mind" (67b–69a). These hypermetrical lines heighten the irony of his situation, for the warrior swoons on the very bed upon which he intended to rape the maiden. Having lost his head to drink, in a double sense he himself is penetrated by the virgin's sharp sword, "hard in the storm of battle" (79a), therefore literally losing his head. But first Judith draws the sword from its sheath in her right hand, seizes him by the hair in a mock loving gesture (98b–99a), then pulls him toward her "shamefully" ("teah hyne folmum wið hyre weard/ *bysmerlice*," 99b–100a). The "b" alliteration in line 100 ("*by*-smerlice, ond þone *bealofullan*") draws attention to *bysmerlice*, which as a verb (*bysmrian*) elsewhere suggests the act of "defiling" (intercourse).[23] In this line what seems shameful is apparently her embrace of the warrior's body while she moves it to a supine position. As in *Beowulf*, the female assumes the superior position; she lays him down so that she may control (*gewealdan*, 103a) him more easily in cutting off his head. The ironic embrace and mock intercourse of this couple parallels that of Beowulf and the *ides āglæcwīf*: the aggressive and sword-bearing "virgin" contrasts with the passive and swordless man (Holofernes, Aeschere, and even Beowulf are all momentarily or permanently swordless). The poet's point in each case is that a perversion of the sexual roles signals an equally perverse spiritual state. Holofernes' impotence is as unnatural in the male as the *wif*'s aggression is unnatural in the female; so the battle with the heroine or hero in each case is described with erotic overtones to suggest the triumph of a right and natural sexual (and social and spiritual) order over the perverse and unnatural one. In the latter case, Grendel's dam and her son pose a heathen threat to Germanic society (the macrocosm) and to the individual (Beowulf the microcosm) as Holofernes and the Assyrians pose a heathen threat to Israelite society (the macrocosm) and to the individual (Judith the microcosm).[24]

In this second part of the adventure of Grendel's Mother, Hygd and Freawaru as queens or cup-passers contrast with the *wīf* just as Hildeburh and Wealhtheow as mothers were contrasted with Grendel's dam in the first part. Hygd, the first woman encountered after the defeat of Grendel's mother, truly fulfills the feminine ideal of *Maxims I*, just as Wealhtheow does. Her name, which means "thought" or "deliberation," suggests that her nature is antithetical to that of the bellicose *wīf* and possibly that of the war-like Thryth, whose actions, if not her name, suggest "Strength" (only in a physical sense; the alternate form of her name, "Mod-Thrytho" or "Mind-Force," implies in a more spiritual sense stubbornness or pride).[25] Although Hygd, like the *wīf* and Thryth, will be lordless after Hygelac's death, she does not desire to usurp the role of king for herself: doubting her son's ability to prevent tribal wars she offers the throne to Beowulf (2369ff). In addition, this gracious queen bestows treasure generously (1929b–31a), unlike the *wīf* and Thryth, the latter of whom dispense only "grim grips" and sword blows upon their "retainers."

The Thryth digression is inserted after Hygd enters to pass the cup upon Beowulf's return to Hygelac. Its structural position invites a comparison of this stubborn princess and the other two "queens," Hygd and the *wīf*. She appears to combine features of both: she begins as a type of the female monster, but upon marriage to Offa changes her nature and becomes a much loved queen. According to the poet, Thryth commits a "terrible crime": she condemns to death any retainer at court caught staring at her regal beauty. That she abrogates her responsibilities as a queen and as a woman the poet makes clear: "Such a custom—that the peace-weaver   after a pretended injury   deprive the dear man of life—is not queenly for a woman to do,   although she be beautiful" ("Ne bið swylc cwēnlic þēaw / idese tō efnanne,   þēah ðe hīo ænlicu sȳ, / þætte freoðuwebbe   fēores onsǣce æfter ligetorne   lēofne mannan," 1940–3). The label "peace-weaver" (*freoðuwebbe*) seems ironic in this context, especially as she does not weave but instead severs the ties of kinship binding her to her people and also the bonds of life tying the accused man to this world. That is, for any man caught looking at her, "the deadly bonds, hand-woven,   were in store; / after his arrest   it was quickly determined / that the sword, the damascened sword,   must shear, / make known death-bale" ("ac him wælbende   weotode tealde / hand-gewriþene;   hraþe seoþðan wæs / æfter mundgripe   mēce geþinged, / þæt hit sceādenmǣl   scȳran mōste / cwealmbealu cȳðan," 1936–40a). If

she weaves at all, then she weaves only "deadly hand-woven bonds"
binding him to a grisly end. The "peace-weaver" cuts these bonds—
imprisoning ropes—with a sword, simultaneously shearing the bonds of
life to "make known death-bale." She resembles that other ironic peace-
weaver, the *wif*, who tried to penetrate the braided breast-net of Beowulf
with her knife.

Both antitypes of the peace-weaving queen behave like kings, using
the sword to rid their halls of intruders or unwanted "hall-guests." Unlike
Thryth, the monstrous *wif* remains husbandless, having lost her son,
"wife" only to the *mere* she inhabits both in life and in death. At this
moment in the poem, both Thryth and Grendel's Mother belong to the
past. If they represent *previous* inversions of the peace-weaver and cup-
passer, and Hygd who is passing the mead-cup to Beowulf's weary men in
celebration signifies a *present* cup-passer, so the poet introduces a final
queen, this time a cup-passer of the *future* who will fail in her role just as
Hildeburh, the first woman, failed in hers.

Freawaru, like Hildeburh, seems innocent of any crime. She is
envisioned by Beowulf as a queen married to Ingeld of the Heathobards in
a digression (2032–69) immediately preceding his summary of the battles
with Grendel and with his mother. She will fail in her role as peace-
weaver because of an underlying hostility—an old Heathobard warrior's
bitterness over ancient Heathobard treasure acquired through previous
wars and worn by a young Danish man accompanying the new queen. The
fragility of this role is heightened even further when, in the third section
involving the dragon, Beowulf inhabits a queenless kingdom and when
Wiglaf must become the cup-passer, pouring water from the "cup" of
Beowulf's helmet in a futile attempt to revive his wounded lord.

Indeed, three female characters appear outside this middle section
to convey dialectically the idea that woman cannot ensure peace in this
world. First, Wealhtheow, unlike other female figures, appears in the first
(or Grendel) section of the poem to pour mead after Grendel's challenge
has been answered by the hero. This first entrance symbolizes the ideal
role of Germanic woman as a personification of peace, as we have seen. In
antithesis, Beowulf's account of the fall of the *wif unhўre* appropriately
ends the poem's second (Grendel's Mother) section which has centered on
this role: the personification of discord, the antitype of feminine ideal, has
been destroyed. But in the poem's third section a synthesis emerges. The
nameless and unidentified Geat woman who appears, like the other
female characters, after a battle—this one between Beowulf and the
dragon—mourns at the pyre. This damaged one-line reference undercuts
the role of the peace-weaver because it broadens the context in which she
appears. That is, the efforts of the peacemaker, while valuable in worldly

and social terms, ultimately must fail because of the nature of this world. True peace exists not in woman's but in God's "embrace" (*fæðm*, 188).

III

This idea is implied in Hrothgar's sermon (1700–84), which occupies a part of the middle section of *Beowulf* dominated by the female monster and which at first glance seems unrelated to it or her. In the sermon Hrothgar describes three Christian vices—envy, pride, and avarice—in distinctly Germanic terms. Impelled by envy, Heremod kills his "table-companions" (1713–14); next, the wealthy hall-ruler in his pride is attacked by the Adversary while his guardian conscience sleeps within the hall of his soul (1740–4); finally, this same hall-ruler "covets angry-minded" (gȳtsað gromhȳdig," 1749a) the ornamented treasures God has previously given him by refusing to dispense any to his warriors. Each of these three sins is personified in the poem by the three monsters: Grendel personifies envy, like Heremod, because he killed the Danish retainers; the dragon personifies avarice, like the hall-ruler he mocks, when he stands guard over a treasure. So the monster that specifically epitomizes pride in *Beowulf*, as does Eve in *Genesis B*, is female—Grendel's Mother—thematically related to Thryth or Mod-Thrytho, whose name (if it can be said to exist in manuscript in that form) means "pride." Grendel's Mother substitutes war-making for the peace-weaving of the queen out of a kind of selfish pride—if she were capable of recognizing it as such. Although the poet portrays the monsters as antitypes of Germanic ideals, his integument conceals a Christian idea. The city of man, whether located in a Germanic or Christian society, is always threatened by sin and failure.

These three sins alienate Christian man from self, neighbor, and God; they alienate Germanic man primarily from other men. Note that although each of the three monsters in *Beowulf* is described as guarding or possessing a type of hall, whether Heorot, a watery cavern, or the treasure of the dragon, each remains isolated from humanity (and from each other—Grendel and his mother live together, but they never appear together in the poem until he is dead). Ideally, when the retainer, the queen, and the gold-lord cooperate they constitute a viable nucleus of Germanic society: a retainer must have a gold-lord from whom to receive gold for his loyalty in battle; the peace-weaver must have a "loom"—the band of retainers and their lord, or two nations—upon which to weave peace.

Despite the poet's realization that these roles cannot be fulfilled in this world, this Germanic ideal provides structural and thematic unity for *Beowulf*. Grendel's Mother does occupy a transitional postion in the poem: as a "retainer" attacking Heorot she resembles Grendel, but as an "attacked ruler" of her own "hall" she resembles the dragon. As a monstrous mother and queen she perverts a role more important socially and symbolically than that of Grendel, just as the queen as peace pledge or peace-weaver ultimately becomes more valuable than the retainer but less valuable than the gold-giver himself.

If it seems ironic that a Germanic ideal that cannot exist in this world *can* exist in art, unifying the theme and structure of the poem, then Grendel's Mother, warring antitype of harmony and peace, must seem doubly ironic. The structural position of her episode in the poem, like woman's position as cup-passer among members of the nations, or as a peace pledge between two nations, is similarly medial and transitional, but successfully so.

Conclusion

THE TERMS used to describe women in Anglo-Saxon society and literature have mushroomed in this study. *"Ides ellenrof," "guð-cwen," "sigecwen,"* among others, typify the brave and usually chaste aristocratic woman, or *ides,* just as *"friðusibb"* and *"freoðuwebbe"* typify the passive and usually married aristocratic woman, *ides.* Complex variations on these terms create a network of images and ideas to portray almost a three-dimensional picture of either type of woman.

In her role as peace-weaver Anglo-Saxon woman weaves together members of differing families or tribes on the biological or physical level and on the emotional or psychological or spiritual levels, love and knowledge. Useful also as an image, "peace-weaver" suggests the role of woman as cloth-maker and hence nurturer. Biblical history reminded an Anglo-Saxon audience of Eve, the first woman and first mother, whom it regarded as a failed peace-weaver who "wove" postlapsarian garments for herself and Adam, and then of Mary, weaver of peace between man and God, as the second Eve. In addition, because the weaving image was used to describe the techniques of the Anglo-Saxon *scop,* dependent as he was on oral-formulaic techniques such as variation and alliteration to render his verse, the role of *scop* and peace-weaver seem to have much in common.

The antithesis of the peace-weaver was also portrayed as a full literary type. She who does not make peace must therefore make war and in acting like a warrior behaves unconventionally for an *ides.* Whether such behavior epitomizes errant Anglo-Saxon queens who attempted to seize control of the throne or merely unconventional women like those speakers in the secular elegies, there is a pejorative cast to this behavior.

Frequently such a woman is portrayed as adulterous, or at least not chaste; she may be considered immoral, pagan, or in some other way allied with the Devil. Most interesting for us is her metaphorical depiction in masculine terms as a retainer or lord, as were Eve of *Genesis B* and the narrators of *Wulf and Eadwacer* and *The Wife's Lament*, a role regarded as monstrous to the Anglo-Saxons. Appropriately, the Anglo-Saxon archetype of such a woman is the monster Grendel's Mother. She is described as a vengeful retainer acting in reaction to the murder of her "lord" and son—yet such behavior ironically twists and inverts woman's role as peace-weaver and was immediately recognizable as an inversion to an Anglo-Saxon audience. She is also the "battle-queen"—almost a direct antithesis of Elene—in battling her "guest" Beowulf.

Taking up the role of the "battle-queen" is not always portrayed as "monstrous" activity. Considered permissible behavior for an extremely chaste and saintly woman in historical documents and in literature, battle allegorically enables the "warriors of Christ," whether male or female, to continue His work and thereby defeat His enemy. The *ides ellenrof, guð-cwen,* or *sigecwen* is metaphorically released from the social demand of peace-weaving because, as a symbol of the human soul or the Church itself she serves a higher "lord" than a human husband. Thus, such figures as the historical Anglo-Saxon Saint Aetheldryth, and the legendary saints Juliana and Elene, along with the Old Testament Judith, serve in these roles as types of the Virgin Mary, who, as Ecclesia, heroically exemplifies the Church Triumphant.

Indeed, the Virgin Mary incarnates all of the positive roles in which women are depicted in Old English literature, as we have seen in *Christ I*. Either appearing as the heroic virgin or the peace-weaving bride—roles one would consider mutually contradictory, if not impossible—she offers a flexible and creative range of possibilities to an Anglo-Saxon audience. She is the Germanic ring-adorned queen or the patristic and allegorical "gate" into the garden of Paradise, the *hortus conclusus;* she is the maid giving birth and the militant Ecclesia stamping on the head of the serpent. One might almost suspect the poet of *Christ I* of being a woman, if not merely sympathetic to the often contradictory demands placed upon woman and to her use as a symbol of the political, cultural, and religious tensions racking Anglo-Saxon society.

Three major biblical models for the Anglo-Saxon woman existed in the figures of Eve, the Virgin Mary, and Judith of the Apocryphal book of the Old Testament. Although each was linked implicitly and explicitly to the other—especially in the patristic writings of the early centuries after Christ's death—each contributed to and was assimilated into the literary culture in a slightly different way. Mary becomes the standard against which the other two figures are measured: Eve represents an antithesis as Judith, as heroic widow, represents a type of Mary in her more militant role. Judith sums up qualities also found in many of the women saints most popular with the Anglo-Saxons.

Secular role models existed primarily in the gnomic poems known as *Maxims* I and II, wherein the good queen was characterized as a peace-making mother. An ideal, if one could be said to exist, might be found in Wealhtheow and Hygd, the two major queens of *Beowulf,* Wealhtheow dominating the first half of the poem concerning the Danes as Hygd dominates the beginning of the second half concerning the Geats. Both women do all that they can to ensure peace, but fail to do so for reasons outside their control (whether a lack of strong leadership or unmitigated enmity). Their role, that is, is interdependent on those of lord and retainer, without whose willingness peace making is futile.

Given that most Anglo-Saxon women were political pawns who did not choose their fates (as we have seen in Chapter 2), what role might an aristocratic woman have chosen, if choose she could? Probably she would have become an abbess, whose presumably chaste and holy life would have as compensation leadership, education, and power both within and outside the abbey (whose schools were the ancestors of the modern university). But she might have married and had children, helping her husband the king rule his nation through her wisdom (as we have seen in Chapter 1), despite raids, battles, and other catastrophes. And it is possible, after his death, that she might have entered a convent to become an abbess, as many widows did. Indeed, it has been speculated that some of the texts discussed in this study were originally written as guides— courtesy books for such widows.

What this study portrays are the exceptions, the exaggerations, the ideals. But it is only through such exceptions and exaggerations that we learn something about what must have been the rule. And the rule for Anglo-Saxon society demanded passivity, rather than leadership and ini-tiative, from most of its women. Those exceptions who became political, social, or religious leaders and models did so only through great wisdom and chastity, virtues which—according to the metaphors used throughout the literature—were themselves considered heroic.

Notes

INTRODUCTION

1. *Beowulf and Judith,* ed. Elliott Van Kirk Dobbie, vol. 4 of 6 vols. of *The Anglo-Saxon Poetic Records* (New York: Columbia University Press, 1953), p. 102.

2. See Doris Mary Stenton, *The English Woman in History* (London: Allen and Unwin; New York: Macmillan, 1957), and Sheila C. Dietrich, "An Introduction to Women in Anglo-Saxon Society (c. 600–1066)," in *The Women of England from Anglo-Saxon Times to the Present: Interpretative Bibliographical Essays,* ed. Barbara Kanner (Hamden, Ct.: Archon Books, 1979), pp. 23–39, a collection that also includes more specific studies on medieval women. A longer unpublished study centering on women ecclesiastics: Carmine Jane Bell, "The Role of Monastic Women in the Life and Letters of Early Medieval England and Ireland" (dissertation, University of Virginia, 1975). Other important studies of women outside England or later than this period have offered new insights about the subsequent and larger development of the roles of women: see for example Susan Mosher Stuard, ed., *Women in Medieval Society* (Philadelphia: University of Pennsylvania Press, 1976); Janet L. Nelson, "Queens as Jezebels: The Careers of Brunhild and Balthild in Merovingian History," in *Medieval Women,* ed. Derek Baker (Oxford: Basil Blackwell, 1978), pp. 31–37; and John F. Plummer, ed., *Vox Feminae: Studies in Medieval Woman's Song,* Studies in Medieval Culture 15 (Kalamazoo, Michigan: Medieval Institute Publications, 1981).

3. See, for example, Elaine Tuttle Hansen, "Women in Old English Poetry Reconsidered," *Michigan Academician* 9 (1976): 109–17; Anne Lingard Klinck, "Female Characterization in Old English Poetry," *Dissertation Abstracts International* 38 (1977): 254A (University of British Columbia), and the epitome of her thesis in "Female Characterization in Old English Poetry and the Growth of Psychological Realism: *Genesis B* and *Christ I,*" *Neophilologus* 63 (1979): 597–610; and Audrey L. Meaney, "The *Ides* of the Cotton Gnomic Poem," *Medium Aevum* 48 (1979): 23–39.

4. Studies of single poems have included the religious poems: see especially Bernice W. Kliman, "Women in Early English Literature: 'Beowulf' to the 'Ancrene Wisse,'" *Nottingham Medieval Studies* 21 (1977): 32–49; Jane Chance Nitzsche, "The Anglo-Saxon Woman as Hero: The Chaste Queen and the Masculine Woman Saint," *Allegorica* 5 (1980):

139–48; and also Alexandra Hennessey Olsen, "Inversion and Political Purpose in the Old English *Judith*," *English Studies* 63 (1982): 289–93. Other studies of women have focused on the elegies, as in the book-length study by James Edward Anderson, "Strange Sad Voices: The Portraits of Germanic Women in the Old English *Exeter Book*" (dissertation, University of Kansas, 1978). Study of the women of *Beowulf* can be found in Jane C. Nitzsche, "The Structural Unity of *Beowulf*: The Problem of Grendel's Mother," *Texas Studies in Literature and Language* 22 (1980); 287–303; see also the review of scholarship contained in Alexandra Hennessey Olsen, "Women in *Beowulf*," in *Approaches to Teaching Beowulf*, ed. Jess B. Bessinger, Jr., and Robert F. Yeager (New York: Modern Language Association of America, 1984), pp. 150–56. Old Icelandic antecedents for some of the women in *Beowulf* and other poems have also recently appeared: for example, Helen Damico, "The Old English Wealhtheow and her Old Icelandic Counterparts" (dissertation, New York University, 1980), and also "The Valkyrie Reflex in Old English Literature," *Allegorica* 5 (1980): 149–67, both of which have evolved into *Beowulf's Wealhtheow and the Valkyrie Tradition* (Madison: University of Wisconsin Press, 1984).

1—PEACE-WEAVER, PEACE PLEDGE

1. For references to *Genesis*, see *The Junius Manuscript*, ed. George Philip Krapp, vol. 1 of *The Anglo-Saxon Poetic Records* (New York: Columbia University Press, 1931). For a discussion of the term *ides* and its West Germanic origins, see Audrey L. Meaney, "The *Ides* of the Cotton Gnomic Poem," *Medium Aevum* 48 (1979): 23–39. I have checked the entry for *ides* in the *Microfiche Concordance to Old English*, ed. Richard L. Venezky and Antonette di Paolo Healey, published by the University of Delaware Press (Newark, 1984); it does not include all the references which follow.

2. For references to *Beowulf*, see the edition by Friedrich Klaeber, ed. *Beowulf and the Fight at Finnsburg*, 3rd ed. with first and second supplements (Boston: D. C. Heath, 1936).

3. See Meaney, p. 23, who notes that OS *idis* and OHG *itis* have been applied to the Virgin Mary, and *idisi* to witch women "who sit working spells of binding and loosing" in the OHG *First Merseburg Charm*. Such contexts allow her to link the antecedents of the Anglo-Saxon word with the Tacitus passage, discussed later in this chapter, concerning the holy and prophetic nature of women.

4. For references to the Riddles, see the edition of *The Exeter Book* by George Philip Krapp and Elliott Van Kirk Dobbie, vol. 3 of *The Anglo-Saxon Poetic Records* (New York: Columbia University Press, 1936). Subsequent references to poems contained within *The Exeter Book* will be listed within the text. For the discussion of Riddle 75 and the line following, see Norman E. Eliason, "Four Old English Cryptographic Riddles," *Studies in Philology* 49 (1952): 553–65, but esp. 554–56. Craig Williamson identifies the *ides* in an even less complimentary way, in *The Old English Riddles of the Exeter Book* (Chapel Hill: University of North Carolina Press, 1977), pp. 110, 352–56.

5. Bernice W. Kliman, "Women in Early English Literature, 'Beowulf' to the 'Ancrene Wisse,'" *Nottingham Medieval Studies* 21 (1977): 32–49, believes that *Beowulf* and *Ancrene Wisse* represent important sign-posts in the change of status for women because *Beowulf* was written at a time when war was constant and women, though lesser in strength, held a significant position because of their intelligence and peace-weaving role. By the early thirteenth century, warfare, and hence strength, was not as prevalent and thus women

ceased to be peace-weavers, becoming anchoresses instead. This change in their importance was founded on Pauline rabbinicism, in which submission to male intellect and sexuality are especially important.

6. See Erika von Erhardt-Siebold, "The Old English Loom Riddles," in *Philologica: The Malone Anniversary Studies,* ed. Thomas A. Kirby and Henry Bosley Woolf (Baltimore: Johns Hopkins University Press, 1949), pp. 9–17.

7. von Erhardt-Siebold, p. 11.

8. Contained in *The Vercelli Book,* ed. George Philip Krapp, vol. 2 of *The Anglo-Saxon Poetic Records* (New York: Columbia University Press, 1932).

9. Tacitus, *On Britain and Germany,* trans. H. Mattingly (West Drayton: Penguin Books, 1948), p. 116; and for the original, *The Germania of Tacitus,* ed. Rodney Potter Robinson, Philological Monographs, no. 5 (Middletown, Ct.: American Philological Association, 1935) (Chapter 14). Subsequent references will appear in the text.

10. Contained in *The Anglo-Saxon Minor Poems,* ed. Elliott Van Kirk Dobbie, vol. 6 of *The Anglo-Saxon Poetic Records* (New York: Columbia University Press, 1942).

11. Meaney, pp. 23–39. She prefers the magical associations and the idea that the woman may be somewhat unchaste, but there is no sure way of resolving the question from the Anglo-Saxon original. For the use of secrecy to avoid damning a reputation, see K. S. Kiernan, "*Cwene:* The Old Profession of Exeter Riddle 95," *Modern Philology* 72 (1975): 387.

12. See the discussions of some of these obscene riddles by Edith Whitehurst Williams, "What's So New About the Sexual Revolution?" *Texas Quarterly* 18.2 (1975): 46–55; and Donald Kay, "Riddle 20: A Revaluation," *Tennessee Studies in Literature* 13 (1968): 133–39. In addition, see also Kiernan, "*Cwene:* The Old Profession of Exeter Riddle 95," for the solution to 95 as "prostitute," or *cwene,* because "prostitution was something of a specialty to the Anglo-Saxons," p. 388, and many words for 'prostitute' exist in the lexicon. This seems a strangely modern idea, one perhaps not convincing given other Anglo-Saxon literary contexts in which women are mentioned.

13. Frederick Norman, "Problems in the Dating of *Deor* and its Allusions," in *Franciplegius: Medieval and Linguistic Studies in Honor of Francis Peabody Magoun, Jr.,* ed. Jess B. Bessinger, Jr., and Robert P. Creed (New York: New York University Press, 1965), p. 213n10.

2—THE VIRGIN MARY OF *CHRIST I* AS SECULAR AND ECCLESIASTICAL FEMININE IDEAL

1. St. Jerome, *Epistola* 22: "Ad Eustochium" nn. 18, 19, 21, 24, 38, in *Hieronymi Opera Omnia, Patrologiae Latinae,* ed. J.-P. Migne, vol. 22 (Paris, 1864), cols. 407–408. All translations are my own unless otherwise indicated. In addition to Judith, other members of Christ's new family included Aman, burned in his own fire, and also James and John, who followed the Savior. Judith, interestingly enough, was not a virgin in the Vulgate; she was merely a chaste widow.

2. *Catechesis* 12.15. *Patrologiae Graecae,* ed. J.-P. Migne (Paris, 1857), vol. 33, col. 741, quoted and translated in Thomas Livius, *The Blessed Virgin in the Fathers of the First Six Centuries* (London and New York, 1893), p. 48.

3. *Contra haereses* 3.22.4, *PG,* vol. 7, col. 959. He also declares that "Eve was disobedient; she did not obey when she was virgin. Likewise she was for her husband Adam,

while still virgin . . . and being disobedient and thereby the cause of her own appropriate death, and that of the human race; similarly Mary, having a husband predestined, and nevertheless being the Virgin, obeyed and became for herself and for the whole human race cause of salvation," my translation of *ibid.*, cols. 958–59.

4. The three patriarchates of Rome, Antioch, and Alexandria were represented by Saint Irenaeus; Saint Justin of Palestine in *Dialogus cum Tryphone Iudaeo* 100, *PG*, vol. 6, cols. 710–11; and the African Tertullian in *De carne Christi*, *PL*, vol. 2, col. 782. Another who contrasts the two women is Saint Gregory Thaumaturgus, *Homilia* 1: *In annuntiatione Virginis Mariae*, *PG*, vol. 10, cols. 1148–49; see also Saint Gregory of Nyssa, Saint Amphilochius, Saint Ephrem, and the many other commentators cited in the first chapter of Livius,

5. My translation of *Origenis in Lucam homiliae interprete S. Hieronymo*, 8, *PG*, vol. 13, col. 1919.

6. "The prominence of a female saint in early medieval England and Ireland depended upon two criteria: (1) her historical significance in the development of national monasticism; and (2) her literary and religious significance as the popular national counterpart of the Virgin Mary." For England the most prominent saint was primarily Aetheldryth; for Ireland, Brigit. See Carmine Jane Bell, "The Role of Monastic Women in the Life and Letters of Early Medieval England and Ireland," *Dissertations Abstracts International* 36 (1975): 2835A (University of Virginia).

7. *De virginitate*, cap. 39–40, in *The Prose Works*, trans. Michael Lapidge and Michael Herren (Cambridge: D. S. Brewer; Totowa, N.J.: Rowman and Littlefield, 1979), pp. 106–107.

8. See *Christ and Satan*, lines 408–40, in *The Junius Manuscript:* she says of Mary, "Hwæt, þu fram minre dohtor,   drihten, onwoca / in middangeard   mannum to helpe," 437–38.

9. Homily No. 1 in *The Blickling Homilies of the Tenth Century*, ed. and trans. Rev. R. Morris, Early English Text Society Nos. 58, 63, 73 (London, 1880), pp. 2–3. Other metaphors and concepts of Mary developed in this homily and found also in early patristic commentaries as well as the *Advent Lyrics* include the meekness of the handmaiden Mary; her womb as tabernacle, as Christ's bride-bower, and as door of heaven's kingdom; and herself as bride with her son as bridegroom. In addition to the Annunciation, her Assumption into heaven functions as another favored topic in the homilies.

10. First discovered by E. Sievers, *Der Heliand und die angelsächsische Genesis* (Halle, 1875).

11. One view of unity traces the Germanic and patristic theme of exile throughout *Christ I:* see Stanley B. Greenfield, "The Theme of Spiritual Exile in *Christ I*," *Philological Quarterly* 32 (1953): 321–28. For the view of the poems as separate lyric units, and for an examination of their dependence on the Church Antiphons, see Jackson J. Campbell, "Structural Patterns in the Old English Advent Lyrics," *ELH* 23 (1956): 239–55, and his edition, *The Advent Lyrics of the Exeter Book* (Princeton: Princeton University Press, 1959). Another view of the unity finds time and the sacramental mode of primary importance: see Roger Lass, "Poem as Sacrament: Transcendence of Time in the *Advent Sequence* from the Exeter Book," *Annuale Mediaevale* 7 (1966): 3–15.

12. In addition to the recent edition by Jackson J. Campbell mentioned previously, which is the one used throughout this study, others include Albert S. Cook, *The Christ of Cynewulf* (Boston, 1900) and George Philip Krapp and Elliott Van Kirk Dobbie, *The Exeter Book*, vol. 3 of *The Anglo-Saxon Poetic Records* (New York: Columbia University Press,

1936). All translations are my own, unless otherwise indicated; line numbers will be mentioned within the text.

13. The original and later conventional attribution of speeches to the two principals in Poem 7 was corroborated by Thorpe, Grein, Assmann, Gollancz, Cook, Krapp and Dobbie, and Campbell in their various editions; a minority view in opposition was offered by Neil D. Isaacs, "Who Says What in 'Advent Lyric VII'? (*Christ*, lines 164–213)," *Papers on Language and Literature* 2 (1966): 162–66; his view was challenged by John Miles Foley, "*Christ 164–213*: A Structural Approach to the Speech Boundaries in 'Advent Lyric VII,'" *Neophilologus* 59 (1975): 114–18. Another minority opinion (this one interpretative, based on the meaning of the text) was offered by Earl R. Anderson, "The Speech Boundaries in Advent Lyric VII," *Neophilologus* 63 (1979): 611–18. Because unorthodox attributions proposed by Isaacs and Anderson do not seem especially convincing or illuminating, this study will rely on the older and more conventional attributions.

14. Two studies exist which focus on her characterization, but only in Poem 7: see Earl R. Anderson, "Mary's Role as *Eiron* in *Christ I*," *JEGP* 70 (1971): 230–40; and Anne Lingard Klinck, "Female Characterisation in Old English Poetry and the Growth of Psychological Realism: *Genesis B* and *Christ I*," *Neophilologus* 63 (1979): 597–610. Much helpful information on Marian typology in the sequence derived partly from the Messianic prophecies, the Song of Solomon, and the Gospel can be found in Robert B. Burlin, *The Old English Advent: A Typological Commentary*, Yale Studies in English, vol. 168 (New Haven: Yale University Press, 1968), esp. pp. 19–22. The study carefully analyzes each lyric in the light of patristic commentary, but without especial attention to Mary as a unifying figure either for the whole sequence or for individual poems.

15. *Sermo 36: De laudibus Mariae ex partu Salvatoris*, in *Appendix ad S. Fulgentii opera, Patrologiae Latinae*, ed. J.-P. Migne, vol. 65 (1861), cols. 899–900.

16. *De virginitate*, cap. 39–40, in *The Prose Works*, trans. Michael Lapidge and Michael Herren (Cambridge: D. S. Brewer; Totowa, N.J.: Rowman and Littlefield, 1979), pp. 106–107.

17. On Canticles 4, 8, cited in Livius, p. 271.

18. On Isaiah 7:14, in *Commentarii in Isaiam Prophetam* 3, PL, vol. 24, cols. 107–108.

19. Burlin, p. 73, points to biblical parallels for the *virga/virgo* from the root of Jesse in Isaiah 11, 1, which also lists the Gifts of the Holy Spirit, seen as a tree. The Gifts in this poem are thus imagined perhaps as seeds planted in the human heart.

20. See Burlin, p. 87.

21. *Contra haereses* 3.22, 4, *PG*, vol. 7, col. 959, trans. Livius, p. 36. For an Anglo-Saxon example of the contrast, see Ælfric's *Catholic Homilies: The Second Series: Text*, ed. Malcolm Godden, Early English Text Society (London, New York, and Toronto: Oxford University Press, 1979), esp. p. 11.

22. *Christ and Satan*, lines 408–40, in *The Junius Manuscript*, ed. George Philip Krapp, vol. 1 of *The Anglo-Saxon Poetic Records* (New York: Columbia University Press, 1931), pp. 148–49.

23. *Catechesis* 12.29, *PG*, vol. 33, col. 761. trans. Livius, p. 48.

24. See, for example, Saint Irenaeus, *Contra haereses*, v. 19n, trans. Livius, pp. 37–38. He declares, "For as Eve was seduced by an angel's word so as to shun God, after she had transgressed His word, so Mary also by an Angel's word had the glad tidings given her, that she might bear God, obeying his word."

25. *Epistola 48: Ad Pammachium*, n. 21, in *Hieronymi opera omnia, PL*, vol. 22, col. 510.

26. Lines 9–12, from Ms. 41, Corpus Christi College, Cambridge, in *The Anglo-Saxon Minor Poems*, ed. Elliott Van Kirk Dobbie, vol. 6 of *The Anglo-Saxon Poetic Records* (New York: Columbia University Press, 1942), p. 125.

27. The metaphor of "victorious women" for the bee-swarm is related to the Teutonic concept of the Valkyrie and *idisi*, according to Helen Damico, "The Valkyrie Reflex in Old English Literature," *Allegorica* 5 (1980): 149–67, esp. 151–52.

28. Jerome lists four reasons in commenting on Matthew 1:18, "When as His Mother Mary was espoused to Joseph," one of several Gospel verses wherein the espousal is mentioned: to show the origin of Mary by means of Joseph's genealogy; to prevent stoning by the Jews as an adulteress; to have the comfort of a husband in her flight to Egypt; and most important, to conceal the birth of Christ from the Devil because she seemed to be a wife and not the Virgin Mother prophesied earlier for the Messiah. For the list of reasons, see Jerome's commentary on Matthew 1:18, in *Commentarii in Evangelium Matthaei* 1.1, *PL*, vol. 26, col. 24: "Quare non de simplici Virgine, sed de desponsata concipitur? Promum, ut per generationem, Joseph, origo Mariae monstraretur. Secundo, ne lapidaretur a Judaeis ut adultera. Tertio, ut in Aegyptum fugiens haberet solatium mariti. Martyr Ignatius etiam quartam additit causam, cur a desponsata conceptus sit: ut partus, inquiens, ejus celaretur diabolo, dum eum putat non de Virgine, sed de uxore generatum." Cited in Livius, p. 121. See also, on Luke 1:27 ("A Virgin espoused to a man whose name was Joseph"), Saint Ambrose in his commentary on Luke, *PL*, vol. 15, cols. 1554–55; and Saint Augustine on Luke 1:26, 27, in *De nuptiis et concupiscentia*, 1.11, 13, *PL*, vol. 44, cols. 419–20, 421–22, who sees the espousal as symbolic of the three goods of marriage—offspring (through Christ), fidelity (because there was no adultery), and sacrament (because there was no divorce).

29. Saint Jerome, in his commentary on Matthew 1:19, in *Commentarii in Evangelium Matthaei* 1.1, col. 24, acknowledged that the law applied not only to the guilty but also to those who knew of his crimes. However, Saint Jerome portrayed Joseph as a man knowing both of the chastity and of the pregnancy but remaining silent out of faith.

30. See Jerome, *Commentarii in Isaiam Prophetam* 3, on Isaiah 7, 14, *PL*, vol. 24, col. 107, and the putative Jerome, *Breviarium in Psalmos*, on Psalm 17:1, *Hieronymi opera omnia, PL*, vol. 26, col. 866: "Christ in Mary as if the Bridegroom in the bridechamber, and the body of Mary as if the tabernacle" ("Christus in Maria quasi sponsus in thalamo, et corpus Mariae quasi tabernaculum").

31. Alvin A. Lee, *The Guest-Hall of Eden: Four Essays on the Design of Old English Poetry* (New Haven: Yale University Press, 1972), pp. 56–57.

32. "Christ comes forth as bridegroom from his nuptial chamber," or, "Procedit Christus quasi sponsus de thalamo suo." Saint Augustine, *Sermo* 120: *In natali domini* 4, *Appendix, Tomi quinti operum*, in *PL*, vol. 39, col. 1987. See also Saint Proclus, *Oratio* 6.17: *De laudibus S. Mariae, PG*, vol. 65, col. 756, on Canticles 5:1, for Mary as Spouse and God as Bridegroom. The idea is a very common one.

33. As the Virgin Spouse of God, Mary typifies the Ark of the Covenant. Jerome declares of the ideal virgin, or Mary, that "The Bride of Christ is the ark of the Testament, within and without made gold, a keeper of the law of the Lord. As in the ark there was nothing except the tables of the Testament, so also in you [Mary] no one from outside should be thought of. Alone this propitiary as though above the cherubim, the Lord wishes to sit." Saint Jerome, *Epistola* 22: *Ad Eustochium*, n. 24, in *PL*, vol. 22, col. 410. The Latin reads: "Sponsa Christi arca est Testamenti, intrinsecus et extrinsecus deaurata, custos legis Domini. Sicut in illa nihil aliud fuit, nisi tabulae Testamenti, ita et in te nullus sit extrinsecus cogitatus. Super hoc propitiatorium quasi super Cherubim, sedere vult Dominus."

34. Saint Ambrose, *Expositio Evangelii secundum Lucam* 2.7, *PL*, vol. 15, col. 1555: "Bene desponsata, sed virgo; quia est Ecclesiae typus, quae est immaculata, sed nupta. Concepit nos virgo de Spiritu, parit nos virgo sine gemitu." On Mary and the Church depicted as virgins, see also (among many others) Saint Augustine, *Sermo* 188: *In Natali Domini* 5.4, *PL*, vol. 38, cols. 1004–5; *Sermo* 191: *In natali Domini* 8.1–3, *PL*, vol. 38, cols. 1009–11; and *Sermo* 192: *In natali Domini*, 9.2, *PL*, vol. 38, cols. 1012–13; and Clement of Alexandria, *Paedagogus*, 1.6, *PG*, vol. 8, col. 301.

35. Saint Ambrose, *De institutione virginis* 1.3.24, *Opera omnia*, *PL*, vol. 16, col. 311: "We declare therefore that through a woman has this heavenly mystery of the Church been implemented, in her grace figured forth, on account of whom Christ descended, and completed that eternal work of human redemption. Whence also Adam called the name of his wife Life (*Gen.* 2.23); for it is through a woman that the series and succession of the human race is spread through the world, and through the Church that eternal life is conferred" ("Advertimus itaque per mulierem caeleste illud impletum esse mysterium Ecclesiae, in ea gratiam figuratam, propter quam Christus descendit, et aeternum illud opus humanae redemptionis absolvit. Unde et Adam vocavit nomen mulieris suae vitam (*Gen.* II, 23); nam et in populis per mulierem successionis humane series et propago diffunditur, et per Ecclesiam vita confertur aeterna").

36. Saint Ambrose, *Expositio super septem visiones libri Apocalypsis, Ad opera appendix*, *PL*, vol. 17, col. 876: "Possumus per mulierem in hoc loco et beatam Mariam intelligere, eo quod ipsa mater sit Ecclesiae: et filia sit Ecclesiae, quia maximum membrum est Ecclesiae. Draco igitur stetit ante mulierem, ut cum peperisset, filium ejus devoraret: quia in exordio nativitatis Chris;i eum per Herodem ministrum suum interficere voluit (*Matth.* II, 13). Stat etiam ante mulierem, id est, Ecclesiam, ut eos quos per baptismum Deo generat, Male suadendo perdat."

37. Saint Ambrose, *De institutione virginis* 1.8.52, 54; 1.9.58, 62, *PL*, vol. 16, cols. 319, 320, 321. The Latin reads: "Et infra dicit propheta vidisse se in monte alto nimis aedificationem civitatis (*Ezech.* XL, 2 *et seq.*), cujus portae plurimae significantur; una tamen clausa describitur. . . . Quae est haec porta, nisi Maria; ideo clausa, quia virgo? Porta igitur Maria, per quam Christus intravit in hunc mundum, quando virginali fusus est partu, et genitalia virginitatis claustra non solvit. . . . Et ut doceamus quia portam habet omnis homo, per quam Christus ingreditur: *Tollite*, inquit, *portas principes vestras, et elevamini portae aeternales, et introbit Rex gloriae* (*Psal.* XXIII, 7). Quanto magis ergo porta erat in Maria, in qua sedit Christus, et exivit? . . . Porta ergo clausa virginitas est: et hortus clausus virginitas. . . . Porta clausa es, virgo, nemo aperiat januam tuam, quam semel clausit Sanctus et Verus, qui habet clavim David, qui aperit, et nemo claudit: claudit et nemo aperit (*Apoc.* III, 7)." See also Saint Jerome, *Epistola* 48: *Ad Pammachium*, *PL*, vol. 22, col. 510, commenting on Canticles 4:12.

38. From Ms. Cotton Caligula A.vii, in *Anglo-Saxon Minor Poems*, ed. Dobbie, vol. 6 of *The Anglo-Saxon Poetic Records*, pp. 116–18.

39. Saint John Chrysostom, *De mutatione nominum* 2, *PG*, vol. 51, col. 129, cited in Livius, p. 65.

3—BRAVE JUDITH, JULIANA, AND ELENE

1. David Chamberlain, in *"Judith: A Fragmentary and Political Poem,"* in *Anglo-Saxon Poetry: Essays in Appreciation for John C. McGalliard*, ed. Lewis E. Nicholson and Dolores Warwick Frese (Notre Dame, Ind.: University of Notre Dame Press, 1975), pp. 135–

59, sums up the critical debate over *Judith* as a poem either fragmentary or on the contrary nearly complete. It is seen as fragmentary because it begins in mid-sentence, omits the first eleven chapters in the Vulgate Judith, and includes section or "lection" numbers X, XI, and XII at lines 15, 122, and 236 of the edited text (that is, more than eight sections appear to be missing). For the view that it is fragmentary, see the editions by Elliott van Kirk Dobbie, *Beowulf and Judith*, vol. 4 of *The Anglo-Saxon Poetic Records* (New York: Columbia University Press, 1953), p. lix *ff;* and B. J. Timmer, *Judith* (New York: Appleton Century Crofts, 1966), p. 2 (all references to the poem will derive from Dobbie's edition; all translations, unless otherwise noted, are my own); and the critical studies of Arthur G. Brodeur, "A Study of Diction and Style in Three Anglo-Saxon Narrative Poems," in *Nordica et Anglica: Studies in Honor of Stefán Einarsson*, ed. Allan H. Orrick (The Hague: Mouton, 1968), p. 105; Alain Renoir, "*Judith* and the Limits of Poetry," *English Studies* 43 (1962): 146; and Jackson J. Campbell, "Schematic Technique in *Judith*," *ELH* 38 (1971): 166. For the view that it is missing at most a few lines, see R. E. Woolf, "The Lost Opening to the *Judith*," *Modern Language Review* 50 (1955): 168–72; Stanley B. Greenfield, *A Critical History of Old English Literature* (New York: New York University Press, 1965), pp. 164*f,* and Bernard F. Huppé, "Judith," *The Web of Words* (Albany: State University of New York Press, 1970), pp. 136–137, 147.

2. For a discussion of the date of *Judith* and the history of the debate concerning that issue, see Timmer, pp. 6–8; for the dates of Cynewulf, see especially Kenneth Sisam, "Cynewulf and his Poetry" (Sir Israel Gollancz Memorial Lecture Read March 8, 1933), *Proceedings of the British Academy* 18 (1932): 303–31.

3. Albert S. Cook, ed., *Judith: An Old English Epic Fragment* (Boston and London: D.C. Heath, 1904), p. ix; he also notes similar phrasings in the *Gifts of Men*, the *Dream of the Rood*, and the *Metrical Psalm*.

4. Timmer, p. 7; see also Rosemary Woolf, "Saints' Lives," in *Continuations and Beginnings: Studies in Old English Literature*, ed. E. G. Stanley (London and Edinburgh: Thomas Nelson, 1966), p. 64, who declares that "the poem shows unmistakably the influence of the life of the virgin martyr."

5. See Woolf, "Saints' Lives," p. 37.

6. *Ibid.*, pp. 38, 62; she cites Aelfric in his Life of St. Edmund for the discussion of Anglo-Saxon saints.

7. "Saints' Lives," p. 45, believes that *Juliana* was intended for a convent of nuns.

8. Saint Jerome, *Epistola* 22: *Ad Eustochium*, n. 24, in *Patrologiae Latinae*, ed. J. P. Migne, vol. 22 (Paris, 1864), col. 410.

9. Woolf, "Saints' Lives," p. 60.

10. Saint Jerome, *Epistola* 48: *Ad Pammachium, PL*, vol. 22, col. 510; Saint John Chrysostom, "De futurae vitae deliciis," *Patrologiae Graecae*, vol. 51, col. 350, notes that virginity was one of the most honored virtues because it had in effect been banished by the Fall of Man, which instituted propagation of the species; therefore Christ freed virginity from banishment and exile by making a Virgin his mother.

11. Michael Lapidge, "The Writings of Aldhelm" and "Introduction to Aldhelm's Prose *De Virginitate*," in *Aldhelm: The Prose Works*, trans. Michael Lapidge and Michael Herren (Cambridge: D.S. Brewer; Totowa, N.J.: Rowman and Littlefield, 1979), p. 14. (for the date), and p. 52 (for the sources).

12. Aldhelm, *De virginitate*, cap. 19, pp. 75–76. The three states of female chastity, including widowhood, are classified by Ambrose, *De virginibus ad Marcellinam sororem suam* 1.10.60, *PL*, vol. 16, col. 205; Jerome, *Commentarii in evangelium Matthaei* 2.13.23, *PL*, vol. 26, col. 89, and Augustine, *De sancta virginitate*, cap. 45, *PL*, vol. 40, col. 423.

13. Lapidge, "Introduction to *De Virginitate*," p. 56.

14. This passage and the next two come from *De virginitate*, cap. 11, p. 68.

15. For a discussion of Judith only as an allegorical type of Holy Church, based on comments by Isidore (*Allegoriae quaedam Scripturae Sacrae* 122, *PL*, vol. 83, col. 116) and Rabanus Maurus (*Opera* [1627] III, 250), see Huppé, pp. 142–45. Huppé does not analyze the Old English *Judith* for resonances of the patristic texts, however. Isidore's comment reads, "Judith et Esther typum Ecclesiae gestant, hostes fidei puniunt, ac populum Dei ab interitu eruunt."

16. For Juliana as a type of Christ and the Church, see especially Joseph Wittig, "Figural Narrative in Cynewulf's *Juliana*," *Anglo-Saxon England* 4 (1975): 37–55.

17. For an examination of *Elene* as a conflict between Ecclesia and Synagogue, see especially Thomas D. Hill, "Sapiential Structure and Figural Narrative in the Old English 'Elene,'" *Traditio* 27 (1971): 159–77; Jackson J. Campbell, "Cynewulf's Multiple Revelations," *Medievalia et Humanistica* N.S. 3 (1972): 257–77, and Catharine A. Regan, "Evangelicalism as the Informing Principle of Cynewulf's 'Elene,'" *Traditio* 29 (1973): 27–52. In addition, one of the most interesting approaches to *Elene* describes the theme as a contrast between the universal Christian ethic and the heroic ethic developed in two spheres—the temporal, represented by Constantine, and the ecclesiastical, represented by Judas (Cyriacus)—to be read on three levels: "as a conflict between Satan and God, as a conflict between hostile clans here on earth, and finally as a conflict within the individual human heart, that of the poet," p. 66 of John Gardner, "Cynewulf's *Elene*: Sources and Structure," *Neophilologus* 54 (1969): 65–76. He sees the central unifying image as the cross and what it did for Constantine, Judas, and the poet. Referring again to tropological and eschatalogical levels in the poem, he regards the relationship between Elene and Constantine as analogous to Christ's redemption of the sin, and Judas' loyalty to his clan rather than universal Christendom as analogous to man's loyalty to the flesh rather than the spirit (pp. 66–67).

18. See the discussion of Origen in Beryl Smalley, *The Study of the Bible in the Middle Ages* (Notre Dame, Ind.: University of Notre Dame Press, 1964), pp. 6–11. The most famous and important late medieval statement of the levels of allegory belongs to Dante in his fourteenth-century Letter to Can Grande commenting on Psalm 93:1–2: "When Israel went out of Egypt, the house of Jacob from a barbarous people, Judea was made his sanctuary, Israel his dominion." Dante distinguishes the three levels in his gloss: "Now if we look at the letter alone, what is signified to us is the departure of the sons of Israel from Egypt during the time of Moses; if at the allegory, what is signified to us is our redemption through Christ; if at the moral sense, what is signified to us is the conversion of the soul from the sorrow and misery of sin to the state of grace; if at the anagogical, what is signified to us is the departure of the sanctified soul from bondage to the corruption of this world into the freedom of eternal glory." From *Literary Criticism of Dante Alighieri*, trans. Robert S. Haller (Lincoln: University of Nebraska Press, 1973), p. 99. In the eighth century it is not clear whether scholars were aware, say, of St. Augustine's very different definition of allegory as three-leveled (analogical, etiological, and allegorical). Bede, for example, identifies as allegory irony, sarcasm, and enigma, for "allegory is a trope in which a meaning other than the literal is indicated." See Robert P. Miller, ed. *Chaucer: Sources and Backgrounds* (New York: Oxford University Press, 1977), p. 42.

19. See Hiram Pflaum, "Der allegorische Streit zwischen Synagoge und Kirche in der europäischen Dichtung des Mittelalters," *Archivum Romanicum* 18 (1934): 243–340; and Margaret Schlauch, "The Allegory of Church and Synagogue," *Speculum* 14 (1939): 448–64.

20. Pflaum cites the pseudo-Augustinian work, *De altercatione Ecclesiae et Synagogae dialogus*, *PL*, vol. 42, col. 1131–40, on p. 255: "Una quibusdam temporibus adulterio deprehensa possessionis nostrae praecoqua pervasione jura temeraverat: alia [*lies:* aliam]

merito castitatis per sententiam donatoris, possidentem illam [*lies*: illa] quae auribus vestris
videtur exacta, nonnulla apud saeculum prius clandestina fraude privaverat" (col. 1131).

21. Aldhelm, *De virginitate*, cap. 57, p. 127.

22. *Ibid.*

23. Aldhelm, *De virginitate*, cap. 57, pp. 126–27. Compare the Vulgate Judith 13: 19.

24. Chamberlain, p. 155, holds the first view, and Alexandra Hennessey Olsen,
"Inversion and Political Purpose in the Old English *Judith*" *English Studies* 63 (1982): 289–93.
holds the second.

25. Holofernes has been interpreted as a tyrant similar to Nebuchadnezzar in
Daniel, to Eormenric in *Deor*, and to Heremod in *Beowulf*, by Alvin A. Lee, *The Guest-Hall
of Eden: Four Essays on the Design of Old English Poetry* (New Haven: Yale University
Press, 1972), p. 49. See also Timmer, pp. 11–12, for a discussion of other Germanic heroic
images used to describe Holofernes and his retainers, feast, armor, and battle. Judith's
bravery, coupled with her wisdom, has also been interpreted as an example of the theme of
sapientia et fortitudo by Jane Mushabac, "*Judith* and the Theme of *Sapientia et Fortitudo*,"
Massachusetts Studies in English 4 (1973): 3–12, although it seems more likely that the
Judith-poet employs aspects of this motif to render a type of the good soldier of Christ rather
than the ideal king.

26. The edition used is that of George Philip Krapp and Elliott Van Kirk Dobbie, vol.
3 of *The Anglo-Saxon Poetic Records* (New York: Columbia University Press, 1936).

27. For *Juliana's* chief source, see *Acta sanctorum, Februarius*, vol. 2, ed. Johannes
Bollandus and Godefridus Henschenius (Antwerp: Ioannes Meursus, 1658), pp. 873–77. For
an analysis of the specific differences between *Juliana* and this source, see Claes Schaar,
Critical Studies in the Cynewulf Group, Lund Studies in English, no. 17 (Lund: C.W.K.
Gleerup; Copenhagen: Ejnar Munksgaard, 1949), pp. 29–31. The most illuminating analysis
of Cynewulf's use of his source regards his artistry as a transformation of "the cluttered and
thematically unfocused account of the Latin *Acta* into a sharply etched ritual drama" through
the perception of a pattern of characterization in the three fathers representing three types of
love (God, Africanus, Satan), three emperors (God, Maximianus, and Satan), three tormen-
tors (Eleusius, the devil, and Juliana), and two bridegrooms (Christ and Eleusius). See
Daniel G. Calder, "The Art of Cynewulf's *Juliana*," *Modern Language Quarterly* 34 (1975):
355–71. Other analyses of the use of the source in *Juliana* include the study of typology in R.
Barton Palmer's "Characterization in the Old English 'Juliana'," *South Atlantic Bulletin* 41
(1976): 10–21; the study of social and legal customs, in Lenore MacGaffey Abraham,
"Cynewulf's *Juliana*: A Case at Law," *Allegorica* 3 (1978): 172–89; and the study of its
rhetorical opening in relation to *Andreas, Elene, Guthlac A* and *B*, in Margaret Bridges,
"Exordial Tradition and Poetic Individuality in Five Old English Hagiographical Poems,"
English Studies 60 (1979): 361–79.

28. For a discussion of the heroic imagery and diction used in *Juliana* and *Elene*, see
Schaar, esp. 31–117; for Anglo-Saxonisms, p. 31; for parallels between *Beowulf* and *Juliana*,
p. 246f.

29. Indeed, Schaar, pp. 30–31, believes that the source for Cynewulf's description of
the righteous man armed by God and of the soul as a fortified city (393–413a) may have been
inspired by Jerome's *Commentarii in epistolam ad Ephesios* 3.6, in *PL*, vol. 26, col. 543ff:
"Ad extremum quasi vir bellator et fortis, omnes sectas contrarias veritati concidet, inter-
ficiet, jugulabit, gladium spiritus, id est, verbum Dei, manu tenens . . . . Si enim absti-
nuerimus nos a corporum voluptate, parum cautos in avaritia [diabolus] capit. Quod si et
avaritiam cum voluptate contemnimus, per luxuriam irrepit, et facit nobis ventrem esse

deum, et per hanc etiam illa quae fortia esse videbantur, expugnat. Et quomodo solent sapientes exercituum principes, ea vel maxime oppugnare urbium loca quae parum munita sunt, ut cum per illa irruperint, facile munita capiantur; ita et diabolus per ea quae patere videt, aut certe non firmiter clausa, quaerit irrumpere, et ad ipsam arcem cordis et animae pervenire."

30. On the runic signatures of Cynewulf, in general (those in *Elene, Juliana, Christ II*, and *Fates of the Apostles*), see Carleton F. Brown, "The Autobiographical Element in the Cynewulfian Rune Passages," *Englische Studien* 38 (1907): 196–233, and Dolores Warwick Frese, "The Art of Cynewulf's Runic Signatures," in *Anglo-Saxon Poetry: Essays in Appreciation for John C. McGalliard*, ed. Lewis E. Nicholson and Dolores Warwick Frese (Notre Dame, Ind.: University of Notre Dame Press, 1975), pp. 312–34, on *Juliana*, pp. 315–19, and on *Elene*, pp. 323–27.

31. For the feast days, see Sisam, "Cynewulf and his Poetry," p. 312. For Elene's chief sources, see the *Acta sanctorum, maius*, vol. 1, ed. Godefridus Henschenius and Daniel Papenrochius (Antwerp, 1680), pp. 450f; and Alfred Holder, ed. *Inventio sanctae crucis* (Leipzig, 1889). For a delineation of the specific differences between *Elene* and its sources, see Schaar, pp. 24–27, and also F. Holthausen, "Zur Quelle von Cynewulfs Elene," *Zeitschrift für deutsche Philologie* 37 (1905): 1–19, and "Zur Quelle von Cynewulfs 'Elene'," *Archiv für das Studium der neueren Sprachen und Literaturen* 125 (1910): 83–88. Selections from documents from A.D. 335 to 500 tracing the growth of the legend on which the poem is based are contained in Albert Stanburrough Cook's edition of *The Old English Elene, Phoenix, and Physiologus* (New Haven: Yale University Press; London: Humphrey Milford / Oxford University Press, 1919), pp. xv–xxiv.

32. Many of the recent studies of *Elene* concentrate on literary aspects of the poem, its imagery and thematic structure, often based on Cynewulf's changes in his sources. See especially John Gardner, "Cynewulf's *Elene:* Sources and Structure," *Neuphilologische Mitteilungen* 68 (1967): 65–76; Robert Stepsis and Richard Rand, "Contrast and Conversion in Cynewulf's *Elene*," *Neuphilologische Mitteilungen* 70 (1969): 273–82; Daniel G. Calder, "Strife, Revelation, and Conversion: The Thematic Structure of *Elene*," *English Studies* 53 (1972): 201–10; and Earl R. Anderson, "Cynewulf's *Elene:* Manuscript Divisions and Structural Symmetry," *Modern Philology* 72 (1974): 111–22. In addition, there have been some rhetorical studies, or studies illustrating how Elene fits into the formulaic tradition. See Donald K. Fry, "Themes and Type-Scenes in *Elene* 1–113," *Speculum* 44 (1969): 35–45, and (also on *Juliana*) Bridges, "Exordial Tradition and Poetic Individuality," pp. 361–79.

33. All references to *Elene* derive from the *Vercelli Book*, ed. George Philip Krapp, vol. 2 of *The Anglo-Saxon Poetic Records* (New York: Columbia University Press, 1932).

4—THE SAINT, THE ABBESS, THE CHASTE QUEEN

1. In *An Old English Martyrology*, ed. George Herzfeld, Early English Text Society No. 116, O.S. (London, 1900), the twenty-two brief lives include Aemiliana, Pega, Prisca, Emerentiana, Felicitas, Patricia and Modesta, Seven Women in Sirmium, Anthia, Zoe, Rufina and Secunda, Julitta, Symphorosa, Christina, Mary Magdalene, Assumption of the Virgin Mary, Sabina, Mary's birth, Eufemia, Fausta, Ethelburga, Hilda; in *Aelfric's Lives of Saints*, ed. Walter W. Skeat, Part 3 of vol. 2, Early English Text Society No. 94 (London, 1890), the Death of Mary of Egypt. For a very different classification of saints' lives, both male and female, see Raymon S. Farrar, "Structure and Function in Representative Old English Saints' Lives," *Neophilologus* 57 (1973): 83–93.

2. In the *Martyrology* including Alexandria, Aetheldryth, Tryphonia, Felicitas; in *Aelfric's Lives of Saints*, ed. Walter W. Skeat, Part 2, in 1 vol., Early English Text Society No. 82, O.S. (London, 1885), including Aetheldryth (Etheldreda); in Part 4 of vol. 2, Cecilia.

3. In the *Martyrology* including Anastasia, Agnes, Agape, Chionia, and Irene, Basilla, Petronella, Lucia, Marina, Anatolia, Theodata, Afra and Hilaria, Thecla, Justina, Cyrilla, Caecilia, Eulalia, Lucia; in *Aelfric's Lives of Saints*, ed. Walter W. Skeat, Part 1 of vol. 1, Early English Text Society No. 76, O.S. (London, 1881), including Agnes, Agatha, and Lucy.

4. Methodius, *Symposium*, 6, 5; 7.1 Cf. Origen, *De oratione*, 17.2, ed. J.-P. Migne, *Patrologiae Graecae*, vol. 11, col. 471; John Climachus, *Gradus*, 29, *PG*, vol. 88, col. 1147. Gregory views the Song of Songs as an ideal guide to philosophy and the knowledge of God, "the breviary of Bride mysticism," in *Super Cantica Canticorum*, ed. J.-P. Migne, *Patrologiae Latinae*, vol. 79, cols. 47–548, and depicts Christ as Agape's archer shooting at the soul with love's arrow in an image that anticipates later courtly love metaphors. Augustine understands love's physical consummation as an analogue for the Trinity: the lover, the object loved, and the love between them as a bond in which the Church participates, in *De trinitate*, lib. 8, cap. 10. 14, *PL*, vol. 42, col. 960. For these references I am indebted to M. J. Swanton, "*The Wife's Lament* and *The Husband's Message*: A Reconsideration," *Anglia* 82 (1964): 276–77.

5. In *The Blickling Homilies of the Tenth Century*, ed. R. Morris, Early English Text Society Nos. 58, 63, 73 (London, 1880), pp. 7, 11. All examples and references are taken from *The Old English Version of Bede's Ecclesiastical History of the English People*, ed. Thomas Miller, Part 1, Early English Text Society Nos. 95–96 (London, 1890–91).

6. Aelfric, "On the Dedication of a Church," *Homilies of the Anglo-Saxon Church: The First Part*, ed. B. Thorpe (London, 1844–46), 2: 583.

7. Aelfric, "On the Nativity of the Holy Virgins," *Homilies of the Anglo-Saxon Church*, 21: 567.

8. In the *Martyrology* including Eufemia, Perpetua, Thecla, Pelagia; in *Aelfric's Lives*, Part 1 in vol. 1. Eugenia; Part 4 of vol. 2, Eufrasia.

9. In the *Martyrology* including Columba; in *Aelfric's Lives*, Part 4, in vol. 2, including Daria.

10. Note the twelfth-century adaptation of this idea in Mythographus Tertius, *De dii gentium et illorum allegoriis* 6.16 in *Scriptores Rerum Mythicarum Latini*, ed. G. H. Bode, 2 vols. (1834; rpt. Hildesheim: Georg Olms, 1968), pp. 182–83: "Animae autem duae sunt vires, una superior, altera inferior. Animus superior vis caelestibus adhaeret et incorruptibilibus, et illa concupiscit, vocaturque rationalitas, spiritus, domina, mens, animus. Inferior est, quae voluptatibus corporis consentit, vocaturque sensualitas, animalitas, famula, mens. Estque superioris, ut inferiorum regat. Sed aliquando ex neglegentia superioris praevalet inferior, et seducit superiorem. Est etiam in hac figura Adam et Eva." See Jane Chance Nitzsche, *The Genius Figure in Antiquity and the Middle Ages* (New York: Columbia University Press, 1975), p. 55.

11. These references, all from Bede, include Byrhte (1.25, p. 58); Aethelbeorg (2.9, p. 120), and Ealhflaed (3.21, p. 220). Recently, a plethora of studies of monastic women has appeared: for Hild of Whitby and Aetheldryth of Ely, in particular, see Carmine Jane Bell, "The Role of Monastic Women in the Life and Letters of Early Medieval England and Ireland," *DAI* 36 (1975): 2835A (University of Virginia), and also, more generally, Joan Nicholson, "*Feminae Gloriosae*: Women in the Age of Bede," in *Medieval Women*, ed. Derek Baker, pp. 15–29.

12. See *Aelfric's Lives of Saints*, Part 2, vol. 1, pp. 432–40 (no. 20). For her popularity and similarity to both St. Brigit and the Virgin Mary, see Bell, "The Role of Monastic Women in the Life and Letters of Early Medieval England and Ireland."

13. References to the chronicles, unless indicated otherwise, come from *The Anglo-Saxon Chronicles*, rev. trans., ed. Dorothy Whitelock, David C. Douglas, and Susie I. Tucker (New Brunswick, N.J.: Rutgers University Press, 1961). Passages in Anglo-Saxon derive from B. Thorpe, ed., *The Anglo-Saxon Chronicles*, vol. 1: *Original Texts*, in Rerum Britannicarum Medii Aevi Scriptores, No. 23-1 (London, 1861). References to the Latin Chronicles ("La") come from A. Campbell, ed., *The Chronicle of Aethelweard* (London and Edinburgh: Thomas Nelson and Sons, 1962).

14. *Chronicle of the Kings of England: From the Earliest Period to the Reign of King Stephen*, trans. J. A. Giles (London, 1847), pp. 33–60. For Latin references, see *Willelmi Malmesbiriensis Monachi De gestis regum Anglorum libri quinque; Historiae novellae libri tres*, ed. William Stubbs, 2 vols., Rerum Britannicarum Medi Aevi Scriptores, No. 90 (London, 1887–89), I, 35 (1.35).

15. *Chronicle*, pp. 35–36, 37; *De gestis regum*, I, 35–36, 39 (1.35–37).

16. *Chronicle*, p. 123; *De gestis regum*, I, 136 (2.125)

17. *Chronicle*, p. 30; *De gestis regum*, I, 32 (132).

18. *The Exeter Book*, vol. 3 of *The Anglo-Saxon Poetic Records*, ed. George Philip Krapp and Elliot Van Kirk Dobbie (New York: Columbia University Press, 1936), p. 159 (lines 83–85).

19. For "daughter of," see years 853ABCDE; 919BCD; 965DF; La785, A787; La854, A853; La855; "sister of," 697DEF; 718; 888 (889C); 922A; 942BCD; 925D; La917(=918); "wife, queen, or mistress of," 697DEF; La672; "Lady, queen, abbess," 888ABDE (889C); 912BC; 913BC; 918E; La680.

20. Eight references to marriages and/or separations occur: 718ABCDE; 792DE; 853ABCDE; 924BCD; 925D; 965DF; La785 (A787); La854 (A853); La855.

21. References to Eormengota occur in 630E and to Aelfgifu in La948 = 944, 946.

22. See 888(889C); 918BCB; 922A; La680; La888, La917(=918); La948 = 944, 946.

23. See 697DEF; 894ABCD; 916BC; and 919BCD.

24. See the discussion of "Sons and Mothers: Family Politics in the Early Middle Ages," by Pauline Stafford, in *Medieval Women*, ed. Baker, pp. 79–100, which centers on historical examples from the late tenth and eleventh centuries both in England and on the continent.

25. See Dorothy Whitelock, ed. and trans., *Anglo-Saxon Wills* (1930; rpt. New York: AMS Press, 1973): of the forty wills included, eight are for the women Wynflæd, Aelfgifu, Aethelflæd, Aelfflæd, Leofgifu, Wulfgyth, and Siflæd.

26. For a discussion of "Land Charters and the Legal Position of Anglo-Saxon Women," see Marc A. Meyer's contribution to *The Women of England: Interpretive Bibliographical Essays from Anglo-Saxon Times to the Present*, ed. Barbara Kanner (Hamden, Ct.: Archon, 1979), pp. 57–82.

27. Benjamin Thorpe, ed. and tr. *Diplomatarium anglicum aevi Saxonici: A Collection of English Charters and Wills* (London, 1865), p. 266.

28. *Ibid.*, pp. 337–38.

29. See, e.g., *ibid.*, pp. 44, 237–41.

30. *Ibid.*, p. 427.

31. *Chronicle*, 71; *De gestis regum*, I, 77 (1.75).

32. *De gestis regum*, I, 262 (2.211).

33. *Chronicle*, p. 106; *ibid.*, I, 118 (2.113).

34. See *Chronicle*, pp. 106–107, and *De gestis regum* I, 117–18 (2.113). See *Asserius De Rebus Gestis Aelfredi*, ed. William Henry Stevenson (Oxford: Clarendon Press, 1904), pp. 11–14 (13–15); it has been translated by L. C. Jane as *Asser's Life of King Alfred* (New York: Cooper Square Publishers, 1966), pp. 10–13.

35. *De rebus gestis*, pp. 17–18.

36. *Saxonis Grammatici Gesta Danorum*, ed. Alfred Holder (Strasbourg, 1886), 8.264. The translation is taken from *The First Nine Books of the Danish History of Saxo Grammaticus*, tr. Oliver Elton (London, 1894), p. 319. Subsequent references to Saxo Grammaticus will appear in the text.

5—EVE IN *GENESIS B*

1. All references in *Genesis B* and other poems of the Junius Manuscript derive from George Philip Krapp, ed. *The Junius Manuscript*, vol. 1 of *The Anglo-Saxon Poetic Records* (New York: Columbia University Press, 1931). For Eve as unfairly deceived and acting out of loyalty to Adam, see Eduard Sievers, *Der Heliand und die angelsächische Genesis* (Halle, 1875), p. 22; and B. J. Timmer, ed. *The Later Genesis* (Oxford: Scrivner Press, 1948), p. 58; for Eve as not innocent but not guilty of vanity and pride, see Robert Emmett Finnegan, "Eve and 'Vincible Ignorance' in *Genesis B*." *Texas Studies in Literature and Language* 18 (1976): 329–39; for Adam as more to blame than Eve see Alain Renoir, "Eve's I.Q. Rating:" Two Sexist Views of *Genesis B*," paper delivered at the Annual Modern Language Association meeting, Houston, Texas, December 28, 1980; for the Devil as chiefly culpable, with Adam and Eve as adversaries of the Devil and hence gently heroic, see Rosemary Woolf, "The Fall of Man in *Genesis B* and the *Mystère d'Adam*," in *Studies in Old English Literature in Honor of Arthur G. Brodeur*, ed. Stanley B. Greenfield (Eugene: University of Oregon Press, 1963), pp. 187–99.

2. Saint Irenaeus, *Contra haereses*, 3.22.4, *Patrologiae Graecae*, ed. J.-P. Migne (Paris, 1857), vol. 7, col. 959, cited in Thomas Livius, *The Blessed Virgin in the Fathers of the First Six Centuries* (London and New York, 1893), pp. 37–38.

3. *Catechesis* 12.5, *PG*, vol. 33, col. 741, cited in Livius, p. 67.

4. See Renoir's well-stated summary in the paper cited above.

5. From *Ad opera Sancti Ambrosii appendix, PL*, 17, col. 692.

6. See Stanley B. Greenfield, *A Critical History of Old English Literature* (1965; rpt. New York: New York University Press, 1968), pp. 151–52. Similarities between *Genesis B* and the fragmentary Old Saxon *Genesis*, aside from language (and the poet has changed details and adapted the lengthy Old Saxon verse-line), include Adam's speech to Eve when he laments the future after the fall (*Genesis B*, 790–816): see Timmer, pp. 55–60. Other changes in the biblical Genesis made either in the Old Saxon original or in *Genesis B* from other sources center on the temptation undertaken by the subordinate devil; the masking of the Tempter as an angel; the tempting of Adam first; the Tree of Knowledge as ugly and dark; Eve's eating of the apple in good faith, thinking she will carry out God's will; her vision of heaven; Adam's eating of the apple in good faith; the disappearance of the vision of heaven and its replacement by a vision of hell: see especially J. M. Evans, "*Genesis B* and its Background," *Review of English Studies*, n.s. 14 (1963), 1–16 and 113–23. Sources and

influences he cites include Augustine in *De civitate Dei* and *De Genesi ad litteram*, Bede's *Hexaemeron*, Alcuin's *Interrogationes et responsiones in Genesin*, and his pupil Raban Maur's *Commentarii in Genesim libri quatuor*, as well as Jewish apocrypha, the earliest Fathers, Christian Latin poets like Avitus, Cyprian, Victor, et al., and Germanic epic. Woolf, pp. 189–99, believes that *Genesis B* and the twelfth-century Anglo-Norman *Mystère d'Adam* probably had a common source from the East.

7. In addition to the brief discussion by Greenfield, *A Critical History*, pp. 150–52, see also the much more extensive examination by Alain Renoir in "The Self-Deception of Temptation: Boethian Psychology in *Genesis B*," in *Old English Poetry: Fifteen Essays*, ed. Robert P. Creed (Providence, R.I.: Brown University Press, 1967), pp. 47–67.

8. See J. R. Hall's literary analysis of the role of the two words in the poem in "*Geongordom* and *Hyldo* in *Genesis B*: Serving the Lord for the Lord's Favor," *Papers on Language and Literature* 11 (1975): 302–307; he does not discuss either the heroic or theological implications of the two words, but only traces their appearance.

9. In *The Homilies of Wulfstan*, ed. Dorothy Bethurum (Oxford: Clarendon Press, 1957), p. 157 (Homily VII).

10. *PG*, vol. 42, col. 728, cited and translated in Livius, p. 51.

11. In *Opera omnia*, *PG*, vol. 65, col. 682, cited and translated in Livius, pp. 220–21.

6—THE ERRANT WOMAN AS *SCOP* IN *WULF AND EADWACER* AND *THE WIFE'S LAMENT*

1. Benjamin Thorpe, *Codex Exoniensis* (London, 1842), p. 527. More modern "non-interpretations" include Alain Renoir, "*Wulf and Eadwacer*: A Noninterpretation," in *Franciplegius: Medieval and Linguistic Studies in Honor of Francis Peabody Magoun, Jr.* (New York: New York University Press, 1965), pp. 147–63; and Neil D. Isaacs, "A Negative Note on *Wulf and Eadwacer*," in his *Structural Principles of Old English Poetry* (Knoxville: University of Tennessee Press, 1968), pp. 114–17.

2. The only study of which I know to interpret the narrator of *Wulf and Eadwacer* as male (and a minstrel as well) was written by Norman E. Eliason, "On Wulf and Eadwacer," in *Old English Studies in Honour of John C. Pope*, eds. R. B. Burlin and E. B. Irving, Jr. (Toronto: University of Toronto Press, 1974), pp. 225–34, who eccentrically believes that this "is a private communication addressed to a colleague, ruefully but playfully protesting about the mishandling of their poetry, which . . . has been separated, some of it being copies in one place of a manuscript and the rest in another, less favorable place." The equally odd vogue for regarding the sex of the speaker of *The Wife's Lament* as male began with Benjamin Thorpe's edition (see the preceding note), for he thought the feminine inflections were scribal errors and therefore assumed the speaker was male. He was followed by L. L. Schücking in 1906 who thought the speaker was a retainer who had lost his first lord, a murderer, but in finding a second lord was regarded as an accomplice to the first and therefore banished, although Schücking changed his view of the narrator's sex to female, in 1917: see "Das angelsächsische Dicht von der *Klage der Frau*," *Zeitschrift für deutsches Altertum und deutsche Litteratur* 48 (1906): 436–49; and Review of *Die altenglische Elegie* by Ernst Sieper, *Englische Studien* 51 (1917–18): 97–115. Two modern views of the speaker as male based on semantic and grammatical evidence belong to Rudolph Bambas, who brings up the scribal error theory once again in "Another View of the Old English *Wife's Lament,*

JEGP 62 (1963): 303–309, and to Martin Stevens, arguing from a grammatical base, in "The Narrator of *The Wife's Lament*," *Neuphilologische Mitteilungen* 79 (1968): 72–90. These arguments have been answered by Angela M. Lucas in "The Narrator of *The Wife's Lament* Reconsidered," *Neuphilologische Mitteilungen* 70 (1969): 282–97. There is simply no satisfactory way of getting around the feminine forms in the first two lines, e.g., *geomorre* (in line 1) and *minre sylfre* (line 2).

3. All references to *The Exeter Book* derive from the George Philip Krapp and Elliott Van Kirk Dobbie edition (New York: Columbia University Press, 1936), vol. 3 of *The Anglo-Saxon Poetic Records*. All translations are my own.

4. Nevertheless, folk poetry spoken by women—in Frauenlieder and Frauenstrophen—has been determined to be in part responsible for the rise of courtly love poetry in the High Middle Ages. For Frauenstrophen and -lieder, French and Provençal, with parallels in Portuguese, Serbian, Russian, Greek, and Chinese, see Theodor Frings, *Minnesinger und Troubadors*, Deutsche Akademie der Wissenschaften zu Berlin, Vorträge und Scriften, Part 34 (Berlin: Akademie-Verlag, 1949); for the discovery of medieval Spanish lyrical poetry, see Leo Spitzer, "The Mozarabic Lyric and Theodor Frings' Theories," *Comparative Literature* 4 (1952): 1–22; and for editions, translations, and commentary on individual works in English, see Kemp Malone, "Two English *Frauenlieder*," in *Old English Studies in Honor of Arthur G. Brodeur*, ed. Stanley B. Greenfield (Eugene: University of Oregon Press, 1963), pp. 106–17. But a more modern study points to the existence of the so-called Latin Cambridge Songs, which include the sexually explicit *Veni, dilectissime*, sung by a woman, contained in Cambridge University Library Ms. Gg. 5. 35, dating from the middle of the eleventh century but probably copied from an early continental original for the monastery of Saint Augustine at Canterbury. For the text, see Karl Strecker, ed., *Die Cambridger Lieder* (Berlin: Weidmann, 1926), p. 107. For a study of their significance and context, especially in relation to *The Wife's Lament* and *Wulf and Eadwacer*, see Clifford Davidson, "Erotic 'Women's Songs' in Anglo-Saxon England," *Neophilologus* 59 (1975): 451–62. In addition, a very recent volume tracing the use of the female voice or *persona* in Latin, Portuguese, English, Irish, German, and French song from the tenth century through the fifteenth has been edited by John F. Plummer in *Vox Feminae: Studies in Medieval Woman's Songs*, Studies in Medieval Culture, 15 (Kalamazoo, Mi.: Medieval Institute Publications, 1981).

5. The word *giedd* or *gidd*, according to Bosworth-Toller, usually denotes either a song, lay, or poem of metrical composition (in Latin, *cantus, cantilena, carmen, poema*) or a formal speech, tale, sermon, proverb, or riddle (in Latin, *elogium, verbum, sermo, dictum, loquela, proverbium,* or *aenigma*). In practice the meanings overlap, largely because much of Old English poetry is homilectic and proverbial and because many Old English sermons and riddles are metrical compositions. See Joseph Bosworth and T. Northcote Toller, eds., *An Anglo-Saxon Dictionary* (1898; rpt. Oxford: Clarendon Press, 1976), p. 474a, and the *Supplement* (1921: rpt. London: Oxford University Press, 1966), p. 462a–b.

6. Of course the term *giedd* or *gidd* can refer to any metrical composition, as in Cynewulf's *Fate of the Apostles* (in "se ðe lufige / þysses giddes," 88b–89a) and in his *Juliana* in *The Exeter Book* ("Bidde ic monna gehwone / gumena cynnes, þe þis gied wræce," 718b–19), both relatively pious accounts. See Vol. 2 of *The Anglo-Saxon Poetic Records, The Vercelli Book*, ed. George Philip Krapp (New York: Columbia University Press, 1932). *Gidd* also translates the Latin *proverbium* (proverb) in the Old English translation of Bede's *Ecclesiastical History*: see *The Old English Version of Bede's Ecclesiastical History of the English People*, ed. Thomas Miller, Early English Text Society Nos. 95, 96, 110, 111 (London, 1890–98), 3.12; for the Latin, see the edition by Bertram Colgrave and R. A. B. Mynors

(Oxford: Clarendon Press, 1969). It also translates the Latin *uaticinium* (prophetical speech) in the Old English glosses: see Arthur S. Napier, *Old English Glosses* (Oxford: Clarendon Press, 1900), line 3708. In *Beowulf* it represents a didactic and gnomic speech in Hrothgar's allusion to Heremod made in his (metrical, of course) sermon on pride (1723): see Fr. Klaeber, ed. *Beowulf and the Fight at Finnsburg*, 3rd ed. (Boston: D. C. Heath, 1936), for all references to *Beowulf*. It even means "riddle" in Riddle 55 (of uncertain solution, possibly a weapon-holder with gallows, or shield, scabbard, sword-rack, cross, or ornamented sword box—see Craig Williamson, ed. *The Old English Riddles of the Exeter Book* [Chapel Hill: University of North Carolina Press, 1977], pp. 300–305): "Nu me þisses gieddes / ondsware ywe," "Now show me an answer to this riddle or song" (14b–15a). It is interesting to note that this riddle appears on folio 114a of *The Exeter Book* manuscript, followed by *The Wife's Lament* on folio 115a—almost linking her *giedd* with the riddles; certainly her history is enigmatic and remains so today. The Seafarer also regards his tale as a *giedd*, "Of myself I can recite a true tale" ("Mæg ic be me sylfum   soþgied wrecan," 1) using similar syntax to that of the Wife, and his experiences share with these other examples of the *giedd* an emphasis on the gnomic, the elegiac, and the enigmatic.

7. In the Lay of Finn, when Hildeburh mourned at the funeral pyre of her son and brother, she lamented with songs, "Ides gnornode / geōmrode giddum" (1117b–18a), and when Beowulf mentions Hæthcyn, who killed his son by accident, he uses an epic simile of an old man who mourned the loss of his son: "hē gyd wrece, / sārigne sang" ("he utters a tale, a sorry song," 2446b–47a).

8. For example, the twelve years of attacks by Grendel become widely known through songs probably recited at banquets ("cūþ / gyddum," "known in lays or songs," 150b–51a). The Lay of Finn is often recited by Hrothgar's *scop*, "gid oft wrecen" (1065b), and after it has been related once again, the poet concludes "Lēoð wæs āsungen, / glēomannes gyd" (1159b–60a). When Beowulf has returned to Hygelac's court and relays his exploits, he describes the song and glee before Grendel's Mother arrived ("Þær wæs gidd and glēo," 2105a); he also mentions the *gomela Scilding* who played the harp and "recited a song / true and sorrowful" ("gyd āwræc / sōð ond sārlic," 2108b–9a). After Beowulf has brought in the treasures Hrothgar has given him, he himself recites a formal speech (apparently in the manner of the *scop*, "gyd æfter wræc," 2154b).

9. *Maxims* I notes that the *giedd* is indeed proper for a gleeman and a wiseman (but presumably not for others?): "word gerisað, / gleomen gied   ond guman snyttro" (165b-66, in *The Exeter Book*). Thus in *Oferhygd* the "word-ready prophet" sang and recited a poem about vainglory ("Þæt se witga song, / gearowyrdig guma,   ond þæt gyd awræc," 50b–51, in *The Exeter Book*), that is, a poet both a wise man, or *se witga*, and also an eloquent man, or *gearowyrdig guma*. Earlier, he "recites a truth-song,   varies with words" ("soðgied wrecað / wordum wrixlað," 15b–16a).

10. According to Kenneth Sisam, *Studies in the History of Old English Literature* (Oxford: Clarendon Press, 1953), p. 292.

11. See H. Bradley's discussion of the first riddle of in his review of *English Writers* in *Academy* 33 (1888): 197–98; as a riddle its solutions have been posited as Cynewulf, riddle, and millstone. See Heinrich Leo, *Quae de se ipso Cynevulfus . . . poeta Anglo-saconicus tradiderit* (Halle, 1857); Moritz Trautmann, "Cynewulf und die Rätsel," *Anglia* 6 (1883): 158–69; and H. Patzig, "Zum ersten Rätsel des Exeterbuchs," *Archiv* 145 (1923): 204–47. When the poem is considered as a riddle, its proper names can be interpreted as ironic nouns: 'Eadwacer' means 'property-watcher' and refers to her lover Wulf, according to John F. Adams, "Wulf and Eadwacer: An Interpretation," *Modern Language Notes* 73 (1958): 1–5. Because Wulf has abandoned her, he does not "watch" his property, the woman and her

child. The poem has also been interpreted as a charm: see Donald K. Fry, "Wulf and Eadwacer: A Wen Charm," Chaucer Review 5 (1971): 247–63.

12. For Wulf and Eadwacer as part of this family of Volsung legends, see William Henry Schofield, "Signy's Lament," PMLA 17 (1902): 262–295, and A. C. Bouman, "Leodum is minum: Beadohild's Complaint," Neophilologus 33 (1949): 103–13; as part of the Odoacer legends, see Rudolf Imelmann, Zeugnisse zur altenglischen Odoaker-Dichtung (Berlin: J. Springer, 1907), and Ruth P. M. Lehmann, "The Metrics and Structure of 'Wulf and Eadwacer,'" Philological Quarterly 48 (1969): 151–65. It is thus possible to see Wulf and Deor as complementary poems, with the male poet in Deor involved with the lamenting woman in Wulf, so that Wulf is the warrior-minstrel in the court that loves the king's sister Hild. For this somewhat implausible interrelationship, see P. J. Frankis, "Deor and Wulf and Eadwacer: Some Conjectures," Medium Aevum 31 (1962): 161–75.

13. For a discussion of the words scop and gleomann and their related functions, see Chapters Eight and Nine of Jeff Opland, Anglo-Saxon Oral Poetry: A Study of the Traditions (New Haven: Yale University Press, 1980).

14. See Terence Keough, "The Tension of Separation in Wulf and Eadwacer," Neuphilologische Mitteilungen 77 (1976): 55–56. Similar hallucinations can be found, according to Keough, in The Wanderer, lines 37–48, and The Wife's Lament, lines 37–41.

15. See Erika von Erhardt-Siebold, "The Old English Loom Riddles," in Philologica: The Malone Anniversary Studies, ed. Thomas A. Kirby and Henry Bosley Woolf (Baltimore: Johns Hopkins University Press, 1949), pp. 9–17.

16. For the implicit connective links (helpful explanatory information) and a convincing overall reading of the poem as a unified vision of the plight of various artists, see James L. Boren, "The Design of the Old English Deor," Anglo-Saxon Poetry: Essays in Appreciation for John C. McGalliard, ed. Lewis E. Nicholson and Dolores Warwick Frese (Notre Dame, Ind.: University of Notre Dame Press, 1975), pp. 264–76.

17. A different view of the structure, also as three-part, has been offered by A. N. Doane in "Heathen Form and Christian Function in 'The Wife's Lament,'" Mediaeval Studies 28 (1966): 77–91: lines 1–5 form the introduction, lines 6–41 the statement of the speaker's situation, and lines 42–53 a gnomic passage.

18. Among the recent hypotheses offered (without tangible evidence) in explanation for the Wife's imprisonment are the following: for adultery, the reason for the kinsmen's plotting, according to Douglas D. Short, "The Old English Wife's Lament: An Interpretation," Neuphilologische Mitteilungen 71 (1980): 585–603; enmity between the relatives of the deceased man murdered by her husband and his kin, according to Lee Ann Johnson, "The Narrative Structure of 'The Wife's Lament,'" English Studies 52 (1971): 492–501.

19. A freond can be a man whom a woman views as a husband or bridegroom, as in Juliana 34–41 when she thinks of God. Freondmynd and freondlufu are both compounds applied to a married relationship in Genesis 1831 and 1834. See also the discussion by M. J. Swanton, "The Wife's Lament and The Husband's Message: A Reconsideration," Anglia 82 (1964): 269–90, but freondmynd and freondlufu do seem to extend the idea of friendship or friendliness into mind and love, transcending mere friendship between men.

20. All references to Genesis B derive from The Junius Manuscript, vol. 1 of The Anglo-Saxon Poetic Records, ed. George Philp Krapp (New York: Columbia University Press, 1931).

21. Although one critic has noted the use of the concept hyldo in the poem, no one has yet noticed Eve's desire to serve heroically. See J. R. Hall, "Geongordom and Hyldo in

Genesis B: Serving the Lord for the Lord's Favor," *Papers on Language and Literature* 11 (1975): 302–307. For a discussion of its sources, among which especially is the Germanic epic, see J. M. Evans, *"Genesis B* and its Background," *Review of English Studies*, n.s. 14 (1963): 1–16 and 113–23. In addition, Alain Renoir touches upon the bond of loyalty between Adam and Eve, which resembles the bond of loyalty between man and God and that between Tempter and master Satan, in "The Self-Deception of Temptation: Boethian Psychology in *Genesis B,"* in *Old English Poetry: Fifteen Essays*, ed. Robert P. Creed (Providence, R.I.: Brown University Press, 1967), 47–67.

22. According to R. F. Leslie, who edited the poem in *Three Old English Elegies: The Wife's Lament, The Husband's Message, The Ruin* (Manchester: Manchester University Press, 1961).

23. The actual "earth-hall" for an Anglo-Saxon audience would have been an "ancient pagan sanctuary that included a cave opening up into other caves, located at the foot or in the side of a cliff or hill, in a wooded area with a great oak on or near the top of the cliff or hill," according to Karl P. Wentersdorf, "The Situation of the Narrator in the Old English *Wife's Lament,"* *Speculum* 56 (1981): 508. See also Joseph Harris, "A note on *eorðscræfleorðsele* and Current Interpretation of *The Wife's Lament,"* *English Studies* 58 (1977): 204–208.

24. See the discussion of the hall-compounds and the ironic queen, Grendel's Mother, in Jane Chance Nitzsche, "The Structural Unity of *Beowulf:* The Problem of Grendel's Mother," *Texas Studies in Literature and Language* 22 (1980): 288, and Chapter 7 of this study.

25. For Grendel as a mock *scop* or ironic retainer, see especially Edward B. Irving, Jr., *"Ealuscerwen:* Wild Party at Heorot," *Tennessee Studies in Literature* 11 (1966): 161–68; and also his *Reading of Beowulf* (New Haven: Yale University Press, 1968), p. 16.

26. Wentersdorf, pp. 609–10.

27. See Nora Kershaw, ed. and trans., *Anglo-Saxon and Norse Poems* (Cambridge: Cambridge University Press, 1922), p. 31. For an analysis of the diction that supports the emotionality of the Wife and mention of the abundance of words that signify misery (32 words or phrases) plus 19 instances of verbs which suggest endlessness, see Robert D. Stevick, "Formal Aspects of *The Wife's Lament,"* *JEGP* 59 (1960): 21–25.

7—GRENDEL'S MOTHER AS EPIC ANTI-TYPE OF THE VIRGIN AND QUEEN

1. The edition used throughout is Frederick Klaeber, *Beowulf and the Fight at Finnsburg*, 3rd ed. (Boston: D. C. Heath, 1936, with supplements in 1941 and 1950).

2. In *Beowulf:* in 620, 1168, and 1649 used of Wealhtheow, lady of the Helmings or Scyldings; in 1075 and 1117 of Hildeburh; in 1941 of Queen Thryth.

3. *The Exeter Book*, vol. 3 of *The Anglo-Saxon Poetic Records*, ed. George Philip Krapp and Elliot Van Kirk Dobbie (New York: Columbia University Press, 1936), p. 159 (lines 83–85).

4. Bosworth-Toller's *Anglo-Saxon Dictionary* lists *hringsele* and *niðsele* as compounds singular to *Beowulf,* underscoring the intentionality of the poet's irony.

5. Masculine pronouns refer to the feminine personifications of Old Age (1887b) and Change or Death (2421a), and to the feminine synecdoche "hand" (1344a).

6. *Āglǣca* apparently means "fierce adversary" in *Juliana* 268b and 319a where the Devil in the garb of an angel brings tidings to the maiden; when she asks who sent him, "Hyre se aglæca   ageaf ondsware," 319, in *The Exeter Book*, p. 122. Because he no longer appears to be a "wretch, monster, miscreant," the term *āglǣca* must denote 'foe' in this passage. Indeed, Juliana addresses him in line 317b as "feond moncynnes," 'foe' or 'enemy of mankind.'

7. Groundwork for this interpretation of the monsters as enemies of man was first laid by Arthur E. Du Bois, "The Unity of *Beowulf*," *PMLA* 49 (1934): 391 (Grendel and his mother become "the Danes' liability to punishment" for the secular sins of weakness, pride, and treachery; the dragon, "a variation upon Grendel," is "internal discord"). More recently they have been understood as adversaries of both man and God: see Richard N. Ringler, "*Him Sēo Wēn Gelēah:* The Design for Irony in Grendel's Last Visit to Heorot," *Speculum* 41 (1966): 64, in which Grendel represents *ofermōd* or *fortruwūng*, "held suspect by both Germanic instinct and Christian doctrine." See also Alvin A. Lee, *The Guest-Hall of Eden* (New Haven: Yale University Press, 1972), p. 186.

8. For this interpretation of Grendel, see especially Edward B. Irving, Jr., "*Ealuscerwen:* Wild Party at Heorot," *Tennessee Studies in Literature* 11 (1966): 161–68, and *A Reading of Beowulf* (New Haven: Yale University Press, 1968), p. 16; also, William A. Chaney, "Grendel and the *Gifstol:* A Legal View of Monsters," *PMLA* 77 (1962): 513–20; Joseph L. Baird, "Grendel the Exile," *Neuphilologische Mitteilungen* 67 (1966): 375–81.

9. Irving, *A Reading*, p. 209; Lee, pp. 215–16.

10. Tacitus, *Germania*, ed. Rodney Potter Robinson, Philological Monographs No. 5 (Middletown, Ct.: American Philological Association, 1935), p. 291 (cap. 14).

11. Recently interpretations have stressed her significance in Germanic social terms, but without developing the implications of such insights: a Jungian analysis views her as symbolic of the "evil latent in woman's function, as Grendel symbolizes the destructive element hidden in Beowulf's *mægen* . . . Grendel's mother symbolizes the feud aspect of the web of peace." Further, as a destroyer she signifies "the obverse of the women we meet in the two banqueting scenes which precede Beowulf's descent into Grendelsmere," both of whom combine to form the dual mother image. See Jeffrey Helterman, "*Beowulf:* The Archetype Enters History," *ELH* 35 (1968): 13–14. To other critics she represents vengeance (Nist, Irving, Hume), false loyalty (Gardner), revenge (Leyerle). See John A. Nist, *The Structure and Texture of Beowulf* (São Paulo, Brazil: Universidad de São Paulo, Faculdade de Filosofía, ciências eletras, 1959), p. 21; Irving, *A Reading of Beowulf*, p. 113, and *Introduction to Beowulf* (Englewood Cliffs, N.J.: Prentice Hall, 1969), p. 57; Kathryn Hume, "The Theme and Structure of *Beowulf*," *Studies in Philology* 72 (1975): 7; John Gardner, "Fulgentius's *Expositio Vergiliana Continentia* and the Plan of *Beowulf:* Another Approach to the Poem's Style and Structure," *Papers on Language and Literature* 6 (1970): 255; and John Leyerle, "The Interlace Structure of *Beowulf*," *University of Toronto Quarterly* 37 (1967): 11–12.

Other recent interpretations have explored not only Jungian but also Scandinavian and Celtic mythic and legendary parallels, sources, or analogues of this figure: for the Scandinavian parallels, see Nora K. Chadwick, "The Monsters and *Beowulf*," in *The Anglo-Saxons: Studies in Some Aspects of their History and Culture Presented to Bruce Dickens*, ed. Peter Clemoes (London: Bowes and Bowes, 1959), pp. 171–203, and Larry D. Benson, "The Originality of *Beowulf*," in *The Interpretation of Narrative: Theory and Practice*, ed. Morton W. Bloomfield, Harvard English Studies, No. 1 (Cambridge, Mass.: Harvard University Press, 1970), pp. 1–43; for the Celtic parallels, see Martin Puhvel, "The Might of Grendel's Mother," *Folklore* 80 (1969): 81–88; and for amalgamated parallels—English,

German, Latin, and Scandinavian—viewing Grendel and his mother as incubus and suc-cubus, see Nicholas K. Kiessling, "Grendel: A New Aspect," *Modern Philology* 65 (1968): 191–201.

12. See "Kentish Glosses" (ca. 9th century) in Thomas Wright, *Anglo-Saxon and Old English Vocabularies*, 2nd ed., Richard Paul Wülcker, (London, 1884) I, 88. For "on idesan" paired with "in virgunculam," see *in iuuenculam* in the gloss on Aldhelm's *De laudibus virginitatis* 29.14, in *Old English Glosses*, ed. Arthur S. Napier (Oxford: Clarendon Press, 1900), p. 57; also for *ides* as *virguncula* see the gloss on Aldhelm's *De laudibus Virginum* 191.7 and 194.14, pp. 181, 183.

13. Used of Grendel's mother in lines 1258b, 1276b, 1282a, 1538b, 1683b, 2118b, and 2139b. In 2932a *mōdor* refers to the mother of Onela and Ohthere.

14. If the poem is regarded as two-part in structure, balancing contrasts between the hero's youth and old age, his rise as a retainer and his fall as a king, his battles with the Grendel family and his battle with the dragon, then her episode (which includes Hrothgar's sermon and Hygelac's welcoming court celebration with its recapitulation of earlier events) lengthens the first "half" focusing on his youth to two-thirds of the poem (lines 1–2199). This view of the structure as two-part has generally prevailed since its inception in J. R. R. Tolkien's "Beowulf: The Monsters and the Critics," in *Proceedings of the British Academy* 22 (1936): 245–95, rpt. in *An Anthology of Beowulf Criticism*, ed. Lewis E. Nicholson (Notre Dame, Ind.: University of Notre Dame Press, 1963), pp. 51–103.

15. This increasingly popular view of the structure as tripartite has been advanced by H. L. Rogers, "Beowulf's Three Great Fights," *RES* N.S. 6 (1955): 339–55, rpt. in Nicholson, pp. 233–56; Gardner, "Fulgentius's *Expositio Vergiliana Continentia* and the Plan of Beowulf," 227–62; and most recently, Hume, "The Theme and Structure of *Beowulf*," 1–27. Hume's fine analysis includes an extensive survey of the various approaches to and inter-pretations of structural and thematic unity in *Beowulf* (see pp. 2–5). She declares, p. 3, "That critics should disagree over whether the structure has two parts or three is hardly surprising. Those concentrating on the hero tend to see two, those on action usually prefer three. But neither camp has produced a structural analysis which does not, by implication, damn the poet for gross incompetence, or leave the critic with a logically awkward position." For example, William W. Ryding, *Structure in Medieval Narrative* (The Hague: Mouton, 1971), first regards the middle of *Beowulf* as "a point of maximum logical discontinuity," p. 40, and then, contradicting himself, as a more difficult, more intense, more exciting combat than the fight with Grendel, illustrating a "varied repetition" of the same narrative motif, therefore implying logical continuity (p. 88).

16. Adrien Bonjour, "Grendel's Dam and the Composition of *Beowulf*," *English Studies* 30 (1949): 117. Other early *Beowulf* studies similarly ignored Grendel's mother or treated her as a type of Grendel. See also Tolkien, pp. 51–104, in which he declares, "I shall confine myself mainly to the monsters—Grendel and the Dragon" in Nicholson, p. 52. Similar treatments occur in T. M. Gang, "Approaches to *Beowulf*," *RES* N.S. 3 (1952): 1–12; Bonjour, "Monsters Crouching and Critics Rampant: or the *Beowulf* Dragon Debated," *PMLA* 68 (1953): 304–12; and even more recently, in Margaret Goldsmith, *The Mode and Meaning of Beowulf* (London: Athlone, 1970), e.g., p. 144; Lee, *The Guest-Hall of Eden*, pp. 171–223; and Daniel G. Calder, "Setting and Ethos: The Pattern of Measure and Limit in *Beowulf*," *Studies in Philology* 69 (1972): 21–37. For a cogent summary of the problem, see Alexandra Hennessey Olsen, "Women in *Beowulf*," in *Approaches to Teaching Beowulf*, ed. Jess B. Bessinger, Jr., and Robert F. Yeager (New York: Modern Language Association, 1984), pp. 150–56.

17. See the stories of the treacherous wife but loyal mother Urse in the twelfth-

century *Saxonis Grammatici Gesta Danorum*, ed. Alfred Holder (Strassburg, 1886), pp. 53–55. (*The First Nine Books of the Danish History of Saxo Grammaticus*, tr. Oliver Elton [London, 1894], pp. 64–65 [2. 53–54]).

18. Dorothy Whitelock, *The Beginnings of English Society* (Harmondsworth: Penguin, 1952), p. 41; on duty to one's kin, see pp. 38–47; on duty to one's lord, see pp. 31ff. Duty to one's lord superseded duty to one's kin (p. 37). See also *Saxonis Grammatici Gesta Danorum*, p. 254 (7), for the retainer's duty to lord; in cases of blood revenge the son remained most deeply obligated to his father, pp. 75, 96 (3), then to his brother or sister, pp. 53, 280 (2, 8), finally to his grandfather, p. 301 (9).

19. The poet uses similar word play in describing the "reception" of the guest Beowulf in the "hall" of the gold-lord dragon. First, Beowulf does not dare attack (or more figuratively, "approach") the gold-lord dragon in his ring-hall (*hringsele*, 2840a, 3053a): Wiglaf admits "he ne grëtte goldweard þone" (3081), literally because of the danger from fire, figuratively because of the dragon's avarice. Instead, *wyrd* will dispense or distribute his "soul's hoard" for which Beowulf has paid with his life (*wyrd* will seek his "sawle hord, sundur gedǣlan / līf wið līce," 2422a–23a; he "buys" the hoard with his life in 2799–800). After this "treasure-giving," the cup-passer—Wiglaf—pours water from the cup—Beowulf's helmet.

20. *The Exeter Book*, pp. 190–91. The sword declares:

> Ic wiþ bryde ne mot
> hæmed habban,　ac me þæs hyhtplegan
> geno wyrneð,　se mec geara on
> bende legde;　forþon ic brucan sceal
> on hagostealde　hæleþa gestreona.
> Oft ic wirum dol　wife abelge,
> wonie hyre willan;　heo me wom spreceð,
> floceð hyre folmum,　firenaþ mec wordum,
> ungod gæleð　Ic ne gyme þæs compes. (27b–35)

For a discussion of the double entendre of this riddle and an alternate solution ("Phallus"), see Donald Kay, "Riddle 20: A Reavaluation," *Tennessee Studies in Literature* 13 (1968), 133–139. Similarly erotic riddles include no. 21, "Plow"; no. 25, "Onion"; no. 44, "Key"; no. 45, "Dough"; no. 53, "Battering Ram"; no. 62, "Poker" on "Burning Arrow"; and no. 91, "Key" or "Keyhole." Some of these erotic riddles and the sexual implications of others have been analyzed in full by Edith Whitehurst Williams, "What's So New about the Sexual Revolution?" *Texas Quarterly* 18.2 (Summer 1975): 46–55: no. 25, "Onion", no. 45, "Dough"; no. 61, "Helmet" or "Shirt"; no. 12, "Leather"; and no. 9, "Key" or "Keyhole."

21. See *An Old English Martyrology*, ed. George Herzfeld, EETS No. 116, O.S. (London, 1900). For example, see the discussion of St. Lucia, p. 218, discussed previously in Chapter 2.

22. Although the poems were written by different poets, *Beowulf* in the late seventh or eighth century and *Judith* in the middle or late tenth century, the second *Beowulf* scribe did transcribe all of the *Judith* fragment, probably in the late tenth century. All references to *Judith* derive from Elliot Van Kirk Dobbie, ed. *Beowulf and Judith*, vol. 4 of *The Anglo-Saxon Poetic Records* (New York: Columbia University Press, 1953).

23. See, again, the life of St. Lucia in the *Martyrology*, p. 218.

24. For a discussion of these planes of correspondence in *Judith*, see James F. Doubleday, "The Principle of Contrast in *Judith*," *Neuphilologische Mitteilungen* 72 (1971): 436–41.

25. See Klaeber's discussion of Thryth's possible prototypes, 1931–62nn. Thryth's name resembles that of Quendrida (Queen Thryth?) and that of the Scottish queen Hermutrude, whose story is related in Saxo Grammaticus' *Danish History*, p. 124. (*Gesta Danorum*, pp. 101–102 [4]). Hermutrude, loved by Amleth, remains unmarried because of her cruelty and arrogance, similar to Thryth's. Finally, note the similarity between the following descriptions and those in *Beowulf*: Offa murdered many without distinction, including King Ethelbert, "thereby being guilty of an *atrocious outrage* against the suitor of his daughter," in William of Malmesbury's *Chronicle of the Kings of England: From the Earliest Period to the Reign of King Stephen*, tr. J. A. Giles (London, 1847), p. 238; in Latin "*nefarium rem* in procum filiae operatus," from *Willelmi Malmesbiriensis Monachi De gestis regum Anglorum libri quinque; Historiae novellae libri tres*. ed. William Stubbs, 2 vols., Rerum Britannicarum Medii Aevi Scriptores, no. 90 (London, 1887), p. 262 (2. 210). Compare *Beowulf*: "Mōdþrȳðo wæg,/fremu folces cwēn, firen' ondrysne," lines 1931b–32. Did the *Beowulf* poet confuse the father of Modhtrytho with the daughter herself?

Bibliography

PRIMARY SOURCES

Aelfric. *Catholic Homilies, The Second Series: Text*. Ed. Malcolm Godden. Early English Text Society. London, New York, and Toronto: Oxford University Press, 1979.

———. *Homilies: A Supplementary Collection*. Ed. John C. Pope. 2 vols. Early English Text Society, nos. 259–60, O.S. London, New York, and Toronto: Oxford University Press, 1967–68

———. *Homilies of the Anglo-Saxon Church: The First Part*. Trans. Benjamin Thorpe. 2 vols. London, 1844–46.

———. *Lives of Saints*. Ed. Walter W. Skeat. Part 1, in vol. 1. Early English Text Society, no. 76, O.S. London, 1881: Part 2, in vol. 2. Early English Text Society, no. 82, O.S. London, 1885; Part 3, in vol. 2. Early English Text Society, no. 94, O.S. London, 1890; Part 4, in vol. 2. Early English Text Society, no. 114, O.S. London, 1900.

Aethelweard. *The Chronicles*. Ed. A. Campbell. London and Edinburgh: Thomas Nelson & Sons, 1962.

Aldhelm. *The Prose Works*. Trans. Michael Lapidge and Michael Herren. Cambridge: D. S. Brewer; Totowa, N.J.: Rowman & Littlefield, 1979.

Asser. *De rebus gestis Aelfredi*. Ed. William Henry Stevenson. Oxford: Clarendon Press, 1904.

———. *Life of King Alfred*. Trans. L. C. Jane. New York: Cooper Square Publishers, 1966.

Bede, Venerable. *Ecclestiastical History of the English People*. Ed. Bertram Colgrave and R. A. B. Mynors. Oxford: Clarendon Press, 1969.

———. *Historia ecclesiastica gentis Anglorum; historia abbatum; epistola ad Ecgberctum*. Ed. Charles Plummer. 2 vols. Oxford, 1896.

———. *A History of the English Church and People*. Trans. Leo Sherley-Price, 1955; rev. ed. R. E. Latham. Harmondsworth: Penguin, 1968.

————. *The Old English Version of Bede's Ecclesiastical History of the English People*, Ed. and trans. Thomas Miller. Part 1. Early English Text Society, nos. 95–96, O.S. London, 1890–91; Part 2. Early English Text Society, nos. 110–111. London, 1898.

————. "Saint Bede's *Martyrologium:* A Translation with an Introduction." Trans. Clarence J. Bogetto. M.A. thesis, De Paul University, 1957.

Bode, George Heinrich, ed. *Scriptores rerum mythicarum latini*. 2 vols. 1834; rpt. Hildesheim: Georg Olms, 1968.

Bollandus, Joannes, and Godefridus Henschenius, eds. *Acta sanctorum*. Vol. 2. Antwerp, 1658.

Campbell, Jackson J., ed. *The Advent Lyrics*. Princeton: Princeton University Press, 1959.

Cook, Albert S[tanburrough] ed. *The Christ of the Exeter Book*. Boston: 1900.

————, ed. *Judith: An Old English Epic Fragment*. Boston and London: D. C. Heath and Co., 1904.

————, ed. *The Old English Elene, Phoenix, and Physiologus*. New Haven: Yale University Press; London: Humphrey Milford, Oxford University Press, 1919.

Cynewulf. *Elene*. Ed. P. O. E. Gradon. London: Methuen, 1958.

————. *Poems*. Ed. and trans. Charles W. Kennedy. London: George Routledge and Sons, Ltd.; New York: Dutton, 1910.

————. *Juliana*. Ed. Rosemary Woolf. London: Methuen, 1955.

Dante Alighieri. *Literary Criticism of Dante Alighieri*. Ed. and trans. Robert S. Haller. Lincoln: University of Nebraska Press, 1973.

Henschenius, Godefridus, and Daniel Papenrochius, eds. *Acta sanctorum, maius*. Vol. 1. Antwerp, 1680.

Herzfeld, George, ed. *An Old English Martyrology*. Early English Text Society, no. 116, O.S. London, 1900.

Holder, Alfred, ed. *Inventio sanctae crucis*. Leipzig, 1889.

Holthausen, F., ed. *Cynewulfs Elene (Kreuzauffindung) mit Einleitung, Glossar, Anmerkungen und der lateinische Quelle*. Alt- und Mittelenglische Texte, series 4. Heidelberg: Carl Winters Universitätsbuchhandlung, 1936.

Kershaw, Nora, ed. and trans. *Anglo-Saxon and Norse Poems*. Cambridge: Cambridge University Press, 1922.

Klaeber, Frederick, ed. *Beowulf and the Fight at Finnsburg*. 3rd ed. Boston: D. C. Heath, 1936, with supplements in 1941 and 1950.

Krapp, George Philip, and Elliott Van Kirk Dobbie, eds. *The Anglo-Saxon Poetic Records*. 6 vols. New York: Columbia University Press, 1931–53.

Leslie, R. F., ed. *Three Old English Elegies: The Wife's Lament, The Husband's Message, The Ruin*. Manchester University Press, 1961.

Migne, J.-P., ed. *Patrologiae cursus completus. Series graeca*. 166 vols. Paris, 1857–1936.

————, ed. *Patrologiae cursus completus. Series latina*. 221 vols. Paris, 1844–64.

Morris, R., ed. and trans. *The Blickling Homilies of the Tenth Century*. Early English Text Society, nos. 58, 63, and 73, O.S. London, 1880.

————, ed. *Old English Homilies of the Twelfth Century.* Second series. Early English Text Society, 1949, no. 53, O.S. London, 1873.

Napier, Arthur S., ed. *Old English Glosses.* Oxford: Clarendon Press, 1900.

Saxo Grammaticus. *Gesta Danorum.* Ed. Alfred Holder. Strasbourg, 1886.

————. *The First Nine Books of the Danish History.* Trans. Oliver Elton. London, 1894.

Strecker, Karl, ed. *Die Cambridger Lieder.* Berlin: Weidmann, 1926.

Tacitus. *The Germania: A Critical Edition.* Ed. Rodney Potter Robinson. Philological Monographs, No. 5. Middletown, Ct.: American Philological Association, 1935.

————. *On Britain and Germany.* Trans. H. Mattingly. West Drayton and Middlesex: Penguin Books, 1948.

Thorpe, Benjamin, ed. *The Anglo-Saxon Chronicle,* vol. 1: *Original Texts.* Rerum Britannicarum Medii Aevi Scriptores, no. 23-1. London, 1861.

————, ed. *Codex Exoniensis: A Collection of Anglo-Saxon Poetry.* London, 1842.

————, ed. and trans. *Diplomatarium Anglicum Aevi Saxonici: A Collection of English Charters and Wills.* London, 1865.

Timmer, B. J., ed. *Judith.* London: Methuen, 1952; rpt. New York: Appleton Century Crofts, 1966.

————, ed. *The Later Genesis.* Oxford: Scrivner Press, 1948.

Warner, Rubie D. N., ed. *Early English Homilies from the Twelfth Century Ms. Vesp. D. XIV.* Early English Text Society, no. 152, O.S. London: Kegan Paul, Trench, Trübner, and Humphrey Milford, Oxford University Press, 1917.

Whitelock, Dorothy, ed. and trans. *Anglo-Saxon Wills.* Cambridge: Cambridge University Press, 1930.

————, David C. Douglas, and Susie I. Tucker. Rev. trans., eds. *The Anglo-Saxon Chronicles.* New Brunswick, N.J.: Rutgers University Press, 1961.

William of Malmesbury. *Chronicle of the Kings of England: From the Earliest Period to the Reign of King Stephen.* Trans. J. A. Giles. London, 1847.

————. *De gestis regum Anglorum libri quinque; Historiae novellae libri tres.* Ed. William Stubbs. 2 vols. Rerum Britannicarum Medii Aevii Scriptores, no. 90. London, 1887–89.

Williamson, Craig, ed. *The Old English Riddles of the Exeter Book.* Chapel Hill: University of North Carolina Press, 1977.

Wright, Thomas. *Anglo-Saxon and Old English Vocabularies.* 2nd ed. Ed. Richard Paul Wülcker. London, 1884.

Wulfstan. *Homilies.* Ed. Dorothy Bethurum. Oxford: Clarendon Press, 1957.

SECONDARY SOURCES

Abraham, Lenore MacGaffey. "Cynewulf's *Juliana:* A Case at Law." *Allegorica* 3 (1978): 172–89.

Adams, John F. "'Wulf and Eadwacer': An Interpretation." *Modern Language Notes* 73 (1958): 1–5.

Anderson, Earl R. "Cynewulf's *Elene:* Manuscript Divisions and Structural Symmetry." *Modern Philology* 72 (1974): 111–22.

―――. "Mary's Role as *Eiron* in *Christ I.*" *JEGP* 70 (1971): 230–40.

―――. "The Speech Boundaries in Advent Lyric VII." *Neophilologus* 63 (1979): 611–18.

―――. "Voices in *The Husband's Message.*" *Neuphilologische Mitteilungen* 74 (1973): 238–46.

Anderson, James Edward. "Strange, Sad Voices: The Portraits of Germanic Women in the Old English *Exeter Book.*" Dissertation, University of Kansas, 1978.

Baird, Joseph L. "Grendel the Exile." *Neuphilologische Mitteilungen* 67 (1966): 375–81.

Baker, Derek, ed. *Medieval Women:* Studies in Church History: Subsidia 1. Oxford: Basil Blackwell, 1978.

Bambas, Rudolph C. "Another View of the Old English *Wife's Lament.*" *JEGP* 62 (1963): 303–309.

Bell, Carmine Jane. "The Role of Monastic Women in the Life and Letters of Early Medieval England and Ireland." *Dissertation Abstracts International* 36 (1975): 2835A (University of Virginia).

Benson, Larry D. "The Originality of *Beowulf.*" In *The Interpretation of Narrative: Theory and Practice.* Ed. Morton W. Bloomfield. Harvard English Studies, 1. Cambridge, Mass.: Harvard University Press, 1970. Pp. 1–43.

Bessinger, J. B., Jr. *A Concordance to the Anglo-Saxon Poetic Records.* Ithaca: Cornell University Press, 1978.

Bleeth, Kenneth A. "*Juliana, 647–52.*" *Medium Aevum* 38 (1969): 119–22.

Bloomfield, Morton W. "The Form of *Deor.*" *PMLA* 79 (1964): 534–41.

Bonjour, Adrien. "Grendel's Dam and the Composition of *Beowulf.*" *English Studies* 30 (1949): 113–24.

―――. "Monsters Crouching and Critics Rampant: or the *Beowulf* Dragon Debated." *PMLA* 68 (1953): 304–12.

Boren, James L. "The Design of the Old English *Deor.*" In *Anglo-Saxon Poetry: Essays in Appreciation for John C. McGalliard.* Ed. Lewis E. Nicholson and Dolores Warwick Frese. Notre Dame and London: University of Notre Dame Press, 1975.

Bosworth, Joseph. *An Anglo-Saxon Dictionary.* 1898; rpt. Oxford: Oxford University Press, 1976. *Supplement* by T. Northcote Toller. London: Oxford University Press, 1966.

Bouman, A. C. "*Leodum is Minum:* Beadohild's Complaint." *Neophilologus* 33 (1949): 103–13.

Bradley, Henry. Review of *English Writers: An Attempt towards a History of English Literature,* vol. 2, by Henry Morley. *Academy* 33 (1888): 197–98.

Bridges, Margaret. "Exordial Tradition and Poetic Individuality in Five Old English Hagiographical Poems." *English Studies* 60 (1979): 361–79.

Brodeur, Arthur G. "A Study of Diction and Style in Three Anglo-Saxon Narrative Poems." In *Nordica et Anglica: Studies in Honor of Stefán Einarsson*. Ed. Allan H. Orrick. The Hague: Mouton, 1968.

Brown, Carleton F. "The Autobiographical Element in the Cynewulfian Rune Passages." *Englische Studien* 38 (1907): 196–233.

Burlin, Robert B. *The Old English Advent: A Typological Commentary*. Yale Studies in English 168. New Haven and London: Yale University Press, 1968.

Calder, Daniel G. "The Art of Cynewulf's *Juliana*." *Modern Language Quarterly* 34 (1973): 355–71.

———. *Cynewulf*. Boston: Twayne, 1981.

———. "Setting and Ethos: The Pattern of Measure and Limit in *Beowulf*." *Studies in Philology* 69 (1972): 21–37.

———. "Strife, Revelation, and Conversion: The Thematic Structure of *Elene*." *English Studies* 53 (1972): 201–10.

Campbell, Jackson J. "Cynewulf's Multiple Revelations." *Medievalia et Humanistica*, N.S. 3 (1972): 257–77.

———. "Schematic Technique in *Judith*." *ELH* 38 (1971): 155–72.

———. "Structural Patterns in the Old English Advent Lyrics." *ELH* 23 (1956): 239–55.

Chadwick, Nora K. "The Monsters and *Beowulf*." In *The Anglo-Saxons: Studies in Some Aspects of Their History and Culture Presented to Bruce Dickens*. Ed. Peter Clemoes. London: Bowes & Bowes, 1959.

Chamberlain, David. "*Judith:* A Fragmentary and Political Poem." In *Anglo-Saxon Poetry: Essays in Appreciation for John C. McGalliard*. Ed. Lewis E. Nicholson and Dolores Warwick Frese. Notre Dame and London: University of Notre Dame Press, 1975.

Chaney, William A. "Grendel and the *Gifstol:* a Legal View of Monsters." *PMLA* 77 (1962): 513–20.

Cross, J. E. "Mary Magdalen in the *Old English Martyrology:* The Earliest Extant 'Narrat Josephus' Variant of her Legend." *Speculum* 53 (1978): 916–25.

Damico, Helen. *Beowulf's Wealhtheow and the Valkyrie Tradition*. Madison: University of Wisconsin Press, 1984.

———. "The Old English Wealhtheow and her Old Icelandic Counterparts: Legend and Art in the Construction of a Beowulfian Character." *Dissertation Abstracts International* 41 (1980): 2594A-95A (University of Wisconsin).

———. "The Valkyrie Reflex in Old English Literature." *Allegorica* 5 (1980): 149–67.

Davidson, Clifford. "Erotic 'Women's Songs' in Anglo-Saxon England." *Neophilologus* 59 (1975): 451–62.

Dietrich, Sheila C. "An Introduction to Women in Anglo-Saxon Society (c. 600-1066)." In *The Women of England from Anglo-Saxon Times to the Present: Interpretive Bibliographical Essays*. Ed. Barbara Kanner. Hamden, Ct: Archon Books, 1979.

Doane, A. N. "Heathen Form and Christian Function in '*The Wife's Lament*'."

Mediaeval Studies 28 (1966): 77–91.

Doubleday, James F. "The Principle of Contrast in *Judith*." *Neuphilologische Mitteilungen* 72 (1971): 436–41.

Du Bois, Arthur E. "The Unity of *Beowulf*." *PMLA* 49 (1934): 374–405.

Dubs, Kathleen Ellen. "*Genesis B*: A Stylistic Analysis." *Dissertation Abstracts International* 35 (1975): 7863A (University of Iowa).

Eis, Gerhard. "Waltharius-Probleme: Bemerkungen zu dem lateinischen Waltharius, dem angelsächsischen Waldere und dem voralthochdeutschen Walthari." In *Britannica: Festschrift für Hermann M. Flasdieck*. Eds. Wolfgang Iser and Hans Schabram. Heidelberg: Carl Winter-Universitätsverlag, 1960.

Eliason, Norman E. "Four Old English Cryptographic Riddles." *Studies in Philology* 49 (1952): 553–65.

———. "On Wulf and Eadwacer." *Old English Studies in Honour of John C. Pope*. Ed. Robert B. Burlin and Edward B. Irving, Jr. Toronto: University of Toronto Press, 1974.

———. "The Story of Geat and Maeðhild in *Deor*." *Studies in Philology* 62 (1965): 495–509.

Ellis, Deborah. "*The Wife's Lament* in the Context of Early English Literature: The Paralysis of Desertion." *Journal of Women's Studies in Literature* 1 (1979): 22–32.

Erhardt-Siebold, Erika von. "The Old English Loom Riddles." In *Philologica: The Malone Anniversary Studies*. Ed. Thomas A. Kirby and Henry Bosley Woolf. Baltimore: The Johns Hopkins University Press, 1949.

Evans, J. M. "*Genesis B* and its Background." *Review of English Studies*, N.S. 14 (1963): 1–16, 113–23.

Fanagan, John M. "*Wulf and Eadwacer*: A Solution to the Critics' Riddle." *Neophilologus* 60 (1976): 130–37.

Farrar, Raymon S. "Structure and Function in Representative Old English Saints' Lives." *Neophilologus* 57 (1973): 83–93.

Finnegan, Robert Emmett. "Eve and 'Vincible Ignorance' in *Genesis B*." *Texas Studies in Literature and Language* 18 (1976): 329–39.

Fitzgerald, Robert P. "*The Wife's Lament* and 'The Search for the Lost Husband.'" *JEGP* 62 (1963): 769–77.

Foley, John Miles. "*Christ 164–213*: A Structural Approach to the Speech Boundaries in 'Advent Lyric VII.'" *Neophilologus* 59 (1975): 114–18.

Frankis, P. J. "*Deor* and *Wulf and Eadwacer*: Some Conjectures." *Medium Aevum* 31 (1962): 161–75.

Frings, Theodor. *Minnesinger und Troubadours*. Deutsche Akademie der Wissenschaften zu Berlin, Vorträge und Schriften, vol. 34. Berlin: Akademie-Verlag, 1949.

Fry, Donald K. "The Heroine on the Beach in *Judith*." *Neuphilologische Mitteilungen* 68 (1967): 168–84.

———. "Imagery and Point of View in *Judith*, 200b-231." *English Language Notes* 5 (1967): 157–9.

———. "Themes and Type-Scenes in *Elene* 1–113." *Speculum* 44 (1969): 35–45.

_____. "*Wulf and Eadwacer: A Wen Charm.*" *Chaucer Review* 5 (1971): 247–63.

Gang, T. M. "Approaches to *Beowulf.*" *Review of English Studies* 3 (1952): 1–12.

Gardner, John. "Cynewulf's *Elene:* Sources and Structure." *Neophilologus* 54 (1970): 65–76.

_____. "Fulgentius's *Expositio Vergiliana Continentia* and the Plan of *Beowulf:* Another Approach to the Poem's Style and Structure." *Papers on Language and Literature* 6 (1970): 227–62.

Goldsmith, Margaret E. "The Enigma of *The Husband's Message.*" In *Anglo-Saxon Poetry: Essay in Appreciation for John C. McGalliard.* Ed. Lewis E. Nicholson and Dolores Warwick Frese. Notre Dame and London: University of Notre Dame Press, 1975.

_____. *The Mode and Meaning of Beowulf.* London: Athlone Press, 1970.

Greenfield, Stanley B. *A Critical History of Old English Literature.* New York: New York University Press, 1965.

_____. "The Theme of Spiritual Exile in *Christ I.*" *Philological Quarterly* 32 (1953): 321–28.

_____, "*The Wife's Lament* Reconsidered." *PMLA* 68 (1953): 907–12.

Hall, J. R. "*Geongordom* and *Hyldo* in Genesis B: Serving the Lord for the Lord's Favor." *Papers on Language and Literature* 11 (1975): 302–307.

Hansen, Elaine Tuttle. "Women in Old English Poetry Reconsidered." *Michigan Academician* 9 (1976): 109–17.

Harris, Joseph C. "A note on *eorðscræf / eorðsele* and Current Interpretation of *The Wife's Lament.*" *English Studies* 58 (1977): 204–208.

Helterman, Jeffrey. "*Beowulf:* The Archetype Enters History." *ELH* 35 (1968): 1–20.

Hill, Thomas D. "The Fall of Angels and Man in the Old English *Genesis B.*" In *Anglo-Saxon Poetry: Essays in Appreciation for John C. McGalliard.* Ed. Lewis E. Nicholson and Dolores Warwick Frese. Notre Dame and London: University of Notre Dame Press, 1975.

_____. "Sapiential Structure and Figural Narrative in the Old English 'Elene.'" *Traditio* 27 (1972): 159–77.

Holthausen, F. "Zur Quelle von Cynewulfs Elene." *Archiv für das Studium der neueren Sprachen und Literaturen* 125 (1910): 83–88.

_____. "Zur Quelle von Cynewulfs Elene." *Zeitschrift für deutsche Philologie* 37 (1905): 1–19.

Howlett, D. R. "*The Wife's Lament* and *The Husband's Message.*" *Neuphilologische Mitteilungen* 79 (1978): 7–10.

Hume, Kathryn. "The Theme and Structure of *Beowulf.*" *Studies in Philology* 72 (1975): 1–27.

Huppé, Bernard F. *The Wed of Words: Structural Analyses of the Old English Poems Vainglory, The Wonder of Creation, The Dream of the Rood, and Judith.* Albany: State University of New York Press, 1970.

Imelmann, Rudolf. *Zeugnisse zur altenglischen Odoaker-Dichtung.* Berlin: J. Springer, 1907.

Irving, Edward B., Jr. "*Eauluscerwen:* Wild Party at Heorot." *Tennessee Studies in Literature* 11 (1966): 161–68.

————. *Introduction to Beowulf.* Englewood Cliffs, N.J.: Prentice-Hall, 1969.

————. *A Reading of Beowulf.* New Haven: Yale University Press, 1968.

Isaacs, Neil D. *Structural Principles in Old English Poetry.* Knoxville: University of Tennessee Press, 1968.

————. "Who Says What in 'Advent Lyric VII'? (*Christ*, lines 164–213)." *Papers on Language and Literature* 2 (1966): 162–68.

Jensen, Emily Ruth. "Narrative Voice in Old English Lyric Poetry." *Dissertation Abstracts International* 33 (1973): 3587A. (Pennsylvania State University).

————. "Narrative Voice in the Old English *Wulf.*" *Chaucer Review* 13 (1979): 373–83.

Johnson, Lee Ann. "The Narrative Structure of 'The Wife's Lament.'" *English Studies* 52 (1971): 497–501.

Kanner, Barbara, ed. *The Women of England from Anglo-Saxon Times to the Present: Interpretive Bibliographical Essays.* Hamden, Ct.: Archon Books, 1979.

Kaske, R. E. "*Sapientia et Fortitudo* as the Controlling Theme of *Beowulf.*" *Studies in Philology* 55 (1958): 423–56. Rpt. in Lewis E. Nicholson, ed. *An Anthology of Beowulf Criticism.* Notre Dame, Ind.: University of Notre Dame Press, 1963.

————. "Weland and the *wurmas* in *Deor.*" *English Studies* 44 (1963): 190–91.

Kay, Donald. "Riddle 20: A Revaluation." *Tennessee Studies in Literature* 13 (1968): 133–39.

Keough, Terrence. "The Tension of Separation in *Wulf and Eadwacer.*" *Neuphilologische Mitteilungen* 77 (1976): 552–60.

Kiernan, K. S. "*Cwene:* The Old Profession of Exeter Riddle 95." *Modern Philology* 72 (1975): 384–89.

Kiessling, Nicolas K. "Grendel: A New Aspect." *Modern Philology* 65 (1968): 191–201.

Kliman, Bernice W. "Women in Early English Literature: 'Beowulf' to the 'Ancrene Wisse.'" *Nottingham Medieval Studies* 21 (1977): 32–49.

Klinck, Anne Lingard. "Female Characterization in Old English Poetry." *Dissertation Abstracts International* 38 (1977): 254A (University of British Columbia).

————. "Female Characterization in Old English Poetry and the Growth of Psychological Realism: *Genesis B* and *Christ I.*" *Neophilologus* 63 (1979): 597–610.

Langenfelt, Gösya. "Studies on *Widsith.*" *Nam och Bygd* 47 (1959): 70–111.

Lass, Roger. "Poem as Sacrament: Transcendence of Time in the *Advent* Sequence from the Exeter Book." *Annuale Mediaevale* 7 (1966): 3–15.

Lee, Alvin A. *The Guest-Hall of Eden: Four Essays on the Design of Old English Poetry.* New Haven: Yale University Press, 1972.

Lehmann, Ruth P. M. "The Metrics and Structure of 'Wulf and Eadwacer.'" *Philological Quarterly,* 48 (1969): 151–65.

Leo, Heinrich. *Quae de se ipso Cynevulfus . . . poeta Anglo-saconius tradiderat.* Halle, 1857.

Leyerle, John. "The Interlace Structure of *Beowulf*." *University of Toronto Quarterly* 37 (1967): 1–17.

Livius, Thomas. *The Blessed Virgin in the Fathers of the First Six Centuries*. London and New York, 1893.

Lucas, Angela M. "The Narrator of *The Wife's Lament* Reconsidered." *Neuphilologische Mitteilungen* 70 (1969): 282–97.

Malone, Kemp. "Two English Frauenlieder." In *Studies in Old English Literature in Honor of Arthur G. Brodeur*. Ed. Stanley B. Greenfield. Eugene: University of Oregon Press, 1963.

———. "Variation in *Widsith*." *JEGP* 45 (1946): 147–52.

Meaney, Audrey L. "The *Ides* of the Cotton Gnomic Poem." *Medium Aevum* 48 (1979): 23–39.

Meyer, Marc A. "Land Charters and the Legal Position of Anglo-Saxon Women." In *The Women of England from Anglo-Saxon Times to the Present: Interpretive Bibliographical Essays*. Ed. Barbara Kanner. Hamden, Ct.: Archon Books, 1979.

Mildenberger, Kenneth. "Unity of Cynewulf's *Christ* in the Light of Iconography." *Speculum* 23 (1948): 426–32.

Miller, Robert P., ed. *Chaucer: Sources and Backgrounds*. New York: Oxford University Press, 1977.

Mirsky, Aaron. "On the Sources of the Anglo-Saxon *Genesis* and *Exodus*." *English Studies* 48 (1967): 385–97.

Mushabac, Jane. "*Judith* and the Theme of *Sapientia et Fortitudo*." *Massachusetts Studies in English* 4 (1973): 3–12.

Nelson, Janet L. "Queens as Jezebels: The Careers of Brunhild and Balthild in Merovingian History." In *Medieval Women*. Ed. Derek Baker. Studies in Church History, Subsidia, 1. Oxford: Basil Blackwell, 1978.

Nicolson, Joan. "*Feminae Gloriosae:* Women in the Age of Bede." In *Medieval Women*. Ed. Derek Baker. Studies in Church History, Subsidia, 1. Oxford: Basil Blackwell, 1978.

Niles, John D. *Beowulf: The Poem and its Tradition*. Cambridge, Mass.: Harvard University Press, 1983.

Nist, John A. *The Structure and Texture of Beowulf*. Faculdade de filosofía, ciências e letras. Boletim no. 229. Lingua e literatura inglêsa, no. 1. Sao Paulo, Brazil: Universidade de Sao Paulo, 1959.

Nitzsche, Jane Chance. "The Anglo-Saxon Woman as Hero: The Chaste Queen and the Masculine Woman Saint." *Allegorica* 5 (1980): 139–48.

———. *The Genius Figure in Antiquity and the Middle Ages*. New York: Columbia University Press, 1975.

———. "The Structural Unity of *Beowulf*: The Problem of Grendel's Mother." *Texas Studies in Literature and Language* 22 (1980): 287–303.

Norman, Frederick. "Problems in the Dating of *Deor* and its Allusions." In *Franciplegius: Medieval and Linguistic Studies in Honor of Francis Peabody Magoun, Jr*. Ed. Jess B. Bessinger, Jr., and Robert P. Creed. New York: New York University Press, 1965.

Olsen, Alexandra Hennessey. "Inversion and Political Purpose in the Old English *Judith.*" *English Studies* 63 (1982): 289–93.

―――. "Women in *Beowulf.*" In *Approaches to Teaching Beowulf.* Ed. Jess B. Bessinger, Jr., and Robert F. Yeager. New York: Modern Language Association of America, 1984.

Opland, Jeff. *Anglo-Saxon Oral Poetry: A Study of the Traditions.* New Haven and London: Yale University Press, 1980.

Palmer, R. Barton. "Characterization in the Old English *Juliana.*" *South Atlantic Bulletin* 41 (1976): 10–21.

Patzig, H. "Zum ersten Rätsel des Exeterbuchs." *Archiv* 145 (1923): 204–47.

Pflaum, Hiram. "Der allegorische Streit zwischen Synagogue und Kirche in des europäischen Dichtung der Mittelalters." *Archivum Romanicum* 18 (1934): 243–340.

Pheifer, J. D. "*Waldere* 1.29–31." *Review of English Studies,* N.S. 11 (1960): 183–86.

Plummer, John F., ed. *Vox Feminae: Studies in Medieval Woman's Songs.* N.S. Studies in Medieval Culture, 15. Kalamazoo, Mich.: Medieval Institute Publications, 1981.

Puhvel, Martin. "The Might of Grendel's Mother." *Folklore* 80 (1969): 81–88.

Raw, Barbara C. *The Art and Background of Old English Poetry.* New York: St. Martin's Press, 1978.

Regan, Catharine A. "Evangelicalism as the Informing Principle of Cynewulf's 'Elene.'" *Traditio* 29 (1973): 27–52.

Renoir, Alain. "Christian Inversion in *The Wife's Lament.*" *Studia Neophilologica* 49 (1977): 19–24.

―――. "Eve's I.Q. Rating: Two Sexist Views of Genesis B." Paper delivered at MLA Conference, December 28, 1980.

―――. "*Judith* and the Limits of Poetry." *English Studies* 43 (1962): 145–55.

―――. "A Reading Context for *The Wife's Lament.*" In *Anglo-Saxon Poetry: Essays in Appreciation for John C. McGalliard.* Ed. Lewis E. Nicholson and Dolores Warwick Frese. Notre Dame, Ind.: Notre Dame University Press, 1975.

―――. "A Reading of *The Wife's Lament.*" *English Studies* 58 (1977): 4–19.

―――. "The Self-Deception of Temptation: Boethian Psychology in *Genesis B.*" In *Old English Poetry: Fifteen Essays.* Ed. Robert P. Creed. Providence, R.I.: Brown University Press, 1967. Pp. 47–67.

―――. "*Wulf and Eadwacer:* A Noninterpretation." In *Franciplegius: Medieval and Linguistic Studies in Honor of Francis Peabody Magoun, Jr.* Ed. Jess B. Bessinger, Jr., and Robert P. Creed. New York: New York University Press, 1965.

Ringler, Richard N. "*Him Sēo Wēn Gelēah:* The Design for Irony in Grendel's Last Visit to Heorot." *Speculum* 41 (1966): 49–67.

Rogers, H. L. "Beowulf's Three Great Fights." *Review of English Studies,* N.S. 6 (1955): 339–55. Rpt. in *An Anthology of Beowulf Criticism.* Ed. Lewis E. Nicholson. Notre Dame, Ind.: Notre Dame University Press, 1963.

Ryding, William W. *Structure in Medieval Narrative.* The Hague and Paris: Mouton, 1971.

Schaar, Claes. *Critical Studies in the Cynewulf Group.* Lund Studies in English, 17. Lund: C. W. K. Gleerup; Copenhagen: Ejnar Munksgaard, 1949.

Schlauch, Margaret, "The Allegory of Church and Synagogue." *Speculum* 14 (1939): 448–64.

Schofield, William Henry. "Signy's Lament." *PMLA* 17 (1902): 262–95.

Schücking, Levin L. "Das Angelsächsiscne Dicht von der *Klage der Frau.*" *Zeitschrift für deutsches Altertum und deutsche Litteratur* 48 (1906): 436–49.

———. Review of Ernst Sieper, *De altenglische Elegie. Englische Studien* 51 (1917–18): 97–115.

Short, Douglas D. "The Old English *Wife's Lament:* An Interpretation." *Neuphilologische Mitteilungen* 71 (1970): 585–603.

Sievers, Eduard. *Der Heliand und die angelsächsische Genesis.* Halle, 1875.

Sisam, Kenneth. "Cynewulf and his Poetry" (Sir Israel Gollancz Memorial Lecture, Read March 8, 1933). *Proceedings of the British Academy* 18 (1932): 303–31.

———. *Studies in the History of Old English Literature.* Oxford: Clarendon Press, 1953.

Sklute, Larry M. "*Freoðuwebbe* in Old English Poetry." *Neuphilologische Mitteilungen* 71 (1970): 534–41.

Smalley, Beryl. *The Study of the Bible in the Middle Ages.* 1952; rpt. Notre Dame: University of Notre Dame Press, 1964.

Spamer, James B. "The Marriage Concept in *Wulf and Eadwacer.*" *Neophilologus* 62 (1978): 143–44.

Spitzer, Leo. "The Mozarabic Lyric and Theodor Frings' Theories." *Comparative Literature* 4 (1952): 1–22.

Stafford, Pauline. "Sons and Mothers: Family Politics in the Early Middle Ages." In *Medieval Women.* Ed. Derek Baker. Studies in Church History, Subsidia, 1. Oxford: Basil Blackwell, 1978.

Stenton, Doris Mary. *The English Woman in History.* London: Allen and Unwin; New York: Macmillan, 1957.

Stepsis, Robert, and Richard Rand. "Contrast and Conversion in Cynewulf's *Elene.*" *Neuphilologische Mitteilungen* 70 (1969): 273–82.

Stevens, Martin. "The Narrator of *The Wife's Lament.*" *Neuphilologische Mitteilungen* 69 (1968): 72–90.

Stevick, Robert D. "Formal Aspects of *The Wife's Lament.*" *JEGP* 59 (1960): 21–25.

Stuard, Susan Mosher, ed. *Women in Medieval Society.* Philadelphia: University of Pennsylvania Press, 1976.

Swanton, M. J. "*The Wife's Lament* and *The Husband's Message:* A Reconsideration." *Anglia* 82 (1964): 269–90.

Tolkien, J. R. R. "Beowulf: The Monsters and the Critics." In *Proceedings of the British Academy* 22 (1936): 245–95. Rpt. in *An Anthology of Beowulf Criticism.* Ed. Lewis E. Nicholson. Notre Dame: University of Notre Dame Press, 1963.

Trautmann, Moritz. "Cynewulf und die Rätsel." *Anglia* 6 (1883): 158–69.

Tripp, Raymond P., Jr. "The Narrator as Revenant: A Reconsideration of Three Old English Elegies." *Papers on Language and Literature* 8 (1972): 339–61.

Ugolnik, Anthony Joseph, Jr. "The Royal Icon: A Structural and Thematic Study of Cynewulf's *Elene*." *Dissertation Abstracts International* 37 (1976): 342–3A (Brown University).

Venezky, Richard L. and Antonette di Paolo Healey, eds. *A Microfiche Concordance to Old English* (Newark, Delaware: University of Delaware Press, 1980).

Vickrey, John F. "*The Micel Wundor* of *Genesis B*." *Studies in Philology* 68 (1971): 245–54.

———. "*Selfsceaft* in *Genesis B*." *Anglia* 83 (1965): 154–71.

———. "The Vision of Eve in *Genesis B*." *Speculum* 44 (1969): 86–102.

———. "The Situation of the Narrator's Lord in *The Wife's Lament*." *Neuphilologische Mitteilungen* 71 (1970): 604–10.

Wentersdorf, Karl P. "The Situation of the Narrator in the Old English *Wife's Lament*." *Speculum* 56 (1981): 492–516.

Whitbread, L. "The Binding of Weland." *Medium Aevum* 25 (1956): 13–19.

Whitelock, Dorothy. *The Beginnings of English Society*. Harmondsworth, England: Penguin, 1952.

Williams, Edith Whitehurst. "What's So New about the Sexual Revolution? Some Comments on Anglo-Saxon Attitudes toward Sexuality in Women Based on Four Exeter Book Riddles." *Texas Quarterly* 18.2 (Summer 1975): 46–55.

Wittig, Joseph. "Figural Narrative in Cynewulf's *Juliana*." *Anglo-Saxon England* 4 (1975): 37–55.

Woolf, Rosemary. "The Fall of Man in *Genesis B* and the *Mystère d'Adam*." In *Studies in Old English Literature in Honour of Arthur G. Brodeur*. Ed. Stanley B. Greenfield. Eugene: University of Oregon Press, 1963. Pp. 187–99.

———. "The Lost Opening to the 'Judith.'" *Modern Language Review* 50 (1955): 168–72.

———. "'Saints' Lives.'" In *continuations and Beginnings: Studies in Old English Literature*. Ed. E. G. Stanley. London and Edinburgh: Thomas Nelson, 1966.

Index

149

Woman as Hero in Old English Literature

was composed in 10-point Mergenthaler Linotron 202 Caledonia and leaded 2 points by
Coghill Book Typesetting Company, Inc.;
with display type in Nordia Bold by Rochester Mono/Headliners;
printed sheet-fed offset on 55-pound, acid-free Glatfelter Antique Cream,
Smyth sewn and bound over 70-point binder's boards in Joanna Arrestox B,
also adhesive bound with paper covers by Maple-Vail Book Manufacturing Group, Inc.;
with dust jackets and paper covers printed in 1 color by Vicks Lithograph & Printing Corporation;
and published by

SYRACUSE UNIVERSITY PRESS
SYRACUSE, NEW YORK 13210